# The Structure of Marx's World-View

# The Structure of Marx's World-View

## JOHN McMURTRY

PRINCETON UNIVERSITY PRESS
Princeton, New Jersey

Copyright © 1978 by Princeton University Press
Published by Princeton University Press, Princeton, New Jersey
In the United Kingdom: Princeton University Press,
Guildford, Surrey

All Rights Reserved

Library of Congress Cataloging in Publication Data will be
found on the last printed page of this book
Publication of this book has been aided by a grant from the
Paul Mellon Fund of Princeton University Press
This book has been composed in VIP Bembo
Printed in the United States of America by Princeton
University Press, Princeton, New Jersey

*"Mankind sets itself only such problems as it can solve."*
    *-Karl Marx*

# Contents

# Acknowledgments

For primary institutional support, this study is indebted to the Canada Council, the University of London, The University of Guelph, and the Princeton University Press. For financial support, it is ultimately indebted to the international citizenry by whom these institutions are sustained.

In the research and writing of the book, Gerald A. Cohen (London) provided continuous, astute comment during its major formative stages.

Painstaking reading of its various drafts, and extended helpful replies, were contributed by Bertell Ollman (New York), Peter Stillman (Vassar), Richard Miller (Cornell), Steven Lukes (Oxford), J. M. Cohen (London), Daniel Goldstick (Toronto) and, last but not least, John Bartkiewicz. Kipling Hunter (Guelph) and Tobias Chapman (Guelph) also helped with important points.

Cynthia McMurtry gave initial typing aid, and the book's major touchstone of value.

Jennifer Sumner provided continuous test readings and personal encouragement, while kind and efficient typing services were supplied by Sheila MacPherson and Judy Martin.

And finally, Sanford G. Thatcher of Princeton University Press provided invaluable editorial assistance and support through the final stages of the book's composition.

# Key to Abbreviations

In each case, the first and last pages of the primary text (including author prefaces) are added in brackets to help the reader locate quotations in other editions. A star (★) indicates that the translator and/or editor is not given.

CI    *Capital* (Volume I), Karl Marx. Trans. Samuel Moore and Edward Aveling, ed. Frederick Engels. Progress Publishers, Moscow, 1965 (7-774).

CII   *Capital* (Volume II), Karl Marx. Trans. I. Lasker, ed. Frederick Engels. Progress Publishers, Moscow, 1967 (25-527).

CIII  *Capital* (Volume III), Karl Marx. Ed. Frederick Engels. Progress Publishers, Moscow, 1954 (23-910).★

CM    *Manifesto of the Communist Party*, Karl Marx and Frederick Engels. Trans. and ed. Frederick Engels and Samuel Moore. Foreign Languages Publishing House, Moscow, 1969 (11-91).

CPÈ   *A Contribution to the Critique of Political Economy*, Karl Marx. Trans. S. Ryazanskaya, ed. Maurice Dobb. Progress Publishers, Moscow, 1970 (18-227).

CW    *The Civil War in France*, Karl Marx. Ed. Frederick Engels. Martin Lawrence Ltd., London, 1933 (21-66).★

EPM   *Economic and Philosophical Manuscripts of 1844*, Karl Marx. Trans. and ed. Martin Milligan. Foreign Languages Publishing House, Moscow, 1961 (20-171).

G     *Karl Marx/Grundrisse*. Trans. and ed. Martin Nicolaus. Penguin Books, Harmondsworth, 1973 (82-893).

GID   *The German Ideology*, Karl Marx and Frederick Engels. Trans. and ed. S. Ryazanskaya. Progress Publishers, Moscow, 1964 (21-596).

GP    *Critique of the Gotha Program*, Karl Marx. Ed. Frederick Engels: Progress Publishers, Moscow, 1966 (10-30).★

18thB *The Eighteenth Brumaire of Louis Bonaparte*, Karl Marx. Progress Publishers, Moscow, 1967 (10-30).★

KMC    *Karl Marx on Colonialism and Modernization*. Ed. Shlomo
       Avineri. Doubleday, New York, 1969 (47-473).

OB     *On Britain*, Karl Marx and Frederick Engels. Lawrence
       and Wishart Ltd. London, 1962 (1-584).★

PofP   *The Poverty of Philosophy*, Karl Marx. Ed. Frederick En-
       gels. Progress Publishers, Moscow, 1966 (25-152).★

Pre-C  *Karl Marx/Pre-Capitalist Economic Formations*. Trans. Jack
       Cohen, ed. E. J. Hobsbawm. Lawrence and Wishart,
       London, 1964 (67-148).

R      *The Revolutions of 1848*, Karl Marx and Frederick Engels.
       Ed. David Fernbach. Random House, New York, 1974
       (62-267).

RZ     *Articles from the Nene Rheinische Zeitung*, Karl Marx and
       Frederick Engels. Trans. S. Ryazanskaya, ed. B. Isaacs.
       Progress Publishers, Moscow, 1964 (21-596).

SC     *Selected Correspondence*, Karl Marx and Frederick Engels.
       Foreign Languages Publishing House, Moscow, 1953
       (25-571).★

S-V I  *Theories of Surplus-Value* (Part I), Karl Marx. Trans. Emile
       Burns, ed. S. Ryazanskaya. Foreign Languages Publishing
       House, Moscow, 1954 (40-400).

S-V II *Theories of Surplus-Value* (Part II), Karl Marx. Trans. and
       ed. S. Ryazanskaya. Progress Publishers, Moscow, 1968
       (15-596).

S-V III *Theories of Surplus-Value* (Part III), Karl Marx. Trans. Jack
       Cohen and S. Ryazanskaya, ed. S. Ryazanskaya and
       Richard Dixon. Progress Publishers, Moscow, 1971 (12-
       540).

WL & C *Wage Labour and Capital*, Karl Marx. Ed. Frederick Engels.
       Foreign Languages Publishing House, Moscow (27-79).★

WPP    *Wages, Prices and Profit*, Karl Marx. Foreign Languages
       Press, Peking, 1970 (1-79).

YM     *Writings of the Young Marx on Philosophy and Society*. Ed. L.
       D. Easton and K. H. Guddat. Doubleday, New York,
       1967 (35-267).

NOTES:  i. Unless otherwise stated, italics within excerpts from the above
        texts are added.

        ii. All further references to the original German of these texts are
        from the *Marx-Engels-Werke* (Volumes 1-39): Dietz Verlag, Ber-
        lin, 1956-1968.

# The Structure of Marx's World-View

# Introduction

Karl Marx's philosophy of the human condition is as celebrated for the charges made against it as for the claims it advances. Four generations of Western economists, philosophers, historians, sociologists, and political scientists—among others—have questioned, criticized, and vilified its formulations. But perhaps the most persistent and discomfiting reproof issued against it is that it is wildly confused.

Marx, it is held, articulated his doctrine ambiguously and loosely, if not incoherently. Thus the British philosopher, H. B. Acton, concludes his definitive critical study, *The Illusion of the Epoch*, with the trenchant decision that Marx's theory is, simply, "a philosophical farrago."[1] In much the same vein, Professor Sidney Hook, who now opposes Marx's doctrine with as much conviction as he once defended it, charges that "Rigorous examination is one thing Marx's ideas will not stand because they were not rigorously formulated."[2] Even the very sympathetic C. Wright Mills laments that Marx's theory is "full of genuine murk" and "contains much that is . . . ambiguous or inadequate."[3]

The range of eminent scholars censuring Marx for muddle and confusion extends across the disciplines. The charge of pervasive "ambiguity," for example, is laid against Marx's conceptual scaffolding by such various figures as Raymond Aron in his *Eighteen Lectures on*

[1] H. B. Acton, *The Illusion of the Epoch* (London, 1955), p. 271.

[2] Sidney Hook, *Marx and the Marxists: The Ambiguous Legacy* (New York, 1955), p. 35.

[3] C. Wright Mills, *The Marxists* (New York, 1962), pp. 102 and 130, respectively.

*Industrial Society*,[4] Bertram D. Wolfe in his *One Hundred Years in the Life of a Doctrine*,[5] and Pitirim Sorokin in his *Contemporary Sociological Theories*.[6] Economist M. M. Bober utters much the same objection when he holds that Marx's work is "obscure, careless in expression and contradictory";[7] while the historian Karl Federn voices his criticism more forcefully still: "The vagueness and indistinctness of Marxian terminology," he remarks, is "deplorable."[8] In short, there exists a broadly established and expert opinion that Marx's theory ruinously wants in clarity and form.[9]

[4] Raymond Aron, *Eighteen Lectures on Industrial Society*, trans. M. K. Bottomore (London, 1967), p. 48.

[5] Bertram D. Wolfe, *Marxism: One Hundred Years in the Life of a Doctrine* (London, 1967), p. xxiii.

[6] Pitirim Sorokin, *Contemporary Sociological Theories* (New York, 1928), p. 527-39.

[7] M. M. Bober, *Karl Marx's Interpretation of History* (Cambridge, Mass., 1950), p. 297.

[8] Karl Federn, *The Materialist Conception of History* (London, 1939), p. 61.

[9] *i*. Marx's abilities as a thinker were not always so discredited in the academy. The leading German philosopher, Moses Hess, had this to say about him in 1842, when he was not yet a revolutionary: "He is the greatest, perhaps the one genuine philosopher now alive and will soon . . . draw the eyes of all Germany. . . . Dr. Marx—that is my idol's name—is still very young (about twenty-four at most) and will give medieval religion and politics their *coup de grace*. He combines the deepest philosophical seriousness with the most biting wit. Imagine Rousseau, Voltaire, Holbach, Lessing, Heine and Hegel fused into one person—I say fused, not thrown together in a heap—and you have Dr. Marx." (Reported in Isaiah Berlin's *Karl Marx: His Life and Environment*, New York, 1959, pp. 72-73.)

*ii*. In recent years, the dismissal of Marx's work by Western scholars has been less monolithic than in the past. Continental "critical theorists" and "structuralists," for example, along with a pluralist Anglo-American "new left," have together constituted a growing academic fifth column against the settled opinion of Marx's irredeemable "confusion." However, the thing most needed here, a direct, propositionally precise delineation of Marx's complete explanatory model, has been altogether missing. We seek to meet this need in the following chapters, adhering rigorously throughout to Marx's own, and not secondary Marxist, work in our reconstruction.

This judgment seems justified by the enormous number and variety of interpretations of Marx's work. Perhaps no corpus since the Holy Scriptures has been so kaleidoscopically construed.

There are radically different opinions, for example, on what Marx's position actually is on ontology (is he really a philosophical materialist, and if so, what kind?), epistemology (is he a naive realist, a pioneering pragmatist, or what?), ethics (what is its nature and place, if any, in his thought?), methodology (positive or normative?), the dialectic (metaphysical or heuristic?),[10] political theory (anarchist, democratic, or totalitarian?), and so on. Then, giving rise to many of these general problems, the focal categories of his historical materialist theory—"forces of production," "relations of production," "superstructure," and so forth—are themselves subject to widely various and, many say, impossible difficulties, as we will presently see.

Any serious inquirer into Marx's thought, then, cannot help but be bemused by the situation on which he finds himself. On the one hand, the texts with which he is concerned are said to be full of conceptual muddle

[10] We take this opportunity to state, from the outset, that this study will not presume acceptance by the reader of dialectical method, but on the contrary will apply its terminology only where nondialectical explanation is already in force. In this manner, passage through a notorious stumbling block to the understanding of Marx's theory will be negotiated, and the sense of controversial dialectical terms (e.g., "contradiction") clarified on the way.

Furthermore, our study will establish that there are limitations to the standard dialectical interpretation of Marx's thought: demonstrating, for example, that laws of correspondence rather than contradiction, and of strict determinism rather than reciprocal interdeterminism, are the primary principles of his theory. In this way, the well-known metaphysics of "dialectical materialism" (a term Marx never once used, but which has dominated Marxist thought for almost a century) will be shown as, at best, an incomplete framework for understanding his science of human society and history.

while, on the other, there seems to be no end of problems associated with his system's fundamental positions
and categories. In approaching his theory, thus, one
might be excused for feeling somewhat like a worker at
the building of Babel. Confusion seems everywhere.

It is for this reason, on the face of it, that Marx's work
has been dismissed by the mainstream of Anglo-Saxon
philosophical thought as unworthy of sober attention.
When a century of scrutiny has failed to understand
what its central categories mean or what its stance is on
the most basic philosophical issues, it must be, the
thought seems to go, because the work in question is a
sham, a fantasy, or, as Acton puts it, an "illusion."
Thus in a summational judgment of this mainstream,
the illustrious index of its fashion, A. J. Ayer, pro-
nounces Marx's philosophy a nonentity. "As for Marxist philosophy," he declares, "it does not exist."[11]

Let us, however, risk dupery, and consider Marx's
thought directly, if only to determine the parameters of
our problem.

Before *The German Ideology* (1845-1846), Marx's
thought is still in a formative stage. The now famous
*Economic and Philosophical Manuscripts*—written in
1844-1845, when Marx was twenty-six years old—is the
most instructive case in point. Though these writings
offer a fascinating insight into Marx's developing
thought, and some of the most poetic and suggestive
remarks he ever utters, they are in the end manuscripts,
and full of the loose ends and conceptual vagary one
might expect of such a form.[12] Even with *The German*

---

[11] This judgment (reported in the British journal, *Radical Philosophy*, No. 7, Spring 1974, p. 1) is by no means atypical of the mainstream in question. Though such judgment might not seem at all in
accordance with this same mainstream's pride in empiric sense, this
does not seem to have inhibited its prevalence.

[12] We do not conclude from this, however, that the *Manuscripts*

*Ideology* and *The Communist Manifesto*, the reader is still
confronted with a somewhat unfinished theory: still
primarily concerned with refuting others, still composed in collaboration with Frederick Engels,[13] still in
the stage of sweeping new principles not yet firmly set.

It is generally agreed that the Preface to *A Contribution
to the Critique of Political Economy*—published in 1859—
gives us the framework of Marx's overview in the most
compressed and lucid form it ever assumes in his work.
By this stage, Marx's theory could be said to have attained a thoroughgoing maturity. It is worth citing
more or less in full:

> The general conclusion at which I arrived and
> which, once reached, continued to serve as the
> guiding thread of my studies, may be formulated
> briefly as follows: In the social production which
> men carry on they enter into definite relations that
> are indispensable and independent of their will;
> these relations of production correspond to a defi-
> nite stage of development of their material powers
> of production. The totality of these relations of
> production constitutes the economic structure of

are somehow out of line with Marx's "mature" work. Though such
a view is widespread among communist party theorists who find the
humanist emphasis of the *Manuscripts* somehow superannuated by
the nomic emphasis of *Capital*, we find no reason to share this view.
On the contrary, we hold the humanist and the nomic emphases of
Marx, his early *Manuscripts* and his later *Capital*, to be inseparable
and complementary aspects of his thought whose disjunction is
theoretically unnecessary and seriously misleading.

[13] Before proceeding further, let us make a position of the study
clear. We have adopted the methodological standpoint that Marx is
not Engels. Though the contrary seems supposed by those who regard their work as one, we infer from their intimate association no
such conflation. Thus, we will include in our reference writings
coauthored by Marx and Engels, but not writings authored by Engels alone. See Chapter 7 for demonstration that Engels, despite his
breadth of learning and sentential pith, is simply not on the same
level as Marx as a thinker.

society—the real foundation, on which the legal
and political superstructure arises and to which
definite forms of social consciousness correspond.
The mode of production of material life determines
the social, political, and spiritual processes of life in
general. It is not the consciousness of men that determines their being, but, on the contrary, their social being determines their consciousness. At a certain stage of their development, the material forces
of production in society come in conflict with the
existing relations of production, or—what is but a
legal expression for them—with the property relations within which they had been at work before.
From forms of development of the forces of production these relations turn into their fetters. Then
occurs a period of social revolution. With the
change of the economic foundation the entire immense superstructure is more or less rapidly transformed. In considering such transformations, the
distinction should always be made between the material transformation of the economic conditions of
production which can be established with the precision of a natural science, and the legal, political, religious, aesthetic or philosophical—in short,
ideological—forms in which men become conscious of this conflict and fight it out. Just as our
opinion of an individual is not based on what he
thinks of himself, so can we not judge of such a period of transformation by its own consciousness;
rather, this consciousness must be explained from
the contradictions of material life, from the existing
conflict between the social forces of production and
the relations of production. No social order ever
disappears before all the productive forces for
which there is room in it have been developed, and

new, higher relations of production never appear before the material conditions of their existence have matured in the womb of the old society. Therefore, mankind always sets itself only such problems as it can solve; since, on closer examination, it will always be found that the problem itself arises only when the material conditions necessary for its solution already exist or are at least in the process of formation.[14]

The structure of Marx's theory that can be analysed out of this passage is constituted of the following essential categories:

1. forces of production (*Produktivkräfte*)
2. relations of production (*Produktionverhältnisse*) or, speaking holistically, the economic structure (*ökonomische Struktur*)
3. legal and political superstructure (*juristischer und politischer Überbau*)
4. ideology (*ideologische Formen*)
5. forms of social consciousness (*gesellschaftliche Bewusstseinsformen*)

[14] This is a reproduction of Bottomore and Rubel's standard translation (*Karl Marx: Selected Writings in Sociology and Social Philosophy*, Harmondsworth, 1961, pp. 67-68), with minor alterations. For example, we have changed their improper translation, "the general character of the social political and ideological processes of life" in the fourth sentence.

It will also be observed that we have deleted Marx's concluding few sentences on the Asiatic, ancient, feudal, and bourgeois modes of production. We have done so for two reasons, the first following from the second: 1. the remarks in question are not relevant to our stated enterprise, and 2. the notion of history falling into four progressive stages of production—what K. Popper mistakenly thinks is the postulation of an inalterable "predetermined path" of history (*Poverty of Historicism*, London, 1955, p. 51)—is one Marx only tentatively suggests here and, as he explicitly insists elsewhere, does *not* involve the postulation of a "general path every people is fated to tread" (*S.C.* 379).

Before advancing our analysis further, it is important to note that we have distinguished "ideology" from "forms of social consciousness," a distinction that is not conventionally made by commentators on Marx, though Marx himself makes it, and though it is of signal significance to his theory (see Chapter 6).

Marx also draws attention in the above passage to several fundamental relationships (relationships that he discusses and elaborates in one way or another throughout his work) that obtain among the five identified classes of phenomena:

i. The relations of production/economic structure correspond (*entsprechen*) to a definite stage of development of the forces of production, except in prerevolutionary periods, when they "fetter" these forces.

ii. The forms of social consciousness correspond (*entsprechen*) with the relations of production/economic structure, as do (as Marx says elsewhere and suggests here) the legal and political superstructure and ideology.

iii. The "mode of production" (that is, for Marx, the forces and relations of production together)[15] determines the social, political, and spiritual processes of life, that is, the legal and political superstructure, ideology, and forms of social consciousness.

For the purposes of economy and simplicity, we reduce, without loss, these three relationships to two:

1) Relationship (i), plus that aspect of relationship (ii) that applies to productive forces alone, together constitute one complex relationship between productive forces and the rest of the categories of phenomena identified in Marx's overall theoretical framework. This

---

[15] Marx sometimes refers only to the forces of production with this phrase. Nonetheless, the term seems usually to refer to both forces and relations of production, and so we have taken such usage as standard.

complex relationship we henceforth designate *technological determinism*.

2) Relationship (ii) which, with respect to the influence of relations of production/economic structure, seems merely repeated in (iii), constitutes the second major complex relationship in Marx's overall theoretical framework: that is, the relationship between relations of production/economic structure and the rest of the general categories of phenomena indicated above. This second, equally important relationship we henceforth designate *economic determinism*.

The resolution of the sociohistorical process into the above five factors and the two fundamental relationships held to obtain between these factors constitutes the essential substance of Marx's historical materialist world-view. Precisely what Marx means by each of his seminal categories, however, and exactly how he construes the two basic relationships are matters that have aroused over a century of claimed bewilderment. Greatly intensifying the general criticisms of extreme confusion in Marx's thought, every one of these central categories has been attacked by critics as ill conceived, while the basic relationships held to exist between their referents have been more vigorously censured still. Very briefly, the standard objections that have been urged against Marx in these connections are as follows.

1. His basic category, "forces of production," is a riddle. To begin with, these forces of production seem to be inseparable from the "relations of production." For example, if we consider a force of production such as a fishing vessel, we can see that it not only involves a complex of technical instruments and skills, but very definite relations as well among the people required to run it—that is, among helmsman, cabin boy, crew, captain, and so forth. Apart from such organizational rela-

tionships, the fishing boat is not really a productive force at all, but a chaotic collection of tools and skills. But if forces of production must in this way involve relations of production, then Marx's central idea, that they are separate factors in the social process, is patently untenable.[16]

On the other hand, there exists as great a difficulty in distinguishing these productive forces from the institutional and ideological "superstructure." For since the productive forces require laws to safeguard their operation, and since they require ideas by virtue of their very existence as agencies of purposive fabrication, they seem thereby ultimately inseparable from the laws and ideology of the superstructure, too.[17] In sum, Marx's "forces of production" category collapses under analysis into intolerable conceptual amorphousness.

2. What the term "relations of production" means is more problematic still. It could mean technological relations of the type indicated in (1); ownership relations, as is suggested in the Preface by Marx's remark that "property relations" are but a "legal expression for" production relations; market-place relations; several of these at the same time, or nothing at all.[18] If it means the first, the problem outline in (1) arises. If it means the second, the distinction between the "essential" production relations and legal superstructure falls to the ground. There is no textual evidence to indicate that it

[16] This is a paraphrase of H. B. Acton's argument in *The Illusion of the Epoch*, pp. 159 ff.

[17] See *ibid.*, pp. 164–67, for an example of this form of criticism.

[18] John Plamenatz (*Man and Society*, II, London, 1968, pp. 280 ff.) argues that Marx's production relations must be equivalent to property relations; H. B. Acton that they also include market-place relations; Irving Zeitlin (*Marxism: A Re-examination*, Princeton, 1967, p. 64) that they involve both work and property relations; and Patrick Gardiner (*Theories of History*, Glencoe, Illinois, 1960, p. 132) that they are simply "not clear."

means the third, and if it means several relations at the
same time or is just obscure, then Marx is guilty of having either confused or bluffed us. In short, the most crucial category of Marx's theory—the relations of production—is a cipher. As Acton puts it, Marx leaves us in
"the devil of confusion."

3. What is meant by the "legal and political superstructure" is also unclear. On the one hand, such a
superstructure overlaps with the relations of production
in the manner described in (2). That is, the property relations prescribed by the superstructure are indistinguishable from the production relations constituting the
economic base.[19] On the other hand, the institutional
superstructure penetrates so deeply into the operation of
the productive forces—every production process is subject to some rules and laws of a nontechnological sort—
that it is not possible to conceive the two as separable.[20]
Because, then, the legal-political superstructure is involved in some way in both the productive forces and
relations, Marx's view of it as a distinct social factor
seems a piece of conceptual conjury.

4. The notion of "ideology" or "ideological forms"
is no less muddled. It could mean all ideas, just unscientific and/or false ideas, those ideas that favor the ruling
class, or both these latter.[21] If the first sense is the one

---

[19] Plamenatz develops this point most successfully in *Man and Society*, p. 280 ff.

[20] This point is made by each of C. Wright Mills (p. 106),
Raymond Aron (p. 48), H. B. Acton (p. 167), and G. H. Sabine (*A
History of Political Theory*, London, 1963, p. 786).

[21] R. N. Carew-Hunt (*The Theory and Practice of Communism*,
London, 1962, p. 48) holds that Marx locates all ideas in the ideological superstructure; Louis Althusser (*For Marx*, trans. Ben Brewster,
London. 1969, p. 231) defines ideology by distinguishing it from
science; and John Plamenatz (p. 323 ff.) claims that Marx variously
describes ideology as ideas in general, just normative or unscientific
ideas, false ideas, and idea favoring the ruling class.

Marx intends, then there is an obvious difficulty in understanding the character of the productive forces, which would seem, thereby, to be construed as arising and functioning in some mysterious manner without the mediation of ideas. If the second, narrower, sense is intended, there is the problem of conceiving how the productive process could carry on without some "unscientific" ideas—of good and bad, for instance—accompanying, guiding, and motivating the actions of the men concerned. If the third sense is meant, then there is the task of determining what criterion is to be employed in ascertaining whether or not an ideological form "favors" the ruling class; for example, under what criterion is the commandment "love thy neighbor as thyself" to be construed as a ruling class idea? And if it is the final sense that Marx has in mind, there is the difficulty of showing that an idea that favors the ruling class is also necessarily false and/or unscientific.[22] In brief, Marx's concept of ideology is (in Professor Plamenatz's words) "extraordinarily confused."

5. What are "forms of social consciousness"? No one, so far as we know, has subjected this concept to analysis, doubtless because it has been assumed to be synonymous with "ideology." But Marx suggests that it is distinct from the latter (*GID*, 37), though he never explains how nor, indeed, gives us any explicit characterization of it at all. So what is its meaning? It may, unlike the other categories, have escaped critical notice; yet as we remain without any sense for it, it is no less problematic.

6. The complex relationship denoted by "technological determinism" is no more illuminatingly conceived. For example, the nature of the "correspondence" be-

---

[22] Carew-Hunt makes the first of these objections (p. 48), Acton the second (p. 178 ff.), and Plamenatz (p. 330 ff.) the last.

tween productive forces and the relations of production/economic structure is unclear. If production relations are interpreted as purely technological relations obtaining between men at work, then there is indeed a correspondence between such relations and the productive forces, but only because the former are included in the latter. Since under this interpretation the claim in question is merely a disguised tautology, Marx must mean something else. But if he means that production relations in another sense—that is, the sense of property relations—"correspond" to the productive forces, he may escape the Scylla of tautology only to end in the Charybdis of error; for, as Raymond Aron among others has argued, "there may be exactly the same technical organization of agricultural production whether the land is the individual property of a great landowner, the collective property of producers' co-operatives or the property of the state."[23] Then there is the further problem of which of the two "corresponding" factors Marx claims as primary. There is sufficient ambiguity to his position that commentators have adopted opposite interpretations.[24] In other words, yet again the general theoretical framework of Marx's work seems shot through with confusion.

7. Finally, the "economic determinism" relational complex—that is, relations of production/economic structure determining the legal and political superstructure, ideology, and forms of social consciousness—is problematic in the extreme. Indeed, one can say without much hesitation that no area of Marx's work has earned

[23] Aron, *Eighteen Lectures*, p. 47.
[24] Sidney Hook, for example (*Towards an Understanding of Karl Marx*, London, 1933, pp. 126 and 156), urges the primacy of the production relations; whereas Georgi Plekhanov (*The Development of the Monist View of History*, Moscow, 1956, p. 207) just as firmly opts for the productive forces.

so much and so vigorous critical attack. To cite all the objections that have been made might require more space than the remainder of this study. However, the standard arguments are that the relationship network in question involves a naive monocausality;[25] that it denies all human freedom and moral responsibility;[26] that it is persistently incompatible with actual history;[27] and that it is committed to logically absurd prediction.[28] In short, this core complex of Marx's thought abounds in reported disorders.

There seems, then, no part of the essential structure of Marx's thought that is not a shambles. However, there is yet another major problem. A prominent part of the critical literature on Marx argues that the theory's very ontological substructure is a vacuity. That is, Marx's mature world-view or general theoretical framework is said to be altogether devoid of a position on the nature of man himself, the ultimate historical agency whose constituting properties underlie everything to which Marx refers. This is the area of what is conventionally called "human nature," and Marx's inquiry into the material foundations of history is said by many—both hostile and sympathetic to his work—to completely extrude from consideration such a factor. Louis Althusser, a self-described Marxist, approvingly calls this extrusion of human nature from his post-1845 work, Marx's "theoretical anti-humanism."[29] Robert Tucker, on the other hand, a non-Marxist who disapproves, agrees that

[25] For example, R. M. MacIver and Charles H. Page, *Society: An Introductory Analysis* (Toronto, 1965), p. 563.

[26] Isiah Berlin articulates the most famous version of this argument throughout his *Historical Inevitability* (London, 1957).

[27] See Chapter 7.

[28] This is Karl Popper's central point in *The Poverty of Historicism* (London, 1961), especially pp. v–vii.

[29] *Lire le Capital*, II, Paris, 1967, pp. 32-34; *For Marx*, pp. 255 ff. Althusser's extremely influential position is that Marx's "mature"

"the very idea of man has seemingly gone out the window."[30] Eugene Kamenka, however, states the paradigmatic case against Marx's liquidation of the human-nature factor. He says that "since Marx's new underlying reality is to be society and no longer man, he is forced—to treat man as no more than a mere reflection or product of social relations." But, Kamenka goes on to say, "what things *are* is prior to their possible adjustments," and hence the mature Marx, in ignoring the "positive character" of human beings underlying socio-historical "adjustments," is left with a self-contradictorily "servile" vision of man who is no more than a passive reflection of his social circumstances.[31]

If there is such theoretical extrusion of the constitutional properties of man in Marx's mature work, it seems a grave deficiency indeed. The main blunders that seem to be involved are as follows. i. The extrusion is grounded on a fallacious inference. That is, even if it is granted that man continuously develops through history, it cannot be inferred that man is thus nothing other than this development. Indeed, since development presupposes something to be developed, to talk about the former without the latter to ground it is unintelligible. ii. Marx's very "forces of production" are left without any explanatory base whatever. As Carew-Hunt puts it, "We are left to suppose that with Marx the productive forces somehow arise and develop automatically."[32] iii. Since there is no human nature, then the capitalist society Marx opposes has no fault other than hindrance of productive forces, and the communist society he envis-

---

theory is scientific precisely because its explanations do not require a concept or postulate of human nature.

[30] *Philosophy and Myth in Karl Marx* (Cambridge, 1961), pp. 165-66.

[31] *The Ethical Foundations of Marxism* (London, 1962), pp. 131, 163.

[32] *The Theory and Practice of Communism* (London, 1962), p. 48.

ages has no human point other than growth of such forces. Hence Marx's vision is wholly technocratic, compatible with a communist society of robots.

Our problem is now defined. The sense of every category and relationship of the structure of Marx's thought has been multitudinously challenged, and its very ontic underpinnings judged void. To the preponderance of his critics, Marx's thought seems a very mutiny against intelligibility.

Marx's work, then, demands systematic clarification: a step-by-step reconstruction of its categorial framework, its determining relationships, and, at bottom, its concept of human nature. Our study assumes this task. We undertake to distill from the enormous and perplexing range of his corpus a clear and integrating structure, which is both propositionally lucid and faithful to his texts. We undertake, in short, philosophy's classic task of underlaborer.

Our intention, however, is not only clarification, or even successful resolution of the host of standard problems we have reported. We attempt all this, certainly. Indeed, we regard the failure to secure any of it a failure of our study. However, to ascertain, as we are setting out to do, the Logos of Karl Marx's vision, is, if he sees aright, to ascertain the Logos of our world. It is this that has most driven us here—to make sense of the human condition through the eyes of its most effective witness.[33]

[33] That Marx's thought provides such witness, if mainly to the world outside the Western academy, is best testified to by the conversion of half the globe to its guidance in the last sixty years. Given this astounding and still increasing influence of his thought, we feel obliged to report our more insistent objections, if only parenthetically, as we move.

# 1

## Human Nature

The final objection to Marx's general theoretical framework cited in our introduction was that there was nothing at all about "human nature," about the properties of man himself, in Marx's post-1845 work. Since this objection claims a radical void at the very foundation of his world-view, we will cater to it first. When we have shown that Marx does, in fact, sponsor in his mature work a definite and substantial position on this ontological substructure of society and history—human nature—we will count this position as constituting the elementary factor in the structure of his world-view.

It is first worth noting that Marx implies an underlying factor of human nature by his very concept of the forces of production. Of the forces of production we may say, in advance, that for Marx they necessarily involve developed labor-power competences, and they are by definition capable of making material use-values. But labor-power competences and material use-values themselves presuppose, respectively, definite capacities and needs of man himself out of which they are developed and to which they are useful. Forces of production therefore presuppose such needs and capacities, and a notion of human nature in these respects is implicit in Marx's theory from the start. And he repeatedly tells us just this. Hence he says, "Man develops his slumbering powers" (*CI*, 177); and "no production without needs" (*G*, 92).

In short, a notion of human nature involving capacities and needs is posited in Marx's theoretical framework by his very concept of the forces of production, and he consistently declares his awareness of this presupposition. But Marx not only presupposes these needs and capacities of human nature. They constitute, as well, the substance of his explicit concept of human nature.

In a rarely observed passage in *Capital*, Marx prescribes a program for dealing with human nature as a factor of history. Arguing against the utilitarianism of Jeremy Bentham who, Marx opines, has a grotesque "shopkeeper" view of man, he says:

> To know what is useful for a dog, one must study dog nature. . . . Applying this to man, he that would criticize all human acts, movements, relations etc. by the principle of utility, must first deal with *human nature in general, and then with human nature as modified in each historical epoch*" (*CI*, 609).

What is of special interest to us in this passage is that the mature Marx—in manifest opposition to what so many have claimed—clearly accepts the legitimacy of a notion of human nature. Indeed, he prescribes such a notion as theoretically necessary to certain systems of thought. Consequently, since his own system of thought is one that "criticizes human acts, movements, relations, etc. by the principle of utility," that is, Marx's essential criticism of the capitalist order is the latter's systematic dedication to exchange-value rather than use-value,[1] his own theory is committed, by his own prescription, to the program of "dealing with" man's nature in both its

---

[1] Marx is not, of course, a utilitarian in the Benthamite sense; but the "principle of utility"—without Bentham's "shopkeeper" calculus and so on—is fundamental to his work, providing the ultimate rationale of his cardinal emphasis on the forces of production.

general and historical aspects.[2] Thus Marx asserts in explicit recognition of this theoretical commitment, "One of the most vital principles of communism" is its "empiric view, based upon a knowledge of man's nature" (*GID*, 593). Not only, then, does Marx accept the validity of a concept of man's nature, but he prescribes it as necessary to his own system of thought.

Working according to the frame of Marx's own declared program, we now outline what his ideas on man's general and historical nature are. But first it is important to clarify the distinction between "human nature in general" and "human nature as modified in each historical epoch." The former refers to the properties of man conceived generally and independently of particular historical forms (for example, man's species need for food or nutrition), whereas the latter refers to the same properties conceived in a definite historical context (for example, the nineteenth-century European man's cultural need for food or nutrition that lives up to the specific established standards of his society). Hence the former's referent is general and constant, whereas the latter's referent is particular and changing.

## HUMAN NATURE IN GENERAL

When he talks about man as a species, Marx pursues the traditional philosophical strategy of distinguishing him from the animal. In one well-known passage from *The German Ideology*, for example, he tells us that men can be distinguished from animals by virtue of their "consciousness," their "religion," or "anything else you

[2] Views like Althusser's, reported in our Introduction, are thus clearly erroneous. The full import of their error will become evident through the remainder of this chapter.

like." But, he goes on to say, man actually raises himself above the animals only when he starts to produce his own means of staying alive: "They [men] distinguish themselves from animals as soon as they begin to produce their means of subsistence. . ." (*GID*, 31). Since for Marx the *differentia specifica* of human behavior is that man alone produces his means of life, it follows that what he construes as the special capacity enabling such productiveness is for him the *differentia specifica* of man's nature.

In a nuclear discussion in *Capital* on the labor process, Marx clearly states what this special capacity is. It is man's creative intelligence. Again in this passage, Marx pursues the traditional procedure of distinguishing man from animal:

> We presuppose labour in a form that stamps it as *exclusively human*. A spider conducts operations that resemble those of a weaver, and a bee puts to shame many an architect in the construction of her cells. But what distinguishes the worst of architects from the best of bees is this: that the architect *raises his structure in imagination before he erects it in reality*. At the end of every labour process, we get a result that already existed in the imagination of the labourer at its commencement. He not only effects a change of form on the material on which he works, but he also realizes a purpose of his own that gives the law to his modus operandi, and to which he must subordinate his will. (*CI*, 179)

It is important to note that in this paragraph Marx explicitly rejects a behaviorist distinction between man and animal. For he says that in terms of actual behavior, the spider and the bee carry out as complex "operations" and "constructions" as an architect. But their activities are mere executions of nature-given "instinct," whereas man's activities express a mentally structured "purpose" or "plan" that is raised by his own "imagination," and then realized in project-commanded activity. In other words, the *differentia specifica* of man has moved from an outward, behavioral difference (in *The German Ideology*) to a difference in intrinsic being itself (*Capital*). Again, contrary to conventional interpretation, Marx here grants more rather than less explanatory status to the immanent nature of man in his mature work.

We shall call this special property of human nature, which for Marx enables man uniquely to "raise a structure in his imagination" and "erect it in reality," the capacity of *projective consciousness*.[3] This phrase is meant not only to draw instructive connection between Marx and Sartre,[4] as well as to represent by the phrase's literal meaning the sense of Marx's position itself, but to link Marx in some way with others in the past, like Aristotle and his notion of man's elevated faculty for *poiesis*— which, ironically, is more suggestive of Marx's position here than the Greek *praxis* he favors, which for Aristotle meant "doing" as opposed to "making" (*Nichomachean Ethics* 1140a2). The kinds of similarity between Marx's concept of a distinctive human capacity to "raise a structure in the imagination" and then "erect it in reality"

[3] Our concept of "projective consciousness" here is to be distinguished from the Feuerbachian or psychoanalytic concept of projection as the attribution of one's own properties to another; the latter is an alienated expression of the former.

[4] The early Sartre's *projet* is, of course, radically individualistic and free (e.g., *Being and Nothingness*, New York, 1956). The later Sartre, however, comes to accept Marx's location of projective consciousness within determining sociohistorical conditions (e.g., *Search for a Method*, New York, 1968). Marx's concept of man defining himself through his projects does not, we might add, prefigure only Sartre, but the entire aiming-at-what-is-not-yet theme of twentieth-century existentialism.

and the whole Western philosophical tradition of mind as the unique feature of man (his "divine element," his "pilot," his "light of reason," and so forth) are too manifest to labor here. But what does deserve attention, what does mark Marx off from most of this tradition is his emphasis on the creative nature of mind, not a Democritean atom system[5] nor a Humean "association" mechanism; as well as his emphasis on the action that mind must issue in to "prove its reality," not essentially comtemplation, as with the ancients, nor retrospection, like Hegel's Owl of Minerva, which "only takes flight when the shades of twilight have fallen."[6]

This species-distinctive capacity for "projective consciousness" that Marx postulates in man is the legislative-executive agency informing all the latter's uniquely human productive feats. It is the human-

[5] Marx, in his 1841 doctoral thesis on Democritus and Epicurus, favors the latter's theory because it allows for a free "swerve" in atoms, in contrast to the former's notion of atomic motion, which is strictly mechanistic. Marx makes it clear in this place that he prefers Epicurus's theory, even though it is less consistent and more dogmatic than Democritus's, solely because it permits on the atomic level some "subjecthood" to matter, some "energizing principle" that can provide a theoretical basis to human freedom or, more specifically, the "freedom of self-consciousness." See Karl Marx and Frederick Engels, *Collected Works*, I (New York, 1975), 25-109, for the complete version of Marx's thesis.

[6] Marx adopts an intransigently antidualist position in two important respects. First, as we have just indicated and as he declares more forcefully in the famous Theses on Feuerbach, mind is to be considered as having "objective truth" or "reality" only insofar as it is *realized in practice* "The dispute over the reality or non-reality of thinking that is isolated from practice," he declares in thesis II, "is a purely scholastic question."

Second, and more fundamentally, he refuses any distinct ontological status or realm for mind (against the tradition manned by Plato and Descartes), regarding it as simply a way of talking about highly developed *"matter which thinks."*

We might characterize the first of these positions as Marx's antidualist epistemology, and the second as his antidualist ontology.

nature cognate of *homo faber*. However it is limited, curtailed, perverted, or otherwise determined, it still is
what specially enables man to be a "toolmaking animal": to be so "many sided" in his constructions, to
wield nature as "one of the organs of his activity," and
to perform all the other constructive negations of production that alter the world from what it is. In his own
words, "the history of industry" is its product, "the
open book of man's essential powers, the exposure to
the five senses of human psychology" (*EPM*, 109). The
capacity for projective consciousness is, in short, the essence of human nature underlying what Marx elsewhere
calls man's "positive freedom." It is for this reason that
he declares, "freedom is thoroughly the essence of
man."[7] Man's freedom is, for him, built in; prescribed
by the agenda of his human nature.

But a few further explications are in order.

1. This special human capacity of "projective consciousness" achieves its "truly human" expression for
Marx in the activity of creative art. For it is in "composition" that he sees the inventive and implementive aspects of this natural capacity most freely and integrally
expressed (*G*, 611).[8] In such creative art (Marx's exam-

---

[7] Eugene Kamenka, *The Ethical Foundations of Marxism* (London,
1962), p. 30.

[8] There may, however, be the objection here that Marx's distinction between the phase of "raising the structure in imagination" and
the phase of "erecting in reality" can plausibly work with the architect's blueprint and the actual building following therefrom, but
manifestly not with the more thoroughgoing art forms of literature,
music, and painting: each of the latter's projective and executive
phases are not typically separate, but part of one integral activity. At
this point, we need to get clear what Marx means by "erecting in
reality." Marx counts as a criterion of something being "erected in
reality" the social character of its materialization. Given this, we can
see that the suspected problem does not arise. The division between
a structure "being raised in the imagination" and "being erected in
reality" can aptly fall between manuscript and publication or, again,

ple is the "composition" of the writer), both the project
and its execution are unconstrained by extrinsic dictate
and united in the same productive agent, unlike the "antagonistic" and "unfree" forms of almost all historical
production. The ultimate end of posthistorical communist society is thus, Marx emphasizes here and elsewhere, to provide those technical and economic conditions whereby all men's activity can achieve precisely
this status of creative art, whereby all men's projective
consciousness or "creative dispositions" can seek "absolute elaboration" (*Pre-C*, 84-85). For Marx, then, Man
the Producer is, in the end, Man the Artist.

2. Marx's position by no means rules out the possibility of collective plans or projects. The operation of such
collective projective consciousness can take either of
two extremes for Marx: production where the "head"
and the "hand" of the social organism altogether "part
company" (extreme division of labor) and become
"deadly foes" (*CI*, 508); or production where the collective laborer is communist and the plans and execution
are performed together: the "tribal community, the
natural commonbody" (*Pre-C*, 68) of man's being,
dialectically fulfilled in the concrete universal of communism. The former of these forms occupies all previous, class-divided history; and the latter constitutes the
"realm of freedom" (*CIII*, 821), the classless utopia. In
the "realm of freedom," the "heads" and "hands" of all
unite in thoroughly cooperative and unantagonistically

---

between musician's score and the playing of it, between studio canvas and its public exhibition. In brief, the two-phase logic Marx imputes to the operation of "projective consciousness" can be maintained intact whatever the productive activity in question may be.
The first phase is the creative preparation period as a whole—
whether the artist preparing the finished form of his canvas or the
factory master preparing his final production plans—and the second
phase is the actual production of the project in material, social form.

integrated production. Here a *social* architect, everyone planning and acting in full community, projects and implements as a completely integrated whole, as the original architect writ huge.[9]

It would be foolish to conclude here, however, that Marx imagined the operation of this collective projective consciousness as the only form in which men could realize themselves in the future society. The individual enterprise assuredly does not disappear here, though some detractors of Marx's vision would have it that way. On the contrary, it becomes ever more materially enabled as technological development, wielded by the

[9] *i*. We can see here the ontological underpinnings of Marx's lifelong commitment to the principles of radical democracy. That is, that all producers ought to participate in the construction of the productive projects in accordance with which they collectively act is entailed by his concept of human nature. For to be fully human, for Marx, is to act in accordance with a self-raised project. Consequently, for him, in any collective productive project, all must share in the raising of that project if all are to realize in their enactment of it their full humanity. Marx's generally misunderstood concept of "the dictatorship of the proletariat" (usually misconstrued as the dictatorship of the Communist party) is just the translation of this ultimate human-natural requirement into an enforceable political program: the dictate of the direct producers to the ruling class that they, the direct producers, henceforth set the projects in accordance with which they act, whatever ruling-class rights of ownership and governance must be nihilated to do so.

*ii*. Marx's revolutionary position here may be instructively compared and contrasted to the traditional position formulated by Aristotle: "For that which can foresee by the exercise of mind is by nature intended to be lord and master, and that which can with its body give effect to such foresight is a subject, and by nature a slave (*Politics*, 1252a4)." Aristotle and Marx, as we can see, both accord a sovereign role to "projective consciousness," and both ultimately derive from its status as natural endowment a program of political rule. But because Marx ascribes this natural capacity to all men (and Aristotle only to a few), his concept of political rule is a transitional inversion of Aristotle's classical concept: a human-nature-based dictatorship of the great majority of producers, in place of a human-nature-based dictatorship of a small minority of nonproducers.

"social architect," progressively reduces the working day and increases "free time" for whatever creative expression the individual chooses to undertake (*CIII*, 820; *G*, 488).

3. The realization of man's special capacity for projective consciousness presupposes, for Marx, man's status as a "social animal": not, of course, in the sense above, but rather in the sense that consciousness of any human sort presupposes social intercourse whereby its currency of language may come to exist. "Consciousness," he says, "is from the very beginning a social product and remains so as long as men exist at all" (*GID*, 42). Hence, for Marx, to say that man has consciousness, as opposed to saying that he can have it, is to imply also his sociality—his situation (if only, as Robinson Crusoe, in the past) amidst the interpersonal connectives of language, conventions, tools, cooperative labor, and so forth, from which stably formed unities of conception can arise.

This is not to say, as some have interpreted Marx as saying, that man is inherently "social" in the sense of being altruistic. Social relationship does not imply social benevolence: though there is in the early Marx good evidence that he believed, with Feuerbach, that man's power to conceptualize others as members of the same species rendered human or "species beings" (*Gattungswesen*) intrinsically empathetic. Indeed, it is his later rejection of this belief in a conceptual communism that constitutes the principal difference between Marx's early and later views of human nature.[10]

[10] It is doubtless true that the later Marx conceived of such a collective outlook coming with communist society. But it is a collective outlook that is historically achieved, rather than, as in the *Manuscripts*, human-naturally given. It finds its place in his overall theory as a key aspect of the historical development of "projective consciousness" and its functionable range, the essential principles of which development we will identify presently.

The theme of man's *differentia specifica*, residing in what we have called "projective consciousness," persists throughout Marx's work. More than twenty years before the above passage on human labor appeared in *Capital*, he said much the same thing in the *Economic and Philosophic Manuscripts*, while discussing, again, how man differs in nature from the animal:

> *Free conscious activity is man's species character.* . . . The animal is immediately identical with its life-activity. . . . Man makes his life-activity itself the object of his will and consciousness. . . . Conscious life-activity directly distinguishes man from animal life-activity. . . . Admittedly animals also produce. They build themselves nests, dwellings, like the bees, beavers, ants, etc. . . . But man in the working up of the objective world . . . duplicates himself not only, as in consciousness, intellectually but also actively, in reality, and therefore he contemplates himself in a world he has created. (*EPM*, 75-76)

Elsewhere Marx talks of man's special "ability to think" (*GID*, 315) "intellectual faculties" (*WLC*, 73) and "natural thinking process" (*SC*, 315), and so forth. And he is quite explicit in *Capital* and other places that the forces of production are the "materialization" of the sovereign workings of this distinctive mental capacity. "Man . . . is . . . a living conscious thing," he says, "and labor is the *manifestation of this power residing in him*" (*CI*, 202) or, in the *Grundrisse*: "Nature builds no machines, no locomotives, railways, electric telegraphs, self-acting mules, etc. . . . These are organs of the human brain, created by the human hand; the power of knowledge, objectified" (*G*, 706).

The material capacity of "projective consciousness" is then, for Marx, the essential feature of human nature: the long-hidden key to understanding his concept of

man from the *Manuscripts* to *Capital*. Why has it so often
been overlooked by Marxists and anti-Marxists alike?
Let us very briefly suggest three reasons. First, there is a
strong tendency in scholarship on Marx to interpret
wrongly what he says about "ideology" being a "reflex" of the forces and relations of production as statements on human consciousness as such (see Chapter 5).
Second, Marx's great emphasis on the influence of
specific material conditions upon men and his correspondingly great scorn for wholly "abstract" conceptions easily but mistakenly leads to the conclusion that
he rejected general conceptions of man, conceptions of
human nature, altogether. The second error, as one can
see, tends to ground the first.[11] And third, reinforcing
both of the above, Marx weaves his account of human
nature so integrally into his post-1845 writings that only
a study of his corpus as a whole can disclose the full substance of his position.

Once we are aware of the essential core of Marx's
concept of human nature—its "species character" of
projective consciousness—we can see how it clearly
underlies his fundamental positions: underlies, for
example, his calls for "conscious plan" in social production, his indignation at the reduction of human work to
dictated and "mindless detail task," his preoccupation

---

[11] Marx's famous sixth thesis on Feuerbach is a standard source
for the claim that he altogether rejected the idea of an intrinsic
human nature: "The human essence is no abstraction inherent in
each single individual. In its reality (*Wirklichkeit*), it is the ensemble
of social relations." However, all that Marx is claiming here is, in a
less refined form, what he claims throughout his subsequent work.
That is, the "base," "structure," "form," "anatomy," or (as here)
"essence" of human affairs is the totality of social relations. He is not
opposing a notion of human nature as such, but an "abstract" version of it. And he is not depriving inherent human properties of
explanatory status, but is saying that "in reality," in practice, the
"human essence" is social rather than atomistic.

with the profit imperative of the capitalist system "blindly" governing human productive activity, his disdain for ideas and thoughts not carried into *praxis*, and so on. Indeed, we question whether it is possible to make sense of his very vocabulary, and its relentless use of such terms as "brutalizing," "alienating," "monstrous," "inhuman," "savage," "ghoulish," and "bestial," unless one acknowledges in such usage a presupposed concept of human nature, unless one discerns an underlying positive notion of what man intrinsically is that makes these terms meaningful and not merely diatribe. To call something "inhuman" presumes, of necessity, an idea of what is "human." And it is difficult to miss Marx's tendency to employ such terms whenever he sees external circumstances as having robbed men of the exercise of their creative intelligence.

But Marx construes the nature of man as characterized not only by an essential *capacity* to construct a project and erect it in reality, but by a corresponding, essential *need* to do so. This need is suggested one way or another from Marx's earliest to his latest writings. Hence we find such phrases as man's "need for his own realization" (*EPM*, 112)[12] or "need for universality" (*PofP*, 125) scattered throughout his work; and similarly, statements indicating that men are driven to liberate themselves from oppressive social conditions by a "definite need" to achieve the freedom for material self-realization (*GID*, 331). When this emancipated social situation is secured, he makes clear on several occasions,

[12] Marx's position here strikingly prefigures the contemporary "human potential" movement in psychology (see, for example, Abraham Maslow's concept of the need for "self-actualization" in *Motivation and Personality*, New York, 1970). Unlike this movement, however, Marx's emphasis is on purposeful work rather than self-expression as such and, correspondingly, on liberation of the work place rather than therapy of the ego.

then creative work will be allowed its proper status as
"*life's prime want*" (*GP*, 17), and the untrammeled realization of "what lies within" will incite men as "an end
in itself" (*Pre-C*, 85). Men's socioeconomic circumstances will, at last, "*be worthy of human nature*" (*CIII*,
821).

In the *Grundrisse*, as elsewhere, Marx attacks the
common conception that productive work must somehow be a "sacrifice," must be something one does
merely instrumentally to secure the means of staying
alive:

> It seems quite far from [Adam] Smith's mind that
> the individual "in his normal state of health,
> strength, activity, skill, facility," *needs* a normal
> portion of work. . . . Smith has no inkling what-
> ever that this overcoming of obstacles is itself a
> liberating activity—and that, further, the external
> aims become stripped of the semblance of merely
> external natural urgencies, and become posited as
> aims which the individual himself posits—hence as
> self-realization, objectification of the subject, hence
> real freedom, whose action is, precisely, labour.
> (*G*, 611)

"He is right of course," Marx goes on to say, "that in its
historic forms as slave-labour, serf-labour and wage-
labour, labour always appears as repulsive, always as external forced labour; and not-labour, by contrast, as
'freedom and happiness.' " But work in which man is
not thus constrained, but freely realizes his subjecthood
in creative *praxis*, this "unadulterated" form of work is
what man needs *qua* man: it is "life's prime want" for
the truly human existence.

The "essence" of man's nature for Marx, then, is not
only the species-distinctive capacity of projective con-

sciousness, but also the cognate need of man to realize such consciousness. This conjunction of capacity and need constitutes the basic—if generally unseen—substance of his concept of man and, as such, comprises the very underpinnings of his world-view.

Marx's position on "human nature in general," however, is not confined to this conjunction. He also makes numerous fleeting references to species needs for (and these seem to be distinct needs for him): food, clothing, habitation (*GID*, 39) and—less obvious—sexual relationship (*EPM*, 101), fresh air and sunlight (*CI*, 265, 426, 465), adequate living and working space (*CI*, 482 and 657-91), cleanliness of person and surroundings (*CI*, 232 and 381), rest from exertion (*CI*, 232 and 527), variation of activity (*CI*, 341, 360, 440, 484-88), aesthetic stimulation (*S-VI*, 392 and *CI*, 232), and play (*GID*, 459).[13] Hardly surprisingly, he also alludes fre-

---

[13] In *The German Ideology*, Marx says: "life involves before everything else eating and drinking, a habitation, clothing and *many other things*. The first historical act is thus the production of the means to satisfy these needs." What we have tried to do above is derive from Marx's texts the needs for the "many other things" to which he refers in this passage: needs that are, as the ones he explicitly identifies here, ontologically prior to man's "first historical act." In most cases, the phraseology he uses—"necessity," "very roots of life," "essential," and so on—demonstrates the human-natural status he grants to the needs in question.

With the needs for "sexual relationship" and "play," however, Marx says very little and, furthermore, he talks of the former only in terms of species-reproductive acts, and the latter only in terms of constructive leisure. Though his narrowness of purview here may be by constraint of his era, which tended to regard eros and playfulness as wicked, we judge this narrowness to be a cardinal limitation of his concept of man. Such deficiency can be overcome, however, by extending the referential range of the categories of "sexual relationship" and "play" past the narrow limits within which his thought is confined. This important theoretical task has been largely performed by Wilhelm Reich in *The Sexual Revolution* (New York, 1945), and Herbert Marcuse in *Eros and Civilization* (Boston, 1955).

quently to the human mechanical capacities associated with the five senses, limbs and organs (the "bodily instruments"). This cluster of other human capacities and needs fleshes out, as it were, his view of man conceived "in general."

It is worthwhile casting this view in summational, schematic form, not only because it deserves considered pause for itself, but because nothing like it has hitherto been reported in literature on Marx:

### HUMAN NATURE IN GENERAL

| | | |
|---|---|---|
| *Essence* | capacity<br>need | for material self-realization (or "to raise a structure in imagination and then erect it in social reality") |
| *Other* | capacities<br>needs | of mechanical limb, organ, and sense abilities ("bodily instruments"): |
| | | food |
| | | clothing |
| | | habitation |
| | | sexual relationship |
| | | fresh air and sunlight |
| | | adequate (living and working) space |
| | | cleanliness of person and surroundings |
| | | rest from exertion |
| | | variation of activity |
| | | aesthetic stimulation |
| | | play |

This schema of "human nature in general" (deliberately drawn from his post-1845 writings)[14] works out, as one

---

[14] One of the standard tactics of those denying that Marx has a concept of human nature is to rule out his early work (where such a concept is undeniable) as "immature." To deprive this tactic of any force against our case, we have, at some pains, adhered more or less exclusively to his post-*EPM* corpus in drawing up our Marxian schedule of needs. As to the question of what exactly is meant by the concept of "need" here, Marx typically provides no definition. However, we offer the following formal criterion, which we think underlies Marx's use of the concept: *x is a need if and only if deprivation of x regularly results in i. discomfort, and ii. reduction of performative power.*

can see, to be a remarkably comprehensive one—especially considering the common view that in his post-1845 years he "threw man out the window," saw him as a "passive reflex" of economic conditions, was a "theoretical antihumanist," and so on. Here, indeed, we see the underlying *dynamis* of Marx's system, the generating power behind all man's technical, economic, legal, political, and ideological activities. How this Promethean agency is and has been bound, in Marx's view, upon the rock of sociohistorical conditions will be the subject of most of the rest of this study.[15] But although Marx certainly saw man's nature as coercively "determined," even "drained," by such material conditions, it is precisely his view of man's nature that underlies his thundering denunciations of such "inhuman" constraints. To miss this is, simply, to miss the ground of his entire *Weltanschauung*.

What is most striking about Marx's concept of human nature is the inherent generative force it imputes to man. Man is, for Marx, by the very needs of his nature impelled to ever more productive undertakings, which his special intrinsic capacities are uniquely able to prosecute. Not only are there the numerous needs for biochemical replenishment and protection to incite him into action, but the many needs for various forms of activity as such: the essential one of these latter being, as we have seen, the need to raise a project in the imagination and execute it in reality, the need to "produce" as an end in itself. Hence man is by his very constitution continually excited into activity, forever pressed by intrinsic demand into vital material expressiveness whose

---

[15] We use "Promethean" advisedly: Prometheus was "the first saint of the philosophical calendar" for Marx; Promethean imagery of "fetters bursting" is his favorite mode of describing social revolution; and the word "Pro-metheus" means literally the fore-sight, which he counted as man's constitutional essence.

most truly human form is work in its "unadulterated" form, or productive activity akin to creative art.

It is certainly true that, for Marx, historical production—slave, serf, or wage—has only been permitted by technical and economic circumstances to exhibit "transitory and inferior forms." But it is precisely because it has frustrated man's intrinsic drive for "truly human" work that Marx considers it "inferior." And it is precisely because he regards it as inferior that he calls for its transcendance in the appropriate material circumstances of nonscarcity and social collectivity, in the projectively and executively unconstrained production of the "realm of freedom." This "realm of freedom" permits the activity of material self-realization "without preconditions," and yields, in the young Marx's words, the "reappropriation of the human essence" (*EPM*, 102). Once this state of affairs is achieved, man cannot cease his restless elaboration of what lies within, even though all his requirements for sustenance are increasingly fulfilled by a "self-acting" or automated productive apparatus (*G*, 704–706). On the contrary, man is for Marx impelled by the very essence of his nature to go on creating, materializing his projects—from, *contra* Kamenka, his material security as springboard—with the "most intense exertion" of the driven artist he seems, for Marx, ultimately to be (*G*, 611).

For Marx, indeed, the secure satisfaction of his "mundane needs" releases man to truly realize his "creative dispositions": the "mere bodily needs" having been the source of "Adam's curse" all along—that is, the demanders of toil, and the levers of exploitation.

In sum, Marx's concept of man, as his great emphasis elsewhere on production, on revolution, and on the epistemology of *praxis* suggest, is above all activist. Man for him can no more relinquish his enabled drive for material self-realization than he can cease to be man. The entire theoretical construct of Marx rests on this human-natural premise.

Considering together all that Marx suggests about "human nature in general," the overall shape is of a dynamic nexus of capacities and needs whose essential spring is the capacity and the need for creative self-realization. In general, the needs of man's nature are what impel him into action ("no one," says Marx, "can ever do anything without doing it for the sake of one or other of his needs"; GID, 276); while the capacities of his nature are what enable him to act. The primary historical expression of these impelling needs and enabling capacities, in turn, is the forces of production, which fulfill, and shape, both. Therein the bridge between potential and actualization, between subject and object, is forged.

## HUMAN NATURE AS
## HISTORICALLY MODIFIED

As we earlier discovered in his remark on Bentham, Marx's program for the analysis of "human nature" prescribes a treatment of this factor not only "in general" but also "as modified in each historical epoch." In many places in his corpus, Marx makes it clear that he regards this historicization of man's nature as continuous and substantial. In the passage in Capital where he defines man's nature as uniquely capable of creative production, he also says, "By thus acting on the external world and changing it man at the same time changes his own nature" (CI, 177). Then, in The Poverty of Philosophy, he remarks: "All history is nothing but the transformation of human nature" (PofP, 128). Because man's inherent properties are viewed as in an increasing process of historical modification, Marx refers in the third volume of *Capital* to man's having "a second nature." (*CIII*, 859). It is, of course, remarks such as these that have tempted the erroneous orthodoxy that Marx viewed human nature as a sort of complex conditioned reflex.

To avoid this and other errors, we now clarify Marx's concept of an historicized human nature:

1. The "modification," "change," or "transformation" of "human nature" of which he speaks is not conceived by him as alteration of man's general nature. As emphasized earlier, "human nature in general" remains the same, all modification of it being in terms of its determinate particulars. For example, the general need for food is unchanging and transhistorical; but its determinate particulars of quality, range, mode of satisfaction, and so on, vary in accordance with specific sociohistorical conditions, in a way we shall describe.

2. As with "human nature in general," "human nature as modified in each historical epoch" is considered in terms of *capacities* and *needs*; the essential capacity and essential need remaining, of course, the capacity and need to raise a structure in the imagination and execute it in reality.

3. This modification of capacities and needs occurs *primarily through the influence of the forces of production*. To compel a treatise into a formula, the forces of production modify natural capacities and needs by: i. the skills they demand; ii. the material products they provide; iii. the human connections they involve; and iv. the alteration of physical environment they effect.

4. The forces of production are viewed by Marx as developing historically in the general direction of increasing complexity and quantity of output—the basis, in Marx's case, of the so-called "illusion of progress."

Hence the capacities and needs of human nature that these forces of production modify develop in a correspondingly progressive direction (to be defined precisely in the remainder of this chapter).

5. Since the productive forces are themselves of man's making, their influence on man is ultimately man's influence on himself: the historicization of human nature is, therefore, the *self-creation* of man ("Man contemplates himself in a world he has created" *EPM*, 76).

Let us now more specifically consider the historical modification of what Marx regarded as the essential capacity of human nature—the capacity of projective consciousness. Here we disinter the basic structure of Marx's philosophy of mind.

As stated, the historical modification of this or any other capacity obtains for Marx primarily through the influence of the forces of production—or, more precisely, in accordance with the development of the productive forces. Hence Marx says: "In reality this [any] barrier to consciousness corresponds to a definite degree of development of the forces of material production" (*G*, 541). The principle of modification that Marx implies here, and elsewhere, is that of limitation of consciousness, extending its domain of permission with the development of the productive forces. In our terminology, the capacity of projective consciousness is historically modified for Marx in terms of its *functionable range*, which increases with technological advancement (that is, development of the forces of production).[16] Such his-

---

[16] Functionable range is to be distinguished from functioning range. A six-year-old child's verbal memory may have the functioning range of 1 to 5 grammatically arranged successive words, but the functionable range of 1 to 1,000 such words (our figures are speculative).

toricization is not in terms of mental content (such as scientific know-how, which belongs to the productive forces themselves; or religion and philosophy, which belong to ideology), but in lower-order terms of under-lying capacity itself and its domain of permission or "functionable range." The following paradigm exem-plifies such historicization of mind.

The rural Indian Hindu has the natural mental capac-ity to master the cognitive moves involved in, say, the technique of butchering and preparing cattle for food. However, this underlying capacity has been "blocked" or rendered unable to function in the appropriate man-ner as the result of the miserable forces of production of the society in which he lives. That is, cattle are virtually the only source of technologically useful nonhuman power available. Consequently, cattle cannot be slaughtered for food without ruinously damaging al-ready meager forces of production. Because, then, of the severe limitations of the latter, and "ideological reflex"—a taboo against killing cattle—is raised. This taboo, in terms of natural capacity, is an historically imposed "limitation" on the functionable range of the Indian's intrinsic capacity of consciousness. Because of this barrier blocking his mental potential, the Indian is unable to operate in the direction of learning the tech-nique in question; the state of his society's productive forces has given rise to cognitive boundaries beyond which he cannot normally go.[17] If, however, the techni-

[17] Marx would not take seriously the claim that this taboo against killing cattle expressed a special Oriental compassion for sentient life. He would point to the same society's egregious unconcern for, say, the suffering of sentient life in the form of women incinerated for surviving their aristocrat husbands, or *sudras* mutilated for defy-ing their lords: sufferings as rigorously prescribed by sacred law as the taboo against killing cattle. Marx specifically refers to the "un-speakable cruelties" of Indian society in *OB*, 397.

cal onslaughts of British imperialism progressively eliminate the material conditions formerly inhibiting the
peasant's ability to use the relevant mental powers, then
the latter's old "frame of mind" on this issue (and many
others) is likely to broaden, and the constitutional capacity to learn the technique will to that extent be freed to
operate in the appropriate way. In such a case, the Indian's inherent mental powers will have increased their
functionable range. Later, the peasant may actually
make operational this mental historicization, and actually learn the technique of killing and preparing cattle
for food. In other words, there are three conceptually
distinct stages to our paradigm:

1. capacity of projective consciousness somehow
*blocked* (retardation)
2. such capacity *released* from the block in question (readiness)
3. new *formulations* of consciousness (learning)

---

However, the question still remains as to Marx's unconcern for
nonhuman nature's suffering under human sway, a suffering that
would seem to increase with technological development (as our
example here is calculated to show).

There can be no doubt that Marx, like most of the Western philosophical tradition, is appallingly indifferent to the agonies of sentient
life subjugated by man. Indeed, his insensitivity here could be
enough to condemn, to a wider view, his entire theory as a brutally
Faustian conceit. On the other hand, his themal concept of man and
nature in "metabolism" supposes *man and nature as one body*, an implication that he persistently emphasizes in his talk of nature as the
"body" and the "organ" of human subjecthood (e.g., *EPM*, 104 and
111; *Pre-C, passim; CI*, 179). Thus his stated ontology is in contradiction to his unstated indifference: for if nature is thus man's body, its
suffering is hardly a matter of unconcern. Marx follows this idea
through to significant extent in his fundamental concern to preserve
natural resources (see pp. 229-30), but not all the way. His underlying ontology of cosmic organism stops short of adequacy, and herein may lie both the greatest promise and the greatest limitation of
his thought.

Marx provides the clue to this underlying structure of his philosophy of mind in an article in the *New York Daily Tribune*, 1852 (*OB*, 397). Here he argues that a "vegetative" mode of production and "miserable" resources bottle up the rural Indian's consciousness: in his own words, "restraining the human mind within the smallest possible compass . . . enslaving . . . depriving it of all grandeur and historical energies." It is largely because British imperialism—despite all its cruelty, greed, and hypocrisy—removes these thought-shackling conditions and allows the mind to range more freely that Marx regards it as a "civilizing force." It is civilizing because it effects a great development in the productive conditions, a change that results in the liberation of mental "energies" that have long been "restrained," "enslaved," and "deprived."

Further examples of this motion of mental barriers imposed or dissolved through the influence of productive conditions are found throughout Marx's work. Thus a "too lavish" natural environment may "keep man in hand, like a child in leading strings," preventing the utilization of his powers—mental and otherwise—by its anesthetizing, Lotusland-like abundance (*CI*, 513).[18] Similarly, conventional productive tasks may contain the mind's powers within a narrow compass—by the "barbarian egotism" of individual plot tillage (*OB*, 397), by the "craft idiocy" of the medieval guild (*PofP*, 125), or by the exclusive "detail tasks" of manufacturing capitalism (*CI*, 363). Advances in the forces of production, on the other hand, can liberate consciousness from its old barriers, "revolutionizing people's minds" (*CI*, 483). Thus the productive forces as they develop and progress from ancient to modern

---

[18] This Protestant-ethic idea, earlier emphasized by Kant and later elaborated by Toynbee, is never seriously pursued by Marx.

forms more and more allow an "imagination freed" from, among other things, mythology (*CPE*, 216). In all such cases, historical modification of man's intrinsic capacity of projective consciousness has to do with erecting and removing blocks (or "limitations") to its functionable range through the influence of developing forces of production.

In other places, Marx puts complementary emphasis on the role of the production relations/economic structure (which "correspond" to the productive forces) in influencing this functionable ambit of man's consciousness. Thus, for example, the capitalist economic form imposes "strict limits" on the normal reach of men's consciousness, on—specifically—their capacity to apprehend the "contradictions" and irrationalities of the obtaining social formation. It is in reference to this limitation of the functionable range of mind by economic form that Marx speaks throughout his work of the narrow "bourgeois horizon" and the "limitations of bourgeois consciousness" (e.g., *CI*, 14 and *18thB*, 11). Even the most outstanding theorists in the capitalist era, he holds, are unable to conceive of an end or alternative to the capitalist order. Their capacity of "projective consciousness" or, as he puts it in physicalist terms, "brain function" (*CI*, 258), has been blocked from operating in the most crucial area of thought of all, consideration of the ubiquitously dehumanizing ruling-class economic system. It is thus Marx's express purpose to break past these cognitive barriers, imposed on the minds of capitalist and working man alike by the massively ensconced economic form, with his new science of human society.[19]

[19] For the precise mechanism whereby the economic structure systematically limits the functionable range of human consciousness, see "Forms of Social Consciousness" (especially pp. 146-55, 167-68).

Marx regards such restrictions by economic form on the functionable range of consciousness as present, in one form or another, in all historical societies. In ancient Greek society, for example, he claims that the obtaining economic order—whose major characteristic was master-slave relations—prevented even a "genius" like Aristotle from comprehending the labor theory of value:

> There was however an important fact which prevented Aristotle from seeing that, to attribute value to commodities, is merely a mode of expressing all labour as equal human labour, and consequently as labour of equal quality. Greek society was founded upon slavery and had, therefore, for its natural basis, the inequality of man and of their labour-powers. The secret of the expression of value . . . cannot be deciphered until the notion of human equality has already acquired the fixity of a popular prejudice. This, however, is possible only in a society in which the great mass of the produce of labour takes the form of commodities, in which, consequently, the dominant relation between man and man is that of owners of commodities. The brilliance of Aristotle's genius is shown by this alone, that he discovered, in the expression of the value of commodities, a relation of equality. The secular conditions of the society in which he lived alone prevented him from discovering what, "in truth" was at the bottom of this equality. (*CI*, 59-60)

Marx holds of course, as we have seen, that this fencing of the mind by economic form is historically defeasible by development of the productive forces. Thus in capitalist society, once the productive forces have "outgrown" their economic form, a scientific and revolutionary theory of society (such as Marx's) becomes capable of conception. In other words, although the economic order imposes certain limits on the "functionable range" of human consciousness in any historical era, these limits are eventually subvertible by the more primary influence of the forces of production (see Chapter 8). [20]

Now in this whole process of various barriers being imposed on and removed from men's inherent powers of consciousness by the influence of productive forces and relations lies much of the substance of Marx's famous remark that men's "social existence determines their consciousness." That is, the functionable range of consciousness is in all historical societies constrained within some bounds (and in this sense "determined") by the technical and economic conditions within which they live. The latter provide the material *frames of reference* to which men's mental powers are more or less confined. The cognitive barriers involved here remain, however, quite consistent with the human mind's raising, and execution of, creative projects. Such barriers simply restrain projective consciousness within certain limitations of range; Marx is not proposing here, as many presume, a mechanistic concept of mind.

[20] We can infer from all this how it is that Marx apprehends a collective outlook arising in the advanced stages of human history. As society's productive forces more and more require and enable people's material cooperation, and as its ownership is correspondingly and necessarily socialized (Chapter 8), the various economic blocks to human awareness confining it within the bounds of self-interest are progressively dissolved, and the functionable range of the human mind thereby opened toward the full scope of communist consciousness: "The communists do not put egoism against self-sacrifice or self-sacrifice against egotism.—On the contrary, they demonstrate the material basis engendering it [this conflict] with which it disappears of itself" (*GID*, 266-67).

Having furnished an outline of how Marx mainly
construes the essential capacity of human nature—"projective consciousness"—undergoing historical modification, we now briefly consider how he construes the
"bodily instruments" themselves—the limbs, organs,
and senses—undergoing such modification. About all
Marx ever says in this respect is in the *Economic and
Philosophical Manuscripts* (*EPM*, 108-109). Here he talks
about a human "sense" being in certain material conditions "a restricted (or 'caught up') sense," and we can
see here the clear homologue to his idea of consciousness being "restrained within a compass." In both cases,
there is the underlying idea of a functionable range to
natural capacity, whose ambit defines the latter's main
form of historical modification. We judge that this line
of thought shows the way to an illuminating account of
the historical modification of man's "bodily instruments": the organs, the senses, and limbs increasing
their functionable range with the development of the
productive forces. However, in accordance with Marx's
reticence, we will not pursue this direction of inquiry
further.[21] Instead, we report the four principles underlying his description of all historical modification of the
capacities of human nature. Together, these principles

[21] Marshall McLuhan partially performs this pursuit for us in *The
Gutenberg Galaxy: The Making of Typographical Man* (Toronto, 1964)
and *Understandia Media: The Extensions of Man* (New York, 1966).
However, McLuhan, who derives Marx's idea here by way of his
mentor H. A. Innis (e.g., *Empire and Communications*, London,
1950), fails to sustain Marx's concept of a progressive broadening of
sentient range through productive force development: conceiving,
instead, man's new technological extensions as alternatives to old
ones. Thus, for example, he conceives electronic media as displacing
print media, though they obviously do not. It is, we think, from this
underlying and erroneous idea of displacement rather than conjunction that the exaggeration and incoherences of McLuhan's judgment
derive.

constitute the general structure of what might be called Marx's philosophical anthropology:

1. The human natural capacity, X, is common to the members of all historical societies (*potential*);

2. X is confined within a certain "functionable range" through the influence of technical and economic conditions (*blocked potential* or *retardation*);

3. X is to some definite extent released from its former "functionable range" through the influence of technical and economic conditions (*released potential* or *readiness*);

4. X, now freed in the above respect, can manifest itself in some new, definite competence (as determinate historical *skill*, to be distinguished from mere potential or capacity.

(1), (2), and (3) refer to the domain of human nature itself; while (4), of course, is outside this domain as, say, a definite labor-power ability (that is, part of the productive forces). As far as the "historical modification" of human nature goes, it is construed in terms of (2) and (3): with (1) belonging to the sphere of human nature "in general." Principles (2) and (3), in short, provide the essential logic of Marx's idea of the historical modification of the capacities of human nature.

Marx's account of man's nature as "historically modified," however, is in terms of needs as well as capacities. Here as well, his remarks are cursory and scattered. But a similar general pattern emerges: namely, that the *scope* of needs—paralleling the functionable range of capacities—expands with the development of the forces of production. As Marx says, "The scope [*Umfang*] of man's so-called necessary needs, as also the mode of satisfying them, is itself the product of historical development and depends there-

fore to a great extent on the degree of civilization of a
country" (*CI*, 171).[22] In this passage from *Capital*,
Marx alludes to the "degree of civilization of a country"
as the factor upon which the extending compass of
needs depends. Elsewhere he is more explicit: "Needs,
poor in the original, only develop with the productive
forces."

How Marx sees men's needs as amplifying their scope
with the development of the productive forces is as follows. The specific objects of such needs extend their
range in accordance with the growth of the production
system that supplies them: "The object of a need is not
an object in general, but a specific object . . . whose
specificity is imposed by production itself" (*G*, 92).
Marx proffers an example here. The need for food is, in
general, always a need for food ("hunger is hunger");
but its specific object broadens its scope from the very
simple diet of the "savage" to the much more extensive
fare of the modern European, *pari passu* with the development of the productive forces of the society in question. That is, historical modification of the need for
food is, in terms of the scope of its need-object, widen-
ing as the productive forces become more and more
fecund in their material yield. It is essentially in this
sense that for Marx "production establishes the need of
the consumer," not only in the case of the need for food
but, where appropriate, all other needs as well. In other
words, men's needs and men's productive forces are in
dialectical relationship with one another. Needs incite
production: "No production without a need" (*G*, 92).
But production, in turn, establishes for need its determinate object, in the direction of a progressively wider

[22] We have changed the English rendering of *Umfang* here from
"number and extent" in the standard translation to the more accurate
"scope" (that is, range).

compass, as a society's technology historically advances. In this way, human nature is "historically modified," while itself impelling that which modifies it.

Given this general schema of historical modification of human natural needs—which is neatly analogous in principle to Marx's concept of the historical modification of human natural capacities—we are now in a position to identify Marx's stance on such questions as standards of living and needs versus wants:

1. Marx consistently emphasizes the social dimension of need-object determination. Need-objects always increase their scope in step with the productive forces of the society that makes them. That is, need-objects always comply with a certain social standard. Hence, Marx says, a person feels "uncomfortable, dissatisfied and cramped" in a home that is "relatively small" compared to the homes in the surrounding society, even though the home in question is adequate in other respects (WLC, 56 ff.).[23] Marx, it is clear, has no sympathy for ascetic renunciation of the fruits of a society's productive development. Indeed, he regards any call for such renunciation as a pious collaboration with ruling-class interests.

2. Although Marx does not directly give any criteria

[23] How does this apply to a Marxian need for an activity as distinct from a thing? Here too, in Marx's schema, it is the scope of the need-object in question that historically is modified. For example, the savage's need for "variety" of pursuit, or for "aesthetic stimulation" is far narrower in its scope than a modern European's. It is on this account that a Marxian explanation for, say, the debilitating boredom of the modern European in a savage environment can be neatly adduced. More important, it is because of this broadening scope of need-object involved in man's need-growth that Marx atypically endorses the latter. For in his view, need-growth thereby increases the range of man's ontic engagement, thereby connects his intentionality and his action to more and more of the world, thereby universalizes him.

whereby historically modified needs can be distinguished from the "depraved fancies," "morbid appetites," and so on, that spring up most of all with
capitalist production—that is, more generally put,
criteria whereby needs can be distinguished from
wants—his writings would seem clearly to yield these
two simple principles of distinction:

a. The "object" of a need is, or is useful for producing, one or other of the need "objects" cata-
logued earlier (that is, food, habitation, clothing,
clean air and surroundings, and so on); whereas the
object of a want (such as "lust for capital," "caprice
of fashion," and so on) is not.

b. A need cannot require what is in excess of the
established social standard (that is, "luxury"),
whereas a want can.[24]

3. The historically modifying influence of production
relations/economic structure on men's needs has not
been treated above because Marx himself regards any
impact it has on human motivation to be a matter of
stirring mere wants—"depraved fancies," "caprices,"
"morbid appetites"—and not needs in his sense at all.
Hence in the case of a capitalist economic order, its
major impact on human motivation is with respect to
encouraging an "unnatural greed" for capital, which
greed is polemically heralded by Marx over and over
again from his earliest to his latest works. In no case—
whether he is talking of dominating this "lust for capi-

---

[24] The corollary of this is that, given qualification under (a), anything that does not exceed the established social standard is the object
of a genuine need. For example, men need mansions if that is the social standard (*WLC*, 56 ff.). This allowance by Marx of unlimited
human need-growth might cause a Diogenes or a Siddhartha to pale,
but it is in keeping with the absolute activism and anthropocentrism
of his vision.

tal" or the more minor swarm of "inhuman, refined, unnatural and imaginary appetites" (*EPM*, 116) that accompany the former—does Marx construe the economic order as promoting need as he conceives it. It is always in terms of non-need cravings of some sort that he talks of such influence. Hence we have here a further, striking symmetry between Marx's schemas of historical modification of human-natural capacity and human-natural need. That is, Marx construes *motivation by mere wants as constituting historically modifying blocks to men's motivation by intrinsic needs*, blocks that are analogous in principle to those retarding limits placed on the functionable range of man's capacities.[25]

4. As needs are historically modified in the direction of increased scope, they necessitate more production to meet them. Hence in this sense, the historicization of needs intensifies the history-old conflict between the "mundane" needs of man's nature and the "essential" need for material self-realization. That is, inasmuch as more production is necessitated by the greater scope of "mundane" needs, just so far is man's "essential" need to work constrained to fulfill itself in a stipulated or unfree way; for example, man must work at food-production and not some other thing of his own choosing. Thus Marx says, "with civilized man's development this realm of physical necessity expands as a result of his wants [read 'needs']." But, Marx immediately adds, "at the same time, the forces of production which

[25] Thus, men's needs for nourishing food, and so forth, are blocked from function by their wants for advertised pasties, and so forth.

We suggest that Herbert Marcuse is, in a different way, after the same point with his famous concern that advanced capitalism's successful creation of artificial wants may have irredeemably bound workers' motivation to its preservation (*One Dimensional Man*, Boston, 1970).

satisfy these wants [read 'needs'] also increase (*CIII*, 820)." So even though the "realm of necessity expands" with the historization of needs, the forces of production also "expand," and thereby one of the fundamental contradictions of human history—between the demands of material survival and the need for free self-realization—is continuously meliorated by technological advance (if also, less so, promoted by it).[26]

Progressively, Marx believes, the forces of production—with an increasingly automated content and planned utilization—will reduce the necessary working day and, correspondingly, increase the free day, until men dwell in a "realm of freedom" where "human energy becomes an end-in-itself" (*CIII*, 820; G, 488). This "realm of freedom" is beyond "the realm of necessity," beyond the dictate of "mundane" needs altogether. And as such, "it is worthy of human nature."

Man only achieves his fully human status for Marx, then, to the extent that the requirements of his historicized needs (that is, his nonessence needs) cease to command and instrumentalize his work. For him, all such needs are to be materially "conquered," to be divested of their imperiousness by the growth of technology. Change in material circumstances thus truly gives rise to a new man who (in Hegelian phrase) "contains within his present all the moments of his past," who remains with all his historically amplified needs, while

---

[26] The possibility that technological advance expands the realm of necessity more than it contracts it—by requiring more labor-time to meet the needs it develops than labor-time it sets free by labor-saving device—never occurs to Marx. Herein lies an unseen potential contradiction in his theory whose importance cannot easily be overestimated. At stake is his most central claim, that technological growth and human liberation proceed hand in hand. See the concluding section of Chapter 8 for resolution of this problem.

at the same time transcending them in liberated activity by virtue of automated, communist forces of production that provide his material base, his platform of unfettered subjecthood.

A final word here. Marx's overall concept of human nature gives the clue both to his persistent normative remarks in a putatively positivist corpus and to the moral indignation he —an apparent despiser of all moral positioning—continually evinces. The entire normative and moral content of Marx's work (and, despite the objections of his orthodox apologists, there is such content in abundance) is based on a hidden first, major ethical premise, which is succinctly this: *Men ought to materially realize themselves.*

Given that Marx sees the nature of man as constituted by the many historical capacities and needs we have outlined, this ethical premise systematically translates into the comprehensive ethical doctrine that anything that promotes or interferes with the material realization of such needs and capacities is good, or bad, respectively. Hence, whenever Marx approves, blames, ascribes duties, or even, on occasion, talks of the "necessity" of revolution, it is because at the bottom of his remarks there stands this underlying ethical imperative, and his positive concept of human nature that gives it flesh.[27]

[27] Marx's ethical imperative is, we also propose, a higher-order generalization of his basic descriptive "law" of technological determinism: thus, an ethical imperative whose "ought" turns out, in the end, to be "is." We examine this arresting metaposition of his theory in the closing pages of our study.

# 2

## Technology

The forces of production are motivated and enabled by, respectively, the needs and capacities of human nature. Their function of embodying or yielding use-value presupposes human need, both as inciter and beneficiary. And their intelligent construction presupposes human capacity, both mental and physical. They are in these ways, for Marx, the *objectifications of human nature*.[1]

Marx never directly defines a "force of production," and he uses a number of terms, such as "conditions of production," "instruments of production," and "means of production," which make it difficult to know whether he intended the formulation in question as a covering term or as one more restricted in meaning (for instance, just labor-power and tools). We will assume —there being no persuasive textual evidence to the contrary—that he intends it as a covering term.

Considering all that Marx says on forces of production, and construing the term in its covering sense, an adequate definition is:

[1] Marx also uses the term "correspond" for the relationship between human nature and productive forces (*EPM*, 109). We emphasize this. "Correspond" (*entsprechen*) is the universal connector term in his theory. That is, implicitly or explicitly, every factor's relationship with every other factor is conceived by Marx as one of "correspondence," except in prerevolutionary or revolutionary periods, when these factors are said to be in multiple "contradiction." Indeed, these sets of "correspondences" and "contradictions" together constitute the relational frame of Marx's entire thought, as we will increasingly discern.

*A force of production is anything that is or can be used to make a material use-value.*[2]

Obvious candidates for forces of production are, then, tools (from hand implements to machines), human labor-power (from manual to scientific), and natural resources (from coal deposits to fish). However, a more systematic and detailed account is required here, and we shall give one presently. Before doing so, it is important to explain the force of the "is or can be used" predication in the above definition. The reason we employ it is to ensure that the definition picks up not only any force of production that is in fact used to make material use-value, but any force that can in fact be so used, but is not on sheerly nontechnological account: that is, those forces of production—for example, unemployed labor-power and unused factory capacities—that are impeded from present use merely by economic obstacles, such as, in capitalism, to use the fashionable euphemisms of the economists, by insufficient "effective demand" or "profit opportunity." These unused forces of production are, for Marx, no less forces of production because of such extrinsic impediment. They thoroughly qualify as forces of production because their immediate utilization for making material use-value is

[2] For Marx's most schematic analysis of productive forces, see *CI*, 177 ff.

Marx counts anything material that anyone wants as a use-value, even pyramids (*G*, 769). However, productive forces used to make use-values like pyramids, which merely serve the fancies of the ruling class, can be used to make use-values like storage houses and dwelling places, which serve the needs of society's membership as a whole. That productive forces are in fact used in the former way rather than the latter is, in Marx's analysis, a matter of ownership impediment, not a matter of the nature of the productive forces themselves. (See the concluding section of this chapter as well as Chapter 8 for development of this pivotal point of Marx's theory.)

frustrated solely by nontechnical barriers raised by the ownership relations of the capitalist economic structure: so, that they are not so used, but are (to use Marx's phraseology) "wasted," "destroyed," "suppressed" by virtue of economic "fetters" does not one whit detract from their status as forces of production. Furthermore, because the ground and index of all social revolutionary possibility is the emergence and growth of just these forces of production that can be used to make material use-value but are not, entirely on account of economic impediments, it is especially important to include such forces in any delineation of Marx's general concept that pretends to adequacy. In short, the "is or can" wording of our definition of the forces of production is required by the concern, basic to Marx's theory, with usable but unused technological powers.

Another point that should be made about our definition of forces of production is that it meets those many objections that hold this category to be indistinguishable from others in Marx's theoretical framework. That is, our definition effectively rules out all human-natural, economic, superstructural, or ideological phenomena from its domain of reference. Thus, a natural capacity or need (as opposed to a definite productive capability), an ownership relation (as opposed to a technological relation), a superstructural law (as opposed to a physical law), an ideological formulation (as opposed to a practical-science formulation)—of none of these may it properly be said that it "is or can be used to make a material use-value." None qualifies, therefore, as a productive force. One or another may indeed be necessary conditions of some sort for forces of production to arise (such as natural capacity and need) or—with the rest—to be appropriated, exchanged, socially apportioned, justified, or in some way appropriately contextualized; and one or other may be used to make something of some sort. But none is or can actually be used to make a material use-value.[3] In this way, then, the definition above secures the required conceptual distinctness of Marx's category of forces of production, and in so doing answers those critics who have claimed its impossible amorphousness.

With Marx's general concept of productive forces clear, we proceed to specific elaboration.

There are for Marx two basic classes of productive force:

1. labor-power (*Arbeitskraft*)
2. means of production (*Produktionsmittel*).

The first constitutes the "subjective factor" of production and the second constitutes the "objective factor." The second, it should be noted, is often further distinguished into natural and man-made means of production, with these latter sometimes being further subdivided into "general conditions" of production (transportation and communication systems),[4] and "instruments" of production (tools and machines). But, in

---

[3] We might cast this point in other terms. Incentives, or bosses, are often conceived as indispensable to production, and even as themselves productive forces. But neither of them is, in fact, a productive force. Incentives may *motivate* people to produce, and bosses may *force* them to produce, but neither *enables* them to produce. Anything, on the other hand, that enables us to produce—tools, education, natural materials, or whatever—is a productive force.

[4] These "general conditions" of production—transportation and communication systems—may at first seem to fail to meet our definition of productive forces as "anything that is or can be used to make a material use-value." But Marx regarded changing the place of something as changing its material use-value: "Here a material change is effected in the object of labour—a spatial change, a change of place—. Its spatial existence is altered and along with this goes a change in its use-value, since the location of this use-value is changed" (*S-V I*, 399). Since to change something from use-value A to use-value B is, clearly, to be used to make use-value B, transportation and communication systems are, in fact, subsumed by our definition.

general, *Produktionsmittel* is the category for nonhuman productive forces, whereas *Arbeitskraft* is the category for all human productive forces. In both cases, the force in question is something that is or can be used to make a material use-value of product—whether it be a human skill, on the one hand, or a natural resource, a public utility, or a technological instrument on the other (see *CI*, 177 ff. and 384).

Of these various sorts of productive force, the primary—because all others are for Marx its products— is labor-power.[5] Marx defines labor-power in *Capital* as "the aggregate of those mental and physical capabilities [*Fahigkeiten*] existing in a human being, which he exercises whenever he produces a use-value of any description" (*CI*, 167). There are a number of points that should be made clear about this characterization of labor-power:

1. "Capabilities" of labor-power are to be distinguished from "capacities" of human nature. The difference between these two is that a capability is the ability to perform a specific work task, whereas a capacity is not: the former are only possible because of the prior existence of the latter (for example, the technical capability of designing bridges presupposes the prior existence of the natural capacity to think), but are distinct from them because any such capacity requires some sort of training or education before it is a labor-power capability (*CI*, 172).

2. Marx's use of the adjective phrase "mental and physical" before "capabilities" should not mislead us

---

[5] Marx regards even natural materials as "products" of labor-power insofar as they are shot through with past labor (such as fertilized land, caught fish, and extracted mineral deposits). His general view that all productive forces are thus products of labor-power is the core of his "labor theory of value," though it does not entail the claims of this theory that trouble economists.

into supposing that he conceives of mental and physical capabilities as different types of competence. On the contrary, there can be for Marx no purely physical labor-power abilities because the latter always involve, technically, rule-governed activities, that is, activities requiring some form of mental mediation. And there can be no purely mental labor-power competence because the latter must terminate in some physical performance if they are to be usable in material production. In other words, the "mental and physical capabilities" of labor-power are forms of *know-how*, involving both mental and physical content in any given case.

3. The formal content of such labor-power "know-how" is practical scientific knowledge, which is for this reason referred to by Marx as the "most solid form of human wealth" (G, 540). This point deserves special emphasis inasmuch as it demonstrates that Marx did not—contrary to wide interpretation—place technological science in the sphere of "ideology," but seated it at the very core of the productive forces. Unlike the ideas of philosophy, religion, politics, and so on, the ideas of practical science very much are or can be used to make material use-values. Indeed, such science is for Marx the force of production *par excellence* in all historical eras, especially the capitalist. And because of its cardinal status as a force of production in all eras, its effective ownership—by Egyptian priesthood or modern business—provides economic-power leverage of the first order: a fact that Marx emphasizes over and over again in his work (e.g., *CI*, 361, 509 ff.).

4. There are two different types of human labor-power—unskilled and skilled. Unskilled labor-power is labor-power that "apart from any special development exists in the organism of every ordinary individual of a society" (*CI*, 44). Exactly what set of capabilities is in-

volved in such unskilled labor-power depends on the
society in question and its level of civilization; but "in a
particular society it is given." Such a set of capabilities
would be the abilities to perform a standard range of
technically useful operations considered "normal" to
the society in question—for example, in present society,
knowing how to read, count, use myriad everyday tools
from shoelaces to telephones, and so on.[6] On the other
hand, skilled labor-power is "multiplied" unskilled
labor-power: that is, labor power that involves more in-
tensive work capabilities than the social standard, "a
given quantity of skilled being equal to a greater quantity of simple labour."[7]

5. Labor-power that "produces a use-value of any description" includes "such labour as produces commodities or directly produces, trains, develops, maintains or reproduces labour-power itself" (*S-V I*, 167).
Such productive labor-power strikingly includes medi-

[6] This point is one we are apt to overlook from habit. But it is
important. Through it, the window is opened to understanding
much of the substance of Marx's concept of "civilization."

[7] Marx's concept of skilled labor-power as a multiple of unskilled
labor-power gives rise to problems of distributive inequality in the
"transitional stage" of socialism, where each is paid "according to
his work," that is, a skilled worker is paid x times more than an unskilled worker.

One of the fundamental differences, and antagonisms, between
the Communist Party of the Soviet Union and the Communist Party
of the People's Republic of China has arisen on this very pont. That
is, the former endorses, and amplifies, the wage-differential system
prescribed by Marx for the "transitional stage" of socialism; whereas
the latter endorses it too, but, according to the former, practices in
fact a "leveller" policy of "distribution according to mouth." In
consequence, China denounces the Communist Party of the Soviet
Union as "capitalist roaders"; while the Communist Party of the
Soviet Union counterdenounces the Communist Party of China as
"antiproletarian." For one of the most revealing accounts of this
great schism, see Lev Delyusin's *The Socio-Political Essence of Maoism*
(Moscow, 1976), pp. 32, 52-60, 80-81. Our sympathy on this issue,
*contra* Marx, lies decisively on the side of China.

cal and educational labor-power (e.g., G, 765 and 774). Just as labor-power that services or adapts machines must be counted as productive, so labor-power that maintains (medical) and develops or trains (educational) human labor-power must count as productive. Indeed, Marx's passage here strictly implies, as he says explicitly elsewhere, that childbearing capabilities also count as productive, inasmuch as they are materially necessary to "produce" and "reproduce" labor-power.[8]

It is crucial here to appreciate fully this embracing referential range of Marx's concept of productive labor-power, not only to achieve more adequate understanding, but—of great contemporary relevance—to gain the conceptual underpinning for Marxian explanations of such currently familiar phenomena as school and university upheavals (an instance of the forces of production—educational labor-power and its "natural resource" student material—"bursting" the relations of production?),[9] health big-business (doctors' monopoly

[8] Though Marx's concept of labor-power thus explicitly subsumes much of woman's traditional role in society's process of material production, it implicitly sumsumes still more. For most of the great range of domestic tasks clearly qualifies as "materially necessary to produce and reproduce labor-power," such as transportation, preparation of food and clothing, and maintenance of dwelling place, for both present and future labor-power. Furthermore, Marx's overall concept of productive force also implicitly subsumes the role of the young in society's process of material production process: for the young are both the raw material and, in part, the trainers and developers of productive labor power, namely, their own.

In this way, as elsewhere, the conceptual framework of Marx's theory outreaches its specific claims, with very substantial and fecund implications. This is a hallmark of good theory, but corresponding important adjustments in Marx's conceptions of the economic structure, the state, and ideology need to be made here in consequence. We will parenthetically propose such adjustments in Chapters 3, 4, and 5.

[9] For an account of the world-wide student revolt of 1968 in these terms, see our "The Student Revolt: Marxism in a New Dimen-

ownership of medical labor-power and special facilities
as qualification for ruling-class status?), and women's
liberation (another instance of the forces of production—here "reproductive" and "maintenance" labor-
power—"bursting" relations of production "fetters"?).

6. Means of subsistence for labor-power are forces of
production in the same way that fuel and storage facilities for machinery are forces of production (*CI*, 527).
But, as we have earlier suggested, such means of subsistence for labor-power undergo historical development;
or, otherwise put, the needs of labor-power that they
meet undergo historical development. Hence insofar as
the means of subsistence for labor-power forces of
production grow with "the degree of civilization of a
country" (*CI*, 171), it is possible—contrary to popular
criticisms of Marx—for labor-power to suffer "immiserization" even as its absolute consumption of means of
subsistence increases.[10]

sion," *Commentator*, XIII, no. 11 (November 1969), 17-23. It is
worthwhile schematising here the structure of a primary argument
in this connection:

i. knowing how to read and write are forces of production; that is,
these skills are or can be used to make material use-values;

ii. contemporary technology requires more and more workers
with these skills, at higher and higher stages of development;

iii. more and more people knowing how to read and write, at
higher and higher stages of development, enables more and more
people, at higher and higher stages of development, to understand
and struggle against ruling-class relations of production.

As to the social "laws" that determine the success or failure of any
such struggle, see our final chapter, "Technological Determinism."

[10] It has, of course, been a favorite claim of critics of Marx that his
theory is obviously mistaken because his repeated prediction of
worker immiserization has not in fact taken place—a claim that has
usually drawn for its only support upon the rising real wages of
workers since Marx's original projection. Such a rebuttal, typically,
is beside the point. Marx emphasizes that whether the worker's
"payment be high or low," his "lot must grow worse" (*CI*, 645),

Having elaborated Marx's concept of labor-power, we now briefly consider the "objective factor" of production: namely, the man-made and natural means of production. As has already been indicated, the former are of two main types—"general conditions" of production (that is, transportation and communication systems), and "instruments" of production (that is, tools, including machines). With the latter, natural means of production—or, in current terminology, "natural resources"—Marx proffers no such division into type. But the following principles hold for both these main sorts of "objective" productive force:

1. Both are seen by Marx as *external organs* of man. Thus of natural resources—indeed, of the whole of Nature—Marx says, "Thus Nature becomes one of the organs of man's activity, one that he annexes to his own bodily organs, adding stature to himself in spite of the bible" (*CI*, 179). And thus of the man-made instruments of production—tools in the broadest sense—Marx invokes the same picture:

Darwin has interested us in the history of Nature's Technology i.e. in the formation of the organs of plants and animals, which organs serve as instruments of production for sustaining life. Does not the history of the productive organs of man, of organs that are the material basis of all social organization, deserve equal attention? (*CI*, 372).

Elsewhere Marx talks of these forces of production as

---

not just because his means of subsistence fail to keep pace with historical development, but—more fundamentally—because the capitalist class owns a greater and greater share of the total material resources of society (by accumulation) and thus, the working class relatively less and less (see below, p. 78).

the "objective body of man's subjecthood" (*Pre-C*, 69) and as "a prolongation of his body" (*Pre-C*, 89). In other words, he persistently identifies natural and constructed forces of production as organic extensions of man, as constituents of human subjecthood. From this basic principle of his materialist ontology, a number of things follow:

i. Since labor-power is for Marx the explicit content of man's subjecthood, the relationship between man and his "external organs" of tools and natural resources is at the same time—on an explicit level—the relationship between labor-power and such "external organs." Hence in the general connection of man to his means of production, we can discern at the same time the more specific technological connection of the "subjective factor" (labor-power) to the "objective factor" (tools and natural resources) of production. This explains why Marx tends to construe man's relationship with his "objective" world in terms of productive forces alone (that is, with no mention of human nature).

ii. Inasmuch as Marx construes the objective means of production of a society as the "external organs" of man, private-property appropriation of these means of production is for him, correspondingly, the dismemberment of those whose "external organs" are cut off by such exclusive appropriation: a kind of ongoing legitimized mutilation of men's objective lives.[11] In this tearing asunder of the social body by private ownership lies, perhaps, the ultimate ground of Marx's concern to eradicate the capitalist order.

iii. Insofar as Nature is an "organ" of man, it pos-

---

[11] Bertell Ollman in personal correspondence has credited this point with striking to "the core of Marx's theory of alienation." For an extended "internal relations" interpretation of Marx's theory of alienation, see Ollman's original and thoughtful study, *Alienation: Marx's Conception of Man in Capitalist Society* (Cambridge, 1972).

sesses no independent value and is wholly a human instrumentality. Marx's position is thereby one of absolute anthropocentrism, with the totality of nonhuman
life and matter on earth conceived as a real or potential
human adjunct.[12]

2. Forces of production—"objective" and "subjective"—are "accumulated" throughout history. That
is, each generation retains and builds upon the productive achievements of the last, to pass onto the next, in a
cumulative gift from the past to the present (SC, 41).[13]
No principle is more emphatically and repeatedly
treated by Marx. One might even claim that in this
principle lies the nub of his "historical materialist" doctrine, as the phrase itself suggests. Because the productive forces are accumulated from one generation to the
next:

i. History exhibits progress of a technological sort
and, from this, other sorts of progress as well (hence
Marx's so-called "illusion of progress").

[12] On the one hand, this position radically devalues Nature by depriving it of any claim to independence from man's use. On the
other hand, it radically revalues Nature by conceiving it at the same
time as man's very body (see also EPM, 104 and 111).

In all, Marx germinally demystifies the ageless concept of Cosmic
Person into historical materialist form. Nature and man are "one
substance," whose head is mankind.

[13] Population growth is a fundamental component and stimulus of
this cumulative growth of productive forces—the more people, the
more labor-power; the more needs, the more productive forces required to meet them (G, 760, 769, 771). Marx therefore takes a fron-
tal stand against Malthusian pessimism about population increase,
regarding it as "a slander against the human race." On the other
hand, his position requires that population, as the basic factor of
production and consumption, be regulated by conscious social plan.
He holds, indeed, that it is because the capitalist order cannot thus
consciously regulate man's material reproduction process that its
supercession is historically necessary.

Today we might add that a society more than reproduces its numbers in direct proportion to the impoverishment of its masses.

ii. Men "are not free to choose their productive forces" because each of them is always born into, and depends for his survival on, a technology that is already more or less formed (hence Marx's so-called "denial of free will").

· iii. The present always contains, in a Hegelian phrase, the "moments of its past" and can only be fully understood in terms of this past (hence Marx's so-called tyrannical idea of "historicism").

iv. Men must or "are obliged to" preserve their forces of production "in order that they may not be deprived of the result attained and forfeit the fruits of civilization" (*SC*, 41): the law-like ground of Marx's claim of "inevitable revolution" against the counter-productive structure of mature capitalist society. [14]

Though the forces of production must be conceived as distinct from, and the material base of, the economic structure, they are by no means unaffected by the latter. Not only does the economic structure dialectically relate to the productive forces as both "stimulus" (for instance, the profit-seeking "law of motion" of capital motivates ever more production) [15] and "fetter" (for in-

[14] Marx here uses the ethical term "obliged" rather than the nomological term "necessitated" to characterize this basic law of his entire theory that a society always preserves its stage of development of productive forces (see pp. 233 ff.). His exchange of term here is not a blunder, however. As we observed at the close of our first chapter, and as we demonstrate at the end of our last, Marx's fundamental ethical imperative is but a higher-order generalization of his fundamental historical law.

[15] Because the capitalist order has contributed so substantially to the development of productive forces, Marx, who subverts here the ubiquitous claim that he is one-sided in his judgment of this order, says: "The bourgeoisie, during its rule of scarce one hundred years, has created more massive and more colossal productive forces than all preceding generations together. —It has been the first to really show what man's activity can bring about" (*CM*, 49 and 51).

stance, the feudal relations of production bind production within "fixed, fast-frozen" limits), but it also importantly distorts the forces of production in intrinsic function and mode of operation, rendering them "destructive forces" (*GID*, 76). That is:

1. It stipulates the material use-values that it is the function of the productive forces to make; for instance, in capitalism, only those use-values that sustain or increase profit for the capitalists, such as cosmetics and weapons.

2. It stipulates the mode of operation of the productive forces; for instance, in capitalism, only such modes of operation that again, sustain or increase profit for capitalists; such as "riveted" division of labor and resource exhaustion.

Marx frequently and passionately observes such distorting effects on the products and procedures of the productive forces by the requirements of the economic structure, though the full implications of such distortions seem not altogether appreciated by him.[16] But in any case, his concern about the distortion by economic influences of the *use-values* made by the productive forces can be distinguished into two kinds:

[16] That the productive forces could become so deformed in these aspects that they are no longer capable of providing the material grounds for and propulsion toward a revolutionary communist society (as opposed to mere centralization of control), never seems seriously to occur to Marx. Though we shall not pursue this point further, it may undermine Marx's projection of the progressive course of human history. When one considers the increasing tendency of capitalist productive forces to produce the "uses-values" of killing-machinery and status commodities, and to apply the methods of resource exhaustion-pollution, exclusive detail-tasks, and administrative policing, it is not easy to see how such distorted productive forces are capable of "bursting" anything but our hearts. From a Marxian standpoint, however, the very force of such considerations argues for the "inevitability" of social transformation (see Chapter 8).

i. Their content is trivialized or in some other way "depraved"; for example, "the murderous, meaningless caprices of fashion" (*CI*, 494).

ii. Their quality is debased; for example, adulterated foodstuffs, inferior dwellings, and unsafe factories.

On the other hand, of the distortions by economic influences of the *mode of operation* of the productive forces, his concern is of three kinds:

i. They are destructive of labor-power: "murdering," "exhausting," "riveting," "brutalizing," and otherwise detracting from its productive potential.

ii. They are destructive of natural resources: "sapping," "despoiling," "polluting," and otherwise destroying the very elements themselves, such as the soil (*CI*, 507).

iii. They are inefficiently used: social coordination of productive forces is "anarchic," labor-power is squandered in "hordes of unproductive workers" (*S-V I, passim*), and outright unemployment of both "subjective" and "objective" factors of production is continuous and, periodically, critical.

The importance of these distortions of the productive forces by the economic structure deserves further emphasis here because it shows the critical force that Marx's analysis has against some fashionable positions of modern social thought. The positions in question are these: 1. advanced technology is the cause of uncontrolled growth; 2. advanced technology requires person-imprisoning division of labor; and 3. advanced technology necessitates hierarchy. To take these in turn, it is quite clear that under a Marxian account, technology is in itself responsible for none of these problems:

1. Uncontrolled growth is a function of the "laws of motion" of capital that systematically enjoin its own self-amplification (that is, profit) without cessation. It is

this economic—not technological—imperative that drives technology in the direction of "uncontrolled growth." Hence, Marx's concern to replace production for private profit by production according to social plan.

2. Person-imprisoning division of labor is a function of the economic structure, which requires the technologically unnecessary exclusive confinement of individuals to places of production. That is, the technological necessity to position labor-power x in place y for $t_1$ . . . . $t_n$—which could be fulfilled in other ways, such as taking turns—is economically constrained to be, in fact, the riveting of just this person to just this job for all of $t_1$ . . . . $t_n$. Hence Marx's concern to supplant capitalism's "fixing" of labor to detail-functions by socialism's "many-sided" alternation of places of production.

3. The necessity of hierarchy is nontechnological, insofar as it cannot properly be said of any component of hierarchy that it "is or can be used to make a material use-value," that is, that it is productively necessary.[17] On the other hand, there is a "necessity of hierarchy" insofar as the economic structure is to be successfully secured and maintained.

We now propose a schematic overview. For Marx, the forces of production, in clear distinction from the economic form within which they are constrained, con-

---

[17] Otherwise put, no technological requirement—including productive-force coordination—implies a ranking or grading of the producers into levels of command. Though it is a common mistake to assume, for example, that "managers" are a technological necessity for all modern forms of production, what is a technological necessity is not "managers" at all, but coordination of productive forces, which coordination could be achieved (*has* to be achieved, Marx holds) by worker self-government (see pp. 121n, 226).

stitute the material foundations of all human existence
and expression: "As individuals express their life, so
they are. What they are, therefore, coincides with their
production, both with what they produce and with how
they produce" (*GID*, 32).

1. The productive forces: i. raise men above the animals; ii. answer to and shape the objects of human
needs; iii. actualize and extend human capacities (Chapter 1).

2. The productive forces: i. set limits to, and ultimately subvert, the economic order; and ii. inform the
legal and political superstructure and ideology with
their content (Chapter 8).

3. The productive forces constitute the basic substance of all human knowledge.[18]

[18] Marx's work is thin on epistemological declaration. But where
he does directly define the nature of knowledge (essentially, in the
"Theses on Feuerbach" and, with respect to the formation of social
science concepts, in "The Method of Political Economy," *CPE*,
205-13), he is fascinating and bold. If his position in the theses can be
distilled into a single proposition, it is this: *A conception, x, is knowledge if, and only if, x is used to materially alter the world in accordance with
human needs*. Although from this Marx might be judged a radical
forerunner of the modern activist epistemologies of pragmatism, in-
strumentalism, and even operationalism, our more immediate concern is to point out the striking similarity between his criteria of
knowledge and productive force. In this similarity, indeed, lies one
of the primary metalinks of Marx's thought. We define it thus:
Knowledge is distinguished from productive force in that it is conception, whereas productive force is this (that is, know-how), but
much more too (that is, tools and resources). More interestingly,
knowledge requires enactment of its content to count as knowledge,
whereas productive force can be such even if it is not used, but can
be. Finally, and perhaps most importantly, the object of knowledge
("to materially alter the world in accordance with human needs") is
broader than the object of productive force ("to make a material
use-value") in that it includes the latter but also the revolutionizing
of the economic order itself within which the production of material
use-value takes place. As Marx's "Theses on Feuerbach" makes
clear, this *revolutionaren Tatigkeit* is the highest form of realization of
knowledge.

4. The productive forces progressively: i. conquer the fundamental limitation of natural and social life, scarcity; and ii. correspondingly liberate man from the struggle for survival and, eventually, class conflict itself.

5. The productive forces ever reduce society's necessary labor, and thereby lift "the curse of Adam" from the shoulders of mankind.

6. The productive forces are the moving power and ultimate determiner of human history, inexorably generating a cumulative second creation, a new cosmic order.

Technology is, in a word, the Marxian Providence.

---

In light of these distinctions, we say that the "productive forces are the basic substance of all human knowledge" because: i. it is the former as applied that constitutes the bulk of human knowledge; ii. it is the former as not applied that constitutes the agenda of much human knowledge to come; and iii. it is the former as a whole that provides the determining premise of all knowledge that is achieved through economic revolution.

For how Marx's theory itself goes from scientific ideology to scientific knowledge, see Chapter 5.

# 3

## The Economic Structure

Relations of production, as a totality, constitute the economic structure. The economic structure, in turn, Marx calls the "anatomy," the "essence," the "form," or the "base" of all historical human society.

Although this category of relations of production/ economic structure seems thus the theoretical linchpin of all Marx's analysis, its precise meaning has been a matter of unresolved controversy for more than a century. Marx himself, as with all the basic categories of his *Weltanschauung*, never proffers a definition. And it is difficult to elicit one from his work because his usage is so rich and elliptical at the same time. Despite these difficulties, however, we can obtain a satisfactory characterization.

The first thing that has to be made clear about Marx's concept of the relations of production/economic structure is that he does not mean—contrary to many interpretations—to refer to the technological relations connecting various human and nonhuman forces of production to one another. It is worth illustrating this point with an example. In a modern factory, technological relations are those relations that must obtain between the various instruments and labor-powers in order to set these forces into some sort of productive coherence. Such relations are as integral to this (or any other) productive mechanism as, in the microcosm, linking and organizing mechanical parts are to a machine. Technological relations are, in other words, wholly within the sphere of productive forces and are stipulated by them.[1]

Relations of production, on the other hand, are extratechnical relations akin to property relations, "property relations" being for Marx, as he says in the Preface to *A Contribution to the Critique of Political Economy* and elsewhere, just "a legal expression" for relations of production. They are relations of production, of course, because the ownership they denote is ownership of productive forces. Thus whereas technological relations are the operating connections implicit in the productive forces, relations of production are the proprietary connections between these productive forces and their owners.[2]

The apparent difficulty with distinguishing relations of production from technological relations is that the former seem thereby to be pushed into the domain of the superstructure. That is, we are now confronted with the new problem of distinguishing relations of production from property relations that are part of the legal superstructure.

To advance straight to the point, the saving distinction here lies in the difference between power and right.[3] A relation of production is a relation of a person to a force of production such that he has *the power to use or exploit it and exclude others from doing so*. A cognate property relation, in contrast, is a relation of a person to

[1] Any relation that "is or can be used to make a material use-value" belongs to the productive forces. Technological relations therefore belong to the productive forces.

[2] Technological relations, on the other hand, never involve persons as such, but only labor-powers. Thus the same technological relations obtain on an assembly line, whether the labor-power places are filled by one set of individuals or by n sets of individuals acting in turn (see p. 69).

[3] For the most extended general discussion by Marx of the distinction between power and right, see *GID*, 357 ff. and 394 ff.

a force of production such that he has the *right* to use or
exploit it and exclude others from doing so. Although
the power and the right to employ a force of production
often, and even generally, coincide, frequently they do
not. The army commander, the criminal chieftain, the
upper bureaucrat, the religious leader, the political
strongman, the monopolist, the party machine, and so
on, may all own the power to use or exploit forces of
production and exclude others from doing so, with no
corresponding right. On the other hand, the penniless,
the conquered and intimidated, the legislatively de-
ceived, and so on, may all have the right to use or
exploit forces of production and exclude others from
doing so, with no corresponding power.[4] The two are
quite distinct.

Having secured a definition of relations of production
that, against objections of its impossibility,[5] distinguishes these relations from both technological relations, which belong to the forces of production, and
cognate property relations, which belong to the legal
superstructure, we are in a position to make explicit the
content of this category:

1. A necessary, though not sufficient, material condition of the power to use or exploit forces of production
and exclude others from doing so is superior physical
force invokable by whoever holds such power, whether
it be the armed force of feudal retinue, police or army,
hired thugs, or whatever. Thus Marx says, "In actual
history, it is notorious that conquest, enslavement, robbery, murder, briefly *force*, play the chief part" (*CI*,
714). Those situations where it is not clearly established
who can, in fact, invoke superior physical violence,
who really has the power to exclude others from productive forces, are situations of open conflict of some

[4] See, for example, *GID*, 79-80.    [5] See Introduction, pp. 12-15.

sort, where the historical testing of economic relations takes place (such as a robbery attempt, a civil insurrection, or an international war). But the results of any such "testing" will be such that superior physical force—and not, say, moral or legal right—will decide who secures effective ownership. For example, in disputes between ruling class and working class, "force decides" (*CI*, 235).[6] As in the nonhuman struggle for survival, availability of ascendent might resolve contrary claims to the means of life. Even where the ability to invoke such force does not seem present as a material condition of economic power—for example, with "naturally just" or "tacitly accepted" relations of production—Marx is concerned to strip away the "mask" or *Schein* of such noncoercive consent to reveal either the physical force upon with such effective ownership can call and has called, or the latter's "merely illusory" quality. Hence his disdain for the traditional concepts, entrenched since Plato's Socrates, of social contract, and revolution by reason alone. Effective ownership in virtually all historical situations requires, for Marx, the owner's ability to bring ascendent physical force to bear on the situation, usually the organized violence of the state.

None of the above, though, is meant to suggest that force is said to be always, or even usually, visible. On the contrary, it is for Marx almost always concealed by a superstructural "veil," and may only occasionally need to be openly exerted.[7]

---

[6] Marx also says, "Indeed is it at all surprising that a society founded on the opposition of classes should culminate in brutal contradiction, the shock of body against body, as its final denouement?" (*PofP*, 152).

[7] Constituents of this superstructural "veil" are precisely the traditional concepts of social contract and ratiocinated revolution mentioned above, which philosophers from Plato to Rawls have

Again, none of the above is meant to suggest that invokability of superior physical force is ever claimed by
Marx to be a sufficient condition of establishing or
maintaining relations of production (hence his repeated
denunciation of revolutionary schemes depending on
violence alone). In addition to the required base of technical conditions (Chapter 8), Marx sees superstructural
overlay as always necessary for ownership relations to
persist (Chapters 4 and 5).

2. Because relations of production involve not only
those members of society who have the power to use or
exploit forces of production, but also those who can be
excluded from the same, they are ultimately triadic in
structure—relating men to productive forces by virtue
of their power to exclude other men from them. Thus
effective ownership of forces of production by some always implies corresponding *"alienation"* of all others
from the same productive forces.[8]

---

studiously fabricated in fulfilment of their roles as ideologists (see
Chapter 5).

Do, then, the intermittently overt exertions of that organized violence protecting all effective ownership relations rend this
superstructural "veil"? No, for it is just such open exertions of
property-protecting force that are most widely sanctified by mass, if
not philosophical, ideology. The omnipresent lawman of contemporary television, for example, exemplifies the overt exertion of organized violence on behalf of proprietary relations; but his state office
ideologically inverts his role of violence into its opposite, "keeper of
the peace."

[8] This principle applies to all ownership, not just ownership of
productive forces. For example, it applies to the ownership of
another's eros prescribed by the institution of marriage. Thus, that
John *has* Mary "to keep and to hold only unto him," entails that all
others are, correspondingly, *alienated from* Mary. Here too, one
party's ownership of x implies all others' alienation from x, which in
the case of marriage is a structuring of the deepest roots of human
life that the Marxian model has to take into account to qualify as
socio-historically adequate. For the required analysis, and incorpora-
tion of such interpersonal orders of ownership into the Marxian

This point is of great importance because:

i. It shows the objective nature of "alienation" for Marx. Alienation is not for him, as contemporary usage mystifies it, some psychological malaise peculiar to modern man, but a necessary material concomitant of all private ownership of productive forces.[9]

ii. It shows why Marx saw private ownership of the forces of production as antihuman. By virtue of every person's or group's private ownership of this sort, every other person or group is by definition cut off from the possibilities of "objective existence" or, otherwise put, from material self-realization through the forces so owned.[10]

iii. It illuminates Marx's claim about increasing "im-

---

model, see our "Monogamy: A Critique" in *Ethics in Perspective*, ed. K. J. and P. R. Struhl (New York, 1975), pp. 319-28; and with an Afterword in *Marriage and Alternatives*, ed. Roger Libby and Robert Whitehurst (Glenview, Ill., 1977), pp. 3-15.

[9] Marx's primary concern is with private ownership of productive forces, which carries with it "the power to subjugate the labor of others" (*CM* 66). However, because all private ownership is the power—backed by invokability of ascendant physical might—to exclude others from what is privately owned, all private ownership entails alienation, whether or not it involves the power to subjugate others' labor. It is certainly the case that step one for Marx is the dissolution of labor-subjugating private ownership; this dissolution is the main advance of human liberation undertaken by "transitional" socialism. But the dissolution of all private ownership is for him the hallmark of the "truly human" relations of communist society. Here the personal usage of goods flourishes—Marx abhors the "leveling-down" vision of "crude, thoughtless communism," which blocks the realization of individual "talent" and "personality" (*EPM*, 98-102). However, such personal usage is guaranteed by cooperative agreement, not by invokability of ascendant physical violence. The animal order of brute territoriality is here, in short, transcended by the human order of conscious community.

[10] We might put this another way. For Marx, the outer world of man is the material "body of his subjecthood" (*Pre-C, passim*). Any fence of others' ownership separating him from this body is, thus, a diminution of his subjecthood.

miserization" in capitalism. Such growing impoverishment is not a matter of decreasing earnings, but
obtains "whether the worker's payment be high or
low" (*CI*, 645) in simple consequence that more forces
of production are owned by the ruling-class capitalists.
That is, since some's ownership always implies others'
alienation, *some's ownership of more implies others' alienation from more*. Hence Marx's "immiserization" doctrine
is clearly not, as conventionally claimed, falsified by rising real wages since the mid-nineteenth century.

iv. It shows why Marx considered communism the
"truly human" social formation. Because there is no
private ownership of the forces of production, there can
be no corresponding alienation from them. Society as a
whole may retain its power to exclude the bodies of nature, or external, ruling-class, societies from the forces
of production in question; but exclusive productive relations within the society in question are dissolved, and
communism, thereby, transcends the "estrangement"
of all previous history.[11]

3. The power to *use* forces of production and exclude
others from doing so is to be distinguished from the
power to *exploit* forces of production and exclude others
from doing so. The latter involves the power to gain
unearned revenue or the benefits of other men's unpaid
labor, whereas the former does not. Such unearned benefits may for Marx take the form of rent-in-kind or corvée labor (feudalism); or money interest, rent, or profit
(capitalism); or other forms not analyzed by him, such
as remuneration for rank in public-sector administra-

---

[11] It is a great mistake to suppose, however, that Marx considered
the end of antagonism over ownership as the end of dialectical ten-
sion. Mankind continues as the site of the world's contradiction between creative consciousness and brute matter, but at a level that
leaves behind ownership interests as, to use the language of Corin-
thians, a man puts away childish things.

tion.[12] On the other hand, the power merely to use forces of production and exclude others from doing so does not involve the power to secure unearned benefits. In cases of purely independent producers—self-employed farmers and artisans, for example—no unpaid labor can be extracted from other men's labor, and so no unearned benefit can be yielded by productive-force ownership (unless it be by peculiar exchange). In most or all other cases of men having such power merely to use forces of production and exclude others from doing so, this turns out in fact to be not really a power at all, but the means whereby one is exploited. For example, the worker's ownership or relation to production extends only to his own personal labor-power, and perhaps some petty possessions, which former must be sold to another or others for their profit in advance of his receiving the means to keep it and himself alive. Or, in the case of the serf, his possession extends only to a personal plot and dwelling, on sufferance, and only to a portion of his own labor-power (say, 5 of 7 days)—relations of production that presuppose that he is exploited by virtue of his in-perpetuity grant by feudal contract of two days' free labor (or its equivalent) to his lord every week. In neither case, then, do the relations of production permit the owners much more than the use of their forces of production for subsistence survival, and in neither case can even this use be secured without at the same time the sufferance of exploitation.[13] In short, in the difference between the power to exploit and the power to use forces of production lies,

[12] See Chapter 8.

[13] It is worth noting that this sense of exploitation—one party extracting unearned benefit from another's labor by virtue of the power of ownership of forces of production—is double-barreled: the power to exploit forces of production being at the same time the power to exploit people.

for Marx, the difference between the power of oppressor and oppressed, excepting slavery, where the slave is not an owner of any productive force but is himself owned as one.

4. The relations of production of a society coincide with its division of labor.[14] That is, what force or forces of production a member of society effectively owns in a society coincides with his position in that society's division of labor. If, for example, one owns nothing but one's own labor-power in a capitalist society, then, correspondingly: i. one's job is as a wage-laborer (employed or unemployed); and ii. one's job is of this or that sort, according to the sort of labor-power that is owned, such as unskilled manual or engineering physics. And if, in the same context, one owns significant forces of production in addition to personal labor-power, then one's position in society's division of labor—whether in the job-place of a small store manager or the job-place of factory master—will similarly coincide with the extent and nature of the additional forces of production so owned. This correspondence between the relations of production and the division of labor of a society, *between its members' ownership places and vocation places*, is repeatedly if cryptically affirmed by Marx. Thus he says, "In the real world . . . the division of labour and all M. Proudhon's other categories are social relations forming in their entirety what is known today as property" (*PofP*, 160). Division of labor is,

---

[14] We must avoid here the confusion, traditional since Adam Smith, of division of task and division of labor. Marx regarded the former as a principal technique of advanced productive forces, the latter as a principal form of ruling-class economic oppression. In communist society, division of task (for example, assembly-line method) is to be retained, while division of labor (confinement of individuals to one "exclusive sphere of activity") is not. In this distinction lies one of the central points of his entire theory (see pp. 69, 224-25).

then, the bridging category between forces of production and relations of production: it mediates between technological relations, whose content is implicit in, but does not enjoin occupational divisions, and economic relations, with which the division of labor coincides. It is their joint expression, just as the operations of a language are the joint expression of its semantics and syntax.[15]

5. Relations of production are more "real," "basic," or "essential" than legal or political relations because, among other reasons, they involve *powers* and the latter involve merely *rights*. As has already been suggested, powers and rights may regularly coincide, but often they do not: as, for example, in any state, whether capitalist or soviet, where the citizen body hold the right(s) of ownership of some or all forces of production, but a small ruling group hold some or all of the power(s) of ownership. Because powers always entail material enablement, whereas rights do not, the powers of relations of production are in this sense for Marx more "real," "basic," or "essential" than the rights of legal and political relations.

6. Relations of production—like human nature, forces of production, and the other general categories of Marx's sociohistorical ontology—are historically concieved. Thus, although all relations of production through successive eras are characterized by the general properties already outlined, they vary from epoch to epoch, inasmuch as:

[15] While we have this comparison before us, we note that Marx's notion of a hidden social "essence" (the economic base), which has earned critical notice as the sin of "essentialism," is no more metaphysical than the grammarian's "essentialist" belief in an underlying structure governing language. The comparison here also illustrates how it is possible for behavior to be governed by laws that the behavioral agent does not himself discern—a claim that has upset many readers of Marx, though not readers of grammar books.

i. the forces of production to which men are so related vary from age to age in content; for instance, artisans' workshops historically give way to modern factories; and, relatedly,

ii. the "laws of motion," that is, laws of exchange and surplus value extraction, of relations of production vary from age to age; for instance, feudal obligations and rent in kind historically give way to cash payment and money profits.[16]

Now that Marx's concept of relations of production has been established, we may consider these relations in their totality: consider, that is, the "economic structure."

For Marx, the essential and defining principle of the economic structure is its ruling-class pattern: that is, the effective ownership of most of society's means of production by a small part of that society (the ruling class), and the effective ownership of few or none of society's means of production by the large majority of that society (the workers).[17] Exactly what means of production

[16] In *Capital* (*CI*, 10), Marx refers to the "economic law of motion" rather than, as we have it, "laws of motion." Though, as it shall be the task of the next pages to point out, there is one covering "law of motion" for all societies in Marx's schema—namely, *every exchange between the ruling class and the producing class yields surplus value to the ruling class*—there are also, for Marx, many complementary specific economic laws (for instance, regarding the rate of surplus value) that have led us to render the term "law of motion" in the plural.

Should the Newtonian nomenclature here dismay the reader by its implicit conflation of natural and social science models, the less provocative "economic laws" may be properly substituted.

Should such substitution still trouble the reader—*because economic laws are not invariant, and thus not laws but law-like social conventions*—then he understands why we henceforth write "laws," not laws.

[17] There are, of course, people—"petty"owners—who are members neither of the ruling class nor of the laboring (or working) class, and our wording permits this.

are involved here—whether the arable land in rural
feudalism, or the factories and machinery in urban
capitalism; who has effective ownership of them—
whether hereditary lords or capitalists; and how such relations of production actually operate—whether by the
economic laws of feudalism or capitalism—are questions to which the answers will provide a more determinate view of the economic structure under consideration.

The ruling-class pattern of the economic structure,
whatever its specific form, renders the nonowning
majority dependent for their survival on the "small part
of society who possesses the monopoly of the means of
production" (*CI*, 235): for the latter are the means
whereby men stay alive. Thus the ruling classes are in
the position, through their monopoly of the means of
production, to extract payment from the nonowning
members of society in exchange for allowing these latter
those benefits from the means of production that they
require to continue living. This payment, in the case of
the productive workers, is *surplus-labor* on the instruments of production owned by the ruling class, above
and beyond what is allocated to keep them alive; which
surplus labor expresses itself in such historical forms as
rent in kind or money profit. Thus, in a definitive passage, Marx says:

> "The specific economic form [Economic Struc-
> ture], in which unpaid surplus-labour is pumped
> out of direct producers . . . the direct relationship of
> the owners of the conditions of production to the
> direct producers . . . reveals the innermost secret,
> the hidden basis of the entire social structure"
> (*CIII*, 791).

In the case of non-productive workers (such as state

functionaries, personal servants, ideologists, and other "parasites"), the payment is labor at mere service functions that directly or indirectly protect the ruling-class economic order, but produce no material use-value.

There are cases, of course, where the nonowners seek to avoid this exploitative arrangement and attempt to stay alive in some other manner—by beggary, for example, or vagabondry or robbery. Marx reports in detail in *Capital*, however, the fate of those who have resorted to such a strategy: whipping, mutilation, slavery, deprivation of children, imprisonment, and execution.[18]

The economic structure is, then, the ruling-class pattern of the totality of the relations of production (that is, a small minority of society effectively owns most of the means of production and a large majority owns few or none of the means of production); and the systematic ruling-class extraction of surplus labor, or service, from this large majority, the nonowning workers (that is, the economic structure's "law of motion").

It is worth adding here that a "ruling-class pattern" embraces for Marx not only those cases in which a ruling class retains its monopolist holdings, but also those cases in which it increases such holdings—for example, in capitalism. So even though there may be continuing changes in relations of production in many respects (in capitalism, for instance, the petty bourgeoisie being

---

[18] Marx reports that people were hanged in the tens of thousands for persistent unemployment after Henry VIII's expropriation of Church manorial lands. He also reports how this process of land seizure and peasant uprooting, initiated by the "Protestant Reformation," continued in various forms (for example, conversion of village commons into sheep farms for the wool business) until the capitalist order was well ensconced. See Marx's electrifying account of the origins of capitalism in "The Primitive Accumulation," *CI*, 713-75.

reduced to wage-laborers and wage-laborers being reduced to lumpenproletarians, not to mention individuals supplanting, and being supplanted by, one another
in economic positions that themselves remain constant),
the economic structure itself and its "law of motion" do
not change. Its ruling-class pattern persists behind the
manifold changes of nonruling-class relations of production, individuals variously switching economic
places, and even the membership of the ruling class itself
dwindling. And the extraction of surplus labor—the
principle of operation of such an economic structure, of
such a ruling-class pattern—remains constant, too; for
example, the feudal lord's exchange of precisely defined
protection for the serf's similarly defined labor service,
the capitalist's exchange of a certain money salary for
the proletarian's weekly labor-power, and so on. It is in
this constancy of the economic structure and its "law of
motion" that Marx perceives the underlying "form" or
"essence" of all historical human society.

   With particular economic structures and "laws of motion," of course, Marx presents a much more specific
picture. For example, in his descriptions of the class
makeup of the capitalist economic structure, he presents
a complex mosaic comprising various groups within the
ruling class, such as "big landed property," "high
finance," and "large-scale industry," and the working
class, such as agricultural, industrial, and service workers; as well as between these two great classes (the
"petty-bourgeoisie"), and beneath them (the "lumpen-
proletariat"). But however determinate and elaborate
Marx's representation of the economic structure's class
makeup may be, classes are such basically by virtue of
*common relations of production*.

   Hence, in an economic structure:

   1. *Members of the ruling class own enough productive forces*

*other than their personal labor-power that they can exploit them to yield*—through the operation of the surplus-labor-extracting "laws of motion" of the economic structure in question—*all the revenue that is required, and more, for subsistence above the social standard*.

Divisions within this ruling class—divisions into subclasses—are, in turn, matters of what sort of surplus-value-yielding external productive forces are so owned, such as landed property, machinery, or fluid capital—that is, ownership of not yet specified forces of production. Such division into subclasses, as with class divisions of any sort in Marx's schema, is only historically meaningful insofar as there is a *contradiction of ownership interests* between the economic groups involved: that is, only when one ruling group's ownership interests or relations of production must be secured through the derogation of the interests of another ruling group; for example, the interests of big landed property in nineteenth-century England demanded tariffs on corn to protect the value of and revenues from their agricultural holdings, whereas the interests of large-scale industry demanded the removal of such tariffs—which must raise food prices—to keep their wage-costs down. When, and only when, such antagonisms of economic interests obtain between class groups does Marx take them into account in his analysis of the economic structure. Herein lies the second criterion for Marx of an economic class, of which more later.

2. Members of *the productive worker class own insufficient productive forces other than personal labor-power to subsist at any level without exchanging the latter for the means to stay alive*; which economic impoverishment of, and exchange by, the productive worker class is at the same time enrichment of, and exploitation by, the ruling class.

Divisions within this laboring class are a matter of what sort of personal labor-power is owned; for instance, in capitalism, skilled or unskilled labor-power, or any gradient of these. However, such divisions in productive worker ownership are rarely historically significant for Marx, inasmuch as there is for him seldom a "contradiction" in ownership interests, seldom an occasion when the securing of one such group's interests must derogate from another's. When there are such antagonisms between working-class owners of different productive labor-powers (such as between Irish immigrant workers and native English workers in nineteenth-century capitalist Britain), then class division within the direct producer class obtains, and subclass analysis becomes important.

Yet even in these cases, because productive worker groups have a greater, common conflict of material interest with the capitalist ruling class and because, besides, their internal subclass conflicts of material interest obtain by virtue of their various labor-powers being owned as commodities for sale to this capitalist ruling class, Marx regards such conflicts of interest between productive worker groups as secondary and derivative—as, that is, symptoms of the capitalist economic structure and its "laws of motion" rather than constituents of it.[19]

[19] Consider, for example, contemporary cases of white working-class members' hostility to black working-class members. A Marxian analysis explains such "racism" as a symptom of an economic order where: i. labor power is a commodity for sale; and ii. more labor power is for sale than is currently being bought. Otherwise put, white workers are hostile to black workers because black workers (such as immigrants from former colonies in Britain and migrants from the South in the United States) compete with and often replace white workers in their jobs, selling their commodity of labor power at a lower price in a labor market that has more labor power for sale than the capitalist class requires to purchase. Were the eco-

3. Other owners of forces of production—for instance, in capitalism, "independent producers," "small
masters," "shopkeepers," and so on—constitute
"petty" classes for Marx insofar as the extent of their
productive force ownership is relatively small, and the
mode of exchange of such productive forces is relatively independent of the surplus-value-extracting laws
of motion of the obtaining economic structure. Hence
Marx more or less ignores such classes in his economic
(as opposed to his political) analysis.

4. Most of the remaining revenue-receiving groups in
capitalist society (lawyers, soldiers, priests, personal
servants, salesmen, bureaucrats, police, entertainers,
judges, lumpenproletarians, and so on) do not own any
significant productive force—no instruments of production, usable natural resources, nor, in practice, productive labor-power—and are to this extent not economic
classes at all. Their economic significance for Marx is
that:

i. They live off the surplus value extracted by the ruling class from the productive laboring class, and are
thereby "parasites" within the economic structure and
upon its "laws of motion."

ii. They typically play some superstructural or
ideological role and are thereby protectors of the
capitalist economic structure (see Chapter 7). Perform-
ing this protective function is, indeed, the earlier-
mentioned "payment" they must make to secure those
benefits from the ruling-class-owned productive forces
they require to stay alive. Marx devotes considerable
time to this motley collection of nonproductive,

nomic order not thus capitalist, and (i) and (ii) therefore not features
of it, there would be, according to the Marxian analysis, no such antagonism of economic interests between producer groups, and hence
no such phenomena of racism.

revenue-receiving, structure-protecting groups in capitalist society—especially in the volumes of his *Theories of Surplus Value*—and he does not seem to have missed the point of their significance in numbers. However, because these groups of "parasites" own no significant forces of production other than the material commodities and labor power they regularly negate as productive forces by unproductive use, Marx refers to them as merely "ideological classes" (e.g., *CI*, 446).

The above framework—constituted of ruling-class and producer-class relations of production, and of antagonistic subclasses within the former, but also of insignificant class and nonclass groups that are, respectively, in the interstices of and dependent on this ruling-class pattern—shows the composition of the economic structure.

We now consider the "laws of motion" of the economic structure. Herein lies, perhaps, the scientific core of Marx's entire post-1845 enterprise. That is, specification of the laws of the capitalist economic structure is the single most extensively treated domain of systematic inquiry of Marx's mature analysis, dominating most of the second two volumes of *Capital*, as well as the three books of *Theories of Surplus Value*. We are not, though, going to venture into the details of this massive literature. Rather, we identify the set of principles that are of general importance in understanding what Marx means by the "laws of motion" of the economic structure— whether it be Asiatic, ancient, feudal, or capitalist.

1. The motion of an economic structure is the circulation or exchange of productive forces that takes place within it—between, essentially, the ruling class and the direct producers. That is, the producers exchange with the ruling class some or all of their productive labor-

power in return for reception from the latter of the material means of subsistence required to keep them alive, the practical necessity of this exchange being what ensures the continuous flow of the "motion" in question. For example, in a capitalist economic structure, there is an unceasing exchange of labor-power and wages between capitalist and proletarian, a perpetual circulation or "motion" of productive forces changing hands, which exchange is and must be continuous in the system—hence Marx's persistent imagery of organism in this connection—for the capitalist to remain a capitalist and for the proletarian to remain productive.

2. The "laws" of this motion, in turn, specify the more or less constant quantities, standard modes, and regularities of circuit of such and such productive forces in repetitive and structure-conforming exchange between the ruling class and the direct producers, but—most important for Marx—with the regular extraction of surplus labor (or surplus value) by the former from the latter that thereby takes place. In the case of capitalism, these "laws of motion" are identified in extended detail by Marx, so that not only does he talk in general terms—as with other economic structures—of such laws necessitating and regulating exchange of certain productive forces between ruling class and direct producers in such a manner that standard forms and amounts of surplus value are continuously "pumped out" to the ruling class; but—unlike his analysis of the "motion" of other economic structures—he formalizes and schematizes this whole process into its main phases of production and of circulation; into its major forms of exploitative extraction (rent, interest, profit); into its precise changes and cycles of composition and turnover; into its rate and accumulation of surplus value expropriation; and so forth. With the particular economic struc-

ture of capitalism, in short, the "laws of motion" governing the ruling-class pattern of production relations constitute a massive theoretical system. But the essential content of these economic laws remains, as always for Marx, the regular extraction of surplus labor by the ruling class from the direct producers.

Of the "laws of motion" specifically of capitalism, it is important to emphasize that Marx sees such "laws" as different from those of any other economic structure in history. For only with capitalism do these "laws of motion" render the growth of exchange value as an end in itself (*CI*, 154). With capitalism, that is, the role of exchange value is no longer, as in other economic formations, that of a simple medium between use-values (use-value → money → use-value), but the final goal for the attainment of which use-values are reduced to mere instrumentality ( money → use-value → more money). That is, the end and aim of production and circulation in capitalism is reversed. Where it was once use-values, or the service of human needs or wants, with money as just a go-between in the circulation of use-values, it is now money as such, with use-values, or the service of human needs or wants, as the mere go-between in the circulation of capital. In other words, the economic laws of capitalism entail, for Marx, the systematic dehumanization of society's process of production and circulation. The service and amplification of men by use-value as the end of the economic process is replaced by the service and amplification of capital by profit as this end. It is for this reason, above all, that Marx conceives the economic order of capitalism to be inhuman. The whole of *Capital*, indeed, may be read as the exposure of a life-and-death struggle between man and capital, in which capital's "laws of motion" of money growth relentlessly "suck the blood" of humankind dry, until the gathering life-throes of human productive forces "burst asunder" their "vampire grip."

When we consider together the class content and "laws of motion" of the economic structure of capitalism, it is not difficult to deduce how a Marxian account can explain, and indeed predict, the well-known social ills that afflict capitalist society today. Thus, briefly:

1. Pollution of the life elements can be explained as the law-like instantiation of the imperative of capital growth exerting its primacy over all considerations of human utility;[20]

2. Economic imperialism can be explained as further predictable instantiation of the same sovereign imperative, "pitilessly" invading wherever and however capital amplification is assured;[21]

[20] That, for example, contemporary capitalist production injects over a thousand food additives into the normal North American daily diet, dumps over a million tons of oil into the oceans every year, poisons countless rivers and lakes with its effluent, pollutes the air of urban settlements across the world by its manufacturing process and products, employs over 500,000 unregulated chemicals in its industries, and so on—all this is well known. (For an advanced analysis of such problems of pollution, see Barry Commoner's *The Closing Circle*, New York, 1972). However, seldom are these systematic phenomena of pollution understood as standard methods of profit maximization. To abet such understanding, we proffer the following syllogism:

Whatever methods of production are used in capitalist production are used to maximize profits.

Polluting methods are used in capitalist production.

Therefore, polluting methods are used in capitalist production to maximize profits.

[21] Capital investment in foreign countries is generally understood by Marxian analysis only in terms of its exploitation of these foreign countries, and its high profit returns to those who have so invested (see, for example, Paul A. Baran and Paul M. Sweezy's *Monopoly Capital*, Harmondsworth, 1966). Less noted is the effect that such foreign investment, and the possibility of such foreign investment,

3. Inflation can be deciphered as the necessary regular devaluation of money: necessary, that is, to maintain the ruling class's structural monopoly of wealth intact in the face of collectively bargained increases in workers' wages;[22] and

4. Replacement of repetitive labor-power by machinery can be understood to pose the social problem of unemployment, as opposed to the social achievement of leisure, because and only because of the capitalist

---

has on the *home* country: blocking regulation of, and working-class gains against, capital by providing "better climates for investment" to which "flights of capital" can be made whenever any limits on profit maximization are raised at home. Indeed, it is this alternative foreign outlet for capital that accounts in large part not only for such blockages in the home country, but for the continual multibillion dollar giveaways the governments of these countries accord to domestic capital in the form of tax exemptions, subsidies, incentives, land grants, depreciation allowances, wage rollbacks, and so on.

[22] If prices did not rise (that is, if inflation did not occur), then regular increases in workers' wages would entail corresponding decreases of capitalists' wealth. For the capitalist economic structure to be maintained intact, then, prices must rise (that is, inflation must occur). Inflation is thus deducible from a capitalist economic structure, in which the price of the commodity of labor is regularly rising.

To reduce such inflation, either: i. wage increases (that is, increases in the price of the commodity of labor) must be held down (by disemployment of workers and/or wage controls); or ii. the productivity of this commodity of labor must be increased (by increases in the intensity or duration of labor); or iii. the structural monopoly of wealth by the capitalist class must be reduced (by a fall in capital holdings or absolute profits). With the Marxian ruling-class model, (i) and/or (ii) is predicted almost certainly to occur, and (iii) is predicted almost certainly not to occur.

Inflation is also deducible from a capitalist economic structure in which state expenditures progressively increase in the maintenance of ownership relations (such as police, army, judicial, and administrative salariats), and in the sustenance of regular circuits of exchange (such as government deficit financing). But such state expenditures do, in fact, progressively increase with some or all capitalist economic structures. Therefore, on these accounts as well, inflation is deducible from some or all capitalist economic structures.

ownership of such machinery and its labor-saving benefits.[23]

In such manner, the comprehension of various problems within capitalist society—more or less mysterious to "bourgeois" economic theory—can proceed employing the Marxian explanatory frame of economic structure and its "laws of motion."

In summary, just as with a particular economic structure Marx presents a much more specific and complex picture of the class setup than merely ruling class and laborers, so—inseparably—he presents a much more specific picture of the "laws of motion" of such an economic structure than merely that of the former "pumping unpaid surplus labor out of" the latter. But whether his concern is general or specific characterization, it is always the case with the mature Marx that he sees in the ruling-class economic structure and its laws the "innermost secret" of this or any other historical society: the "secret" that is systematically "hidden" by the legal and political superstructure, the ideology, and the forms of social consciousness of the society in question, and the "secret" that his work is most of all dedicated to telling.

Before concluding this section, it is worth making a

[23] Replacement of labor power by machinery can disemploy in two ways: some workers lose their jobs, or many workers gain a shorter working day. The former poses the social problem of more unemployment; the latter poses the social achievement of more free time. With capitalist ownership of labor-saving machinery, that which reduces costs to capital is always preferred to that which increases benefits to workers. Therefore, with capitalist ownership of labor-saving machinery, the social problem of unemployment is always preferred to the social achievement of more free time. Herein lies one of Marx's major arguments against capitalist ownership and for social ownership of the means of production of a technologically advanced society.

few final remarks on Marx's central and traditionally problematic concept of "economic class."

1. All classes constitutive of the economic structure—generally speaking, the ruling class, the productive laborer class, and any remaining classes, as well as the subclasses within all these—are only economic classes: that is, each is (to use Marx's term) merely a class, or subclass, "in itself." Whether any is organized or conscious of itself as a class (or subclass), whether any is "for itself," is a matter of superstructural "reflex" to the economic situation: it is not an economic matter. Hence Marx says, "Economic conditions had first transformed the mass of the people of the country into workers. The combination of capital has created for this mass a common situation, common interests. This mass is already a class as against capital, but not yet for itself. In the struggle . . . this mass becomes united and constitutes itself as a class for itself. . . . [And this] struggle of class against class is a *political* struggle" (*PofP*, 150).

2. Economic classes, as we have already indicated, not only require common relations of production to count as classes, but also require—to be historically meaningful—"*contradiction*" between the common ownership interests so involved (that is, one set of such interests is securable only at the expense of another set). The basic contradiction of this sort is always, for Marx, that between the ownership interests of the ruling class and the ownership interests of the direct producers: a contradiction that is implicit in the very notion of an economic structure, in the very notion of a "ruling-class pattern" in the relations of production. But whatever is treated as a real class phenomenon by Marx, whether basic or peripheral, whether referring to general classes or particular classes, involves some "contradiction" between the

common relations of production or interests of the classes and subclasses involved. This dimension of contradiction is essential to all groups that Marx counts as real economic classes, as opposed to sets of people united only by common relations of production— "classes" only in name. This further criterion of what counts as an economic class—that is, that the latter is such not only by virtue of common relations of production, but by virtue of "contradiction" with other common relations of production—deserves special emphasis, because it shows the way to complete the famous unfinished manuscript on classes in *Capital*, Volume III;[24] as well as, more generally, pointing up the inherent antagonism of material interests involved for Marx in economic class division, which antagonism is the spring of the entire legal-political superstructure or state (see Chapter 4).

3. The ruling-class pattern of the economic structure implies, as we have emphasized, the basic contradiction between the interests of the ruling owners and the interests of the direct producers from whom surplus labor (value) is extracted. This bears repeating, inasmuch as

[24] Here is the passage in question (*CIII*, 886): "The first question to be answered is this: what constitutes a class? . . . At first glance, the identity of revenues and sources of revenues. For example, in a capitalist society there are three great social groups whose members, the individuals forming them, live on wages, profit and ground rent respectively, on the realisation of their labour-power, their capital, and their landed property. However, from this standpoint i.e. conceiving classes in terms of common revenues and courses of revenues, physicians and officials, e.g. would also constitute two classes, for they belong to two distinct social groups, the members of each of these groups receiving their revenue from one and the same source. The same would also be true of the infinite fragmentation of interest and rank into which the division of social labour splits labourers as well as capitalists and landowners—the latter, e.g. into owners of vineyards, farm owners, owners of forests, mine owners and owners of fisheries . . ." (here the manuscript breaks off).

there should be no doubt of Marx's view of all further class antagonisms as quite secondary, such as antagonisms between particular subclasses within the ruling class. Classes are real classes for Marx by virtue of the contradiction of their common interests with some other economic group's common interests, but the "basic" or "essential" classes and class contradiction involves for him the ruling owners and the direct producers because:

i. These two classes between them own all or almost all the material means (that is, productive forces) whereby the society reproduces its life (hence their "basic" or "essential" status *qua* relations of production).

ii. From the exchanges of these two classes, all or almost all the surplus value extraction (that is, exploitation) of the society is generated (hence their "basic" or "essential" status *qua* "contradictory" relations of production). It is on these accounts, then, that any other conflicts of class interest count for Marx as less central, and dependent.[25]

[25] What about the conflicts of class interest between adults and the young (such as parents and offspring), male and female (such as man and wife)? In both cases, more the former than the latter, a monopoly ownership of one class's material means of life is held by the other class, by which ruling-class pattern of ownership domination can, and does, infamously proceed. Marx recognizes and identifies these "age" and "sex" class antagonisms, if only parenthetically (e.g., *CI*, 489-90). But he holds these further "economic bases" of domination to be dependent on the ruling-class conflict between capitalists and proletarians. That is, he holds that insofar as the underclasses in question themselves become proletarians (that is, join the capitalist work-force), they thereby lay the foundations of their economic independence from their respective adult and male overclasses, and, simultaneously, enter one "collective working group" struggling against a single, common ruling-class enemy, the capitalists.
We find this interstitial analysis illuminating, and applicable to a

From this description of the economic structure and its "ruling-class pattern," we can understand at least by negation what sort of society Marx had in mind when he talked about communism—obviously no ruling-class ownership or "laws of motion" of exchange whereby a surplus value can be extracted from the direct producers for rulers and parasites' revenues, nor any other form of class antagonism. Indeed, one of the most interesting features of the communist society Marx sketches is—in addition to and corresponding with its communal ownership of the forces of production—its new "law of motion" of exchange: namely, in Marx's own famous words, "From each according to his ability, to each according to his needs" (*GP*, 37). Here, we can see, not only is the exploitative aspect of all historical modes of exchange transcended (that is, there is no surplus value extraction by one class from another by virtue of ownership monopoly); but exchange itself takes on a new character. It surpasses the principle of *quid pro quo* altogether. The radical quality of Marx's vision here cannot be overestimated. Exchange is no longer a matter of giving in order to take, but giving according to one's abilities (independently of payoff) and receiving according to one's needs (independently of contribu-

---

significant extent even where young people and women occupy wage-dependent productive labor positions in domestic and school workplaces, rather than factories or offices (see Chapter 2). It is also applicable to ruling-class state-socialist societies, not just capitalist ones (see Chapter 7). On the other hand, Marx's account is so thin here, and the issues so fecund and important, that we judge this area to be a fundamental blind spot of his thought.

We think, however, that much of the solution here lies in the systematic extension of Marx's principle of communal, democratic use of the material means of life: to, for example, the entire "private" realm of upbringing. In this extension, indeed, may lie the long-missing link of society's successful transformation to truly classless community.

tion). Exchange in the communist utopia is thus organic (that is, there is no division of interest), and free (that is, it is determined by individual "abilities" and "needs"). Strictly speaking, it is not really "exchange" as we know it at all, because giving and receiving are not yoked. Rather, it is the arrangement of love socially construed.

*193635*

# 4

## The State

Above the economic structure stands the state or, as Marx more precisely puts it, "the legal and political superstructure" ("the police, the army, the courts and bureaucracy," *RZ*, 193-94). This state or superstructure is the "official stratum" of society, which "arises upon" the economic structure as its sanctioned and coercive regulator.[1]

In general, what distinguishes the legal and political superstructure or state from the "underlying" economic structure to which it "corresponds" is that all its content is or has been consciously constructed by some form or other of recognized social authority.[2] On the other hand, the more fundamental content of the economic structure obtains "independently of the will of individuals" (*GID*, 357),[3] and is only "scientifically discoverable" (*CI*, 542). Marx maintains this general distinction

[1] Sometimes Marx uses the term "superstructure" to refer to just legal and political institutions, and sometimes he uses it to apply more broadly to these as well as ideology and forms of social consciousness as a unitary whole. We use the term in the same permissive way, with the context rendering its precise referent evident.

[2] Even the "gradual accretions" of law are consciously constructed, each accretion itself being the result of a process of formal deliberation, judgment, and codification. It is by virtue of being a conscious construction *on top of* the "hidden" mechanisms of the economic order that Marx uses the term *super*structure.

[3] This favorite claim of Marx that relations of production obtain "independently of the will of individuals" is often wrongly interpreted as a denial of free will. Marx is, however, making no such metaphysical claim, but is merely stating the empirically incontrovertible truth that the economic order carries on independently of the will (as opposed to actions) of individuals (as opposed to groups). See *GID*, 357 ff.

in all his discussions of the legal-political superstructure and the economic base.

Clarifying this general distinction between the economic structure (E) and the legal-political superstructure (S) is a set of specific distinctions. These are:

1. The relations S involves are in terms of formal *rights* and *obligations*; whereas the relations E involves are in terms of effective *powers* and *constraints* (*GID*, 80 and 352-59).

2. S is the *de jure* representative of "the general interest"; whereas E is the *de facto* organization of particular material interests (*GID*, 45-46, 78).

3. S's form is visible and institutional; whereas E's form is concealed and unacknowledged (*CII*, 791).

We can see, then, that the conventional criticism of Marx's distinction between economic substructure and legal-political superstructure is false. The distinction here, contrary to standard objections (see the Introduction), is both precisely securable and substantial in character. The really contentious point here is not Marx's distinction *per se*, but the relationship that he supposes between the factors that he distinguishes. Why, the question is repeatedly put, is the economic order conceived as the "base" and the state its "superstructure"? Why does he conceive the former as primary, and the latter as secondary?

Marx suggests a number of mutually reenforcing answers to this query, which we can summarize by the following propositions:

1. *The legal and political superstructure arises in whole and in part only upon already existing antagonisms of material interest inherent in the production relations/economic structure* (which it "expresses" and "regulates") *and does not obtain independently of these economic antagonisms* (*PofP*, 151).[4]

---

[4] Note here the similarity in principle to Locke's notion of the state as an "umpire" arising to resolve disputes over individual prop-

Thus, says Marx, the legal and political superstructure is the "official, active and conscious expression of the economic structure of society" (*YM*, 350) wherein (among other, secondary antagonisms) the material interest of the ruling class—to sustain its expropriation of the surplus labor of others—is systematically antagonistic to the material interest of the producer class from whom this surplus labor is expropriated. If, Marx holds, there were no such systematic antagonisms of material interest inherent in the economic order, as in the projected communist society, where there would be no private power to exploit society's forces of production, then there would be no legal and political superstructure required to preside over such divisions; just as, Marx contended, there was no state before such ruling-class ownership of the productive forces came into being.[5] Because the necessary material ground of the superstructure—antagonistic relations of production that it is historically constructed to meet—would no longer exist, it would "wither away." Insofar as the legal and political superstructure is thus dependent for its existence on the divisions of ownership in the economic sys-

---

erty. Like Marx, Locke (not to mention Hobbes and others) takes it as obvious that the erection of the state depends upon already existing antagonisms of interest. However, unlike Marx, these philosophers do not discern a ruling-class pattern to such antagonisms of interest, which for Marx renders the "umpire" or "Leviathan" of the state ultimately subordinate rather sovereign in its function.

[5] Marx's theory of the genesis of the state seems superior to the Social Contract theory of Hobbes, Locke, and others inasmuch as the latter cannot explain how individuals first come to submit to this body, except by an as-if fiction of universal consent. Marx's theory, on the other hand, requires no such as-if posit. People's submission to the state is originally accomplished by organized force, whose function is to protect a ruling-class economic order (cf. the early Rousseau's less developed, but similar account in the *Discourse on the Origin of Inequality*). As for Marx's reasons why others' fictitious account of the origins of the state may be preferred to his empirical one, see our chapter, "Ideology."

tem, it is derivative and the latter is primary. The two are related, in a phrase, as problem-raiser and problem-responder (thus Marx's term "reflex" for superstructure).

Marx's claim here of exhaustive dependency of the state or superstructure on antagonistic relations of production/economic structure does not, we might add, rule out a central planning and distributing agency for production in communist society. Such an agency is not a state or superstructure because it is wholly integral to the dynamic of needs and production. Distribution, for instance, is not dictated by ownership or juridical right, but by the principle of "to each according to his needs."[6]

2. Except in revolution (where the economic base is proximately altered by the operations of the legal and political superstructure), *any conflict between the requirements or laws of the class-patterned relations of production/economic structure and the requirements or laws of the legal and political superstructure is resolved in favor of the former*. For example, the established civil rights of the superstructure will be suspended or ignored if their operation represents a threat to the ruling-class monopoly of productive forces, or to the "law of motion" of the economic base. The requirements of the latter take precedence over the requirements of the former in this, or any other, case of nonrevolutionary disjunction. In this sense too, then, the economic structure has primacy over the legal and political superstructure (for a detailed discussion of this and other forms of economic determinism, see Chapter 7).

3. Since men cannot live on the content of the legal

[6] Marx's theory of communist society must, however, be rigorously distinguished from the subsequent putative practice of it in "communist countries." See our Marxian critique of state socialism in Chapter 7.

and political superstructure, whereas they can and do live on the productive-force content of the relations of production/economic structure, they act in accordance with the latter rather than the former:

> Material interests preponderate. . . . The Middle Ages could not live on Catholicism, nor the ancient world on politics. On the contrary, it is the mode in which they gained a livelihood that explains why here politics and there Catholicism played the chief part (*CI*, 82).

Insofar as men act in accordance with their relations to the material means of human life rather than their relations to the stuff of law and politics as such, the relations of production/economic structure are more "basic" than the legal and political superstructure. In this sense, which underlies sense (2), the former, again, has primacy.

To this point we have seen that Marx distinguishes the legal and political superstructure, or state, from the production relations/economic structure in a number of ways, and that on empirical grounds he regards it as a superstructure in its relationship to the latter.

The superstructure arises because, and only because, of antagonisms of material interest inherent in the economic base. It is a social mechanism for dealing with the problems of these antagonisms and would disappear or "wither away" with the removal of these latter in a communist society. We now ask, precisely how does the superstructure or state relate to the economic antagonisms it is "raised" to deal with? Marx's answer, reduced to formula, is this: *Except in revolutionary periods, the superstructure or state relates always to the problems engendered by the economic structure and its "laws of motion" so as to maintain these latter intact.*

That is, far from being the resolving mechanism of common interest it is conventionally held to be, the state, for Marx, merely maintains the collective interests of the ruling class intact and, thereby, perpetuates the economic antagonisms it is raised to deal with by protecting their underlying structural cause from alteration or change. What it is claimed to be is thus an "upside-down" version of what it is. Thus, says Marx, the state is "a fraud." And thus, he says in defining its "real" as opposed to "pretended" function, "The bourgeois state is nothing but a mutual *insurance pact* of the bourgeois class both against its members taken individually and against the exploited class."[7]

There is a wide variety of ways in which the state is conceived by Marx as protecting the ruling-class economic base and its inherent antagonisms of material interest. We can resolve his myriad descriptions and asides in this connection into the following set of propositions:

1. It *validates* some or all existing relations of production (powers) as legal property relations (rights) and, thereby, validates the ruling class's ownership monopoly and extraction of surplus value.

2. It *enforces* some or all existing relations of production by virtue of enforcing legal property relations that "express" the former, and again enforces the ruling class's monopolistic ownership and extraction of surplus value.

3. It *adjusts* whatever requires adjusting to perpetuate the ruling class's monopoly of ownership and extraction of surplus value; for example, in a capitalist social formation, by periodically regulating wages, imposing protective duties, forcing sale of labor power, funding capitalist ventures, waging imperialist wars, and persecuting dissidents.

[7] Note the telling satire of Social Contract theory informing Marx's declaration here (*Marx-Engels-Werke*, VII, 288).

4. It *adjudicates* individual and group disputes over proprietary claims, which disputes arise from the inherent antagonisms of the ruling-class economic order,[8] in a manner always consistent with the perpetuation of the latter.

5. It *misleads* some or all of the people of a society into acceptance of the ruling class's monopoly of ownership and extraction of surplus value by certain "mystifying" and "concealing" characteristics of its formally articulated content:

i. by its voluntaristic language, which masks economic compulsion by a vocabulary of personal "will" and "agreement" (that is, men do not personally "will" or "agree" to enter their various economic relations, as the voluntaristic language of legal and political contract pretends. On the contrary, they are generally "compelled" to enter such relations as a matter of practical necessity);

ii. by the "abstract" nature of its legal and political rights, which imply universal equality (capitalism) or mutuality (feudalism), while in fact permitting the opposite of these; that is, the abstract and equal right of all to private property in capitalist society permits in fact the virtual propertylessness of the vast majority (see *CI*, 583 ff.); while the universal mutuality of obligation in feudal society permits, in fact, the lord's extraction from

[8] What about proprietary disputes among productive workers themselves?

i. These proprietary disputes constitute a small fraction of the proprietary disputes that the state adjudicates because productive workers' ownership is for the most part confined to ownership of personal labor-power, and because the costs of state adjudication are generally beyond productive workers' means to pay. Therefore, the domain of cases is minimal.

ii. Where there are proprietary disputes among productive workers themselves, these derive from the inherent antagonisms of the ruling-class economic order in the manner outlined in Chapter 3.

the serf of surplus labor "without any compensation" (*CIII*, 790 ff.).

iii. by the community of interest or "illusory community" (*GID*, 45-46) it purports to represent, when a minority or ruling-class interest is in fact what it protects; that is, the modern state purports to be securing the "public interest," when in fact its law is merely "the will of the bourgeois class made into a law for all" (*CM*, 67), and its political mechanisms "merely the organized power of one class oppressing another" (see *CM*, 74).

As (i), (ii), and (iii) suggest, the legal and political superstructure has an important ideological dimension. That is why Marx describes it as "practico-idealist" in nature (*GID*, 85). However, because the ideological factor as a whole encloses considerably more area than that covered by (5), Marx generally extends separate treatment to it (which we analyze in Chapter 5).

Before proceeding further with our exposition of Marx's theory of the state, we attend to what has often been highlighted as a problem. That is, how can the superstructure be conceived of as an "expression" or "reflex" of the economic base, when it itself may have been a necessary condition of the latter's formation? For example, how can the capitalist legal and political superstructure be said to be an expression or reflex of capitalist economic structure when (as Marx himself indignantly affirms throughout his section on the "Primitive Accumulation" in *Capital*) "legal enactments" played a central role in forming this very economic base?

The answer is that the political and legal superstructure is related to the economic structure and its "laws of motion" in a different way *between* historical epochs (for example, the transition period from feudalism to capitalism) than it is *within* these epochs. In such transition periods, Marx holds, the productive forces have "outgrown" the economic structure and its laws, and thereby transformed the latter's historical status from a "form of social development" to a "fetter" on such development. In this situation, and only in this situation, the state cannot both maintain the economic structure and its laws intact, and allow for the preservation and development of the productive forces. It is, on such occasions, confronted with what Marx called a "fundamental contradiction" in the mode of production. In this situation, and, again it must be stressed, only in this situation, the state operates as an agency for the qualitative alteration (as opposed to maintenance) of the economic order, in accordance with the requirements of productive-force development.[9]

But once this period of epochal transition is achieved, once the economic order is so transformed that it is no longer a "fetter" on the productive forces, but a new "form of their development," then the superstructure is *ipso facto* deprived of the material grounds of its revolutionary potential, and reverts to its normal function of maintaining the economic base intact.

In summary, the legal and political superstructure operates always as an "expression" or "reflex" of the eco-

---

[9] These requirements of productive force development are what enable a new ruling class to supplant the old. The state does not cease to be a "class weapon" here. It changes from the "class weapon" of an old ruling class (such as feudal or capitalist), whose rule does not correspond to the technological requirements of the day, to the "class weapon" of a new ruling class (capitalist or proletarian, respectively) whose rule does correspond to the technological requirements of the day. Revolutionary political class struggle, then, is only the social medium whereby a necessary transfer of state power occurs in accordance with productive force requirements. It remains, thus, superstructural, even in its revolutionary function (a point that "Marxists" who fix only on class struggle have perilously, and we think world-historically, missed for a century).

nomic infrastructure, except in periods of epochal transition, such as that between feudalism and capitalism or that between capitalism and socialism. Here, exceptionally, but in strict accordance with the "laws" of technological determinism, it is "seized" by a rising new class and used to alter the old economic order into "another, higher form" that conforms to society's current stage of productive force development. Once this revolution occurs, the rising new class becomes society's ruling class, with the state, again, as the mechanism whereby the underlying economic order is maintained intact.[10]

There is another *prima facie* paradox that arises out of Marx's concept of the legal and political superstructure and its relationship to the economic base. The seeming paradox is this: how can the superstructure be held to be the mechanism for the ruling class to maintain its economic hegemony intact, when this same superstructure, as often noted by Marx, passes laws that seem to be explicitly against the present interests of ruling-class members? For example, English factory legislation limiting the working day of laborers to ten hours (a piece of legislation that earns considerable notice from

[10] Society's revolution from a capitalist to a socialist economic order is historically unique for Marx in that: i. the new ruling class is constituted of the "immense majority of society" (its productive workers), not, as in the past, "a small minority"; ii. its ruling-class order is only "transitional," not, as in the past, epochal; and iii. the legal and political superstructure that protects this rule of the productive workers does not remain, but, with the dissolution of society's "bourgeois remnants," withers away altogether. In short, with the full achievement of communal ownership of the forces of production, there are no classes and, thus, no state required to protect the ownership of one. (For our analysis of the precise requirements of this movement, and the failure to meet them in state-socialist societies, see Chapter 7.)

Marx in *Capital*) compromised, on the face of it, the interests of factory owners. Because such legislation limited the time per day that the factory laborer could work for the owner's profit (so that economists such as Oxford's Nassau Senior claimed the "last hour"—the profit hour—was being eliminated), it seemed very much against at least some ruling-class members' economic interests. So how, when the bill was passed, could the superstructure still be held by Marx as the executor of ruling-class interests?

The first thing to be made clear here is that Marx claims only that the state superstructure maintains *collective* ruling-class interests intact. So it is perfectly consistent with this claim that this or that member or group of members have their particular interests derogated for the good of the class as a whole. In this case, the collective interests of the ruling class were served by, *inter alia*, the better preservation of the endangered "golden goose"—the labor force—which the bill in question secured. Only by understanding this collective sense of ruling-class interests can one understand Marx's concept of the state and its relationship to the economic base. To recite the famous remark in the *Communist Manifesto*: "The bourgeois state is nothing but a mutual insurance pact of the bourgeois class both taken against its members individually and against members of the exploited class."

However, Marx emphasizes in this case that not even the particular interests of a ruling-class sector (albeit a preeminent sector) were in fact compromised by this or any other form of factory legislation. Despite the ideological rhetoric of a number of industrial capitalists (such as earthenware manufacturers), press organs (such as *The Economist*), academic apologists (such as Oxford's Nassau Senior), and others who opposed such legislation as "impossible," what the latter's passage in fact meant (insofar as it was effectively worded and applied)[11] was merely the "intensification of labor" by, mainly, the improvement of machinery. Thus the economic position and surplus-value appropriation rate of even the particular interests of the industrial bourgeoisie were maintained intact. Indeed, Marx suggests such and similar legislation actually benefits the interests of this particular section of the ruling class, as well as the ruling class generally:

1. by requiring greater capital outlays for the improved machinery, and thereby "hastening on the decline of small masters, and the concentration of capital" (*CI*, 477); and

2. by "directly depreciating the value of labor power" (*CI*, 406), and thereby "setting free" laborers replaced by machinery to swell the "industrial reserve army" available to the ruling class, both for new ventures and for disciplining those already employed.

So what appears to be the derogation by the superstructure (that is, factory legislation) of the interests of a central ruling-class sector is here, in fact, the maintenance and, indeed, promotion of its interests. In this case, ruling-class interests are distributively as well as collectively secured by superstructural phenomenon. Such a course of affairs is typical, in Marx's view. Hence, even though a crucial distinction must be made between the collective and particular interests of the ruling class, with the former, as always, primary in the relationship between base and superstructure, both sorts of interest

---

[11] Marx frequently draws attention to the inadequate formulation and application of parliamentary legislation (e.g., *CI*, 479-80, 494-95), which ensures that little or nothing is, in fact, changed by such except official documents. This is one of the common duping features of the legal-political superstructure that occasions Marx's general description of the latter as "illusory."

are, in Marx's view, typically held intact, despite appearances to the contrary.[12]

So far we have focused upon the way in which Marx conceives the state as reflecting ruling-class economic interests. Now we look at the way in which he conceives the state as indispensable to the maintenance of these ruling-class economic interests. Consider his metaphor of "reflex" here. A "reflex" not only reflects the anatomy of the organism out of which it arises, but it is also indispensable to the maintenance of this anatomy. (Marx, we note, not only conceives of the state superstructure as "reflex," but of the economic infrastructure as "anatomy.") Thus, though Marx regards the "reflex" mechanism of the state as depending for its very existence upon a ruling-class economic "anatomy," he considers the persistence, though not existence, of this "anatomy" as, in turn, requiring the "reflex" mechanism of the state to preserve it.

Leaving aside Marx's explanatory model of "reflex" and "anatomy," we now identify the two general requirements of any stable ruling-class economic order, which Marx conceives the state to systematically fulfill:

1. social appearance of sanctity; and
2. collective agency of enforcement for ruling-class interests.

We have already treated these in finer detail above. What we are concerned to do here is to consider them briefly from the point of view of their necessity as de-

[12] This is not to say, certainly, that Marx is suggesting that legislation such as the ten-hour bill should have been opposed by the working class, or was even possible without their militant pressure for it. On the contrary, Marx's dialectical position here is that it is in precisely this sort of way that the seed of revolution is nourished within the bosom of the established order: what is good for the latter is also at the same time nurturing the agencies of its future destruction.

fense mechanisms for the stability of the economic order, from which we will be in a better position to make
sense of the central role Marx ascribes to the superstructural phenomenon of class struggle.

The first requirement provides the protection of
"mask" to the economic base (a mask that ideology
compounds). It constitutes for Marx the overall "illusory" quality of the legal-political superstructure, which
in all societies of man's history conceals the true nature
of its ruling-class economic system. Though he never
directly says so, Marx generally implies this sanctifica-
tion by the legal-political superstructure to be a required
cover-up mechanism for the persistence of any ruling-
class economic order, without which it would be exposed (in the long run, ruinously) for the systematic
exploitation system it is. Though in considering this indispensable "veil" function of the superstructure we unavoidably introduce ideology into our ambit of inquiry,
the mere official institutionalization of economic power
by the state organization must be appreciated as itself a
hallowing of that power. That is, the state's very nature
as a ceremonialized bureaucratic system officering the
whole of society accords the economic order it overlays
the mystique of elevated, awful status. This sanctifica-
tion of the economic order by the state is, indeed, a fundamental, if unremarked, component of the routine of
mystification Marx analyzes in "The Fetishism of
Commodities" (*CI*, 71-83): the apparent magical au-
tonomy of commodities deriving from the very nature
of the state as a vast, consecrated order of ranks, regulations, offices, and protocols standing like the armies of
Yahweh over the ownership and exchange of goods.[13]
We have here, in other words, the phenomenology of

[13] Consider here the standard inscription on American coinage:
"In God We Trust."

Kafka in historical materialist form. Sanctified by the terrifying aspect of the state, the economic system grinds as if by the ordinance of the Lord, and its products shuttle and move in inexorable pattern as if ruled by His "invisible hand."

The second requirement, on the other hand, is a straightforward organizational requirement. The ruling-class economic structure requires more than the particular relations of ownership constituting it in order to survive intact. Some additional collective coordinator, adjudicator, adjuster of enforcement in the interests of the ruling class as a whole must exist—that is, a legal and political superstructure—or the economic order in question will be ill equipped to maintain its hold for long. In the first place, individual interests of the ruling class are not necessarily consistent with the interests of this class as a whole; therefore, some way of resolving possible conflicts between these particular interests must be established "on top of" the production relations/economic structure. The state or superstructure that thus arises is, in traditional terminology, the expression of a "Social Contract" among ruling-class members to be governed by a common representative of their interests as a whole in order to protect themselves from class-destructive internecine strife.

In the second place, individual economic powers of members of the ruling class are easier to resist or usurp than these powers enlarged in a collective form; therefore, some combination of these powers in the unified body of a superstructure is necessary to ensure the maximum security required to sustain the systematically exploitative and antagonistic economic order beneath. The state might that is thereby raised is, to sustain the language of Social Contract theory, the "Leviathan" of the ruling class: the latter's combination

of power into a single, sovereign body presiding over
the economic system underneath as the unbrookable
"organized power of one class for oppressing another"
(*CM*, 74).

"Social appearance of sanctity" and "collective
agency for enforcement of ruling-class interests" would
seem, then, coincident requirements for the persistence
of the ruling-class economic order. Otherwise put, they
are the indispensable shields of any durable system of
exploitation—holist "fraud" and "force," respectively.
Of course, Marx believed that a nonclass economic
order would require no such superstructure or state, insofar as there would be no intrinsic antagonisms of material interest to mystify or enforce. But so long as the
economic order is class-ruptured, an "active, conscious,
and official expression" of this base contradiction, the
state, must for Marx preside over the former to ensure
the preservation of its ruling-class ownership pattern
and "laws of motion" of surplus-labor extraction.[14]

It is only when this indispensability of the legal-

___

[14] It is also implied by Marx (e.g., *CI*, 15) that the *extent of the
state's mechanisms of "fraud" and "force" increases in direct proportion to
the extent of the struggle between the ruling and ruled classes*: so that, for
example, the more proletarians organize as a class against capitalists
as a class, the greater will be the state's mechanisms of "fraud" and
"force." Thus, to apply this principle to post-Marxian circumstances, to the extent that the struggle between proletarian and
capitalist classes increases (for instance, in prewar Germany) to just
that extent will the state's mechanisms of "fraud" and "force" increase (prewar German fascism, for instance); and, conversely, to
the extent that such class struggle diminishes (such as in postwar
Germany), to just that extent will the state's mechanisms of "fraud"
and "force" be reduced (as in postwar German parliamentary democracy). Contrary then to liberal-democratic theory, which sees
fascism as an inexplicable aberration of the state's normal functions,
Marxist theory, as we have it, explains fascism as a paradigmatic
exemplification of these functions, obtaining in law-governed correspondence to struggle between the proletariat and capitalist classes.

political superstructure to the preservation of the ruling-class economic order is clearly comprehended that we can understand why Marx counts superstructural class struggle—and all class struggle for Marx is "political" or superstructural[15]—as so important in history: "The history of all hitherto existing society is the history of class struggle" (*CM*, 45). We can formulate Marx's argument here as follows:

1. The legal and political superstructure is the indispensable general protector of the ruling-class economic order.

2. Therefore, to maintain the ruling-class economic order, the legal and political superstructure must be under the control of the ruling class. Otherwise the former will be insecure to the extent that its essential mechanism of defense is insecure. Conversely, to alter the ruling-class economic order, the legal and political superstructure must be seized from the control of the ruling class. Otherwise the former will remain secure to the extent that its essential mechanism of defense is secure.

3. The only effective way either to keep or to seize

---

[15] Thus Marx says such things as "the struggle of class against class is a political [i.e., superstructural] struggle" (*PofP*,150); and, more elaborately:

> On the other hand, however, every movement in which the working class comes out as a class against the ruling classes and tries to coerce them by pressure from without is a political movement. For instance, the attempts in a particular factory or even in a particular trade to force a shorter working day out of individual capitalists by strikes etc., is a purely economic movement. On the other hand, the movement to force through an eight-hour, etc., law is a political movement. And in this way out of the separate economic movements of the workers there grows up everywhere a political movement, that is to say a movement of the class, with the object of enforcing its interests in a general form, in a form possessing general, socially coercive force (*SC*, 328).

control over the legal and political superstructure is
through class-for-itself (that is, political) action. This
class action necessarily involves some form or other of
class struggle insofar as the existence of a class presupposes the existence of another class or classes with antagonistic material interests (see Chapter 3). Such class-
for-itself action—"class struggle"—is alone effective in
keeping or seizing control of the protective superstructure, because it alone possesses the realized "general
form" (great social group aware of itself, and committed to acting, as a great social group) and the material-
interest content (common economic stake) together required to achieve disposition over state machinery.
Without this realized general form, attempts to keep or
sieze control of the superstructure will be too par-
ticularistic to be socially effective. And without the content of common material interests, this general form, in
turn, will be too "idealist" to endure through the pres-
sures of unshared relations to the means of life. Political
class action or class struggle is, thus, the key to control
of the state or superstructure—demonstrably in the past;
probably, therefore, in the future.

4. From (1), (2), and (3), class struggle must more or
less certainly be considered as the sole effective agency
for keeping or seizing control of the legal and political
superstructure and thereby, since the latter is the necessary general protector of the economic order, the only
mode of action whereby maintenance or change of the
real "anatomy" or "form" of a society can be effected.

This underlying argument of Marx's theory of the
state and class struggle is guided by several important
supportive beliefs that it is crucial to identify. Assuming
(1) to be true, for example, (2) as a whole is true only if
one believes, further, that there is no other practicable
way of altering the ruling-class economic order than by

seizing its indispensable mechanism of defense, the
state. Yet the ruling class itself, or its superstructural
agents, or some combination of these, might evolve the
state away from its historical function of ruling-class
protection and into conformity with its long-pretended
general interest function, with no such seizure "from
beneath" required (a possibility in which social demo-
crats believe). Or, again, the economic order might be
altered by bypassing superstructural mediation altogether—with state repression at the same time effectively resisted and negated—through workers and
others taking over, slowly or rapidly, the means of production directly (a possibility to which anarchists are
commited). Or whatever. There are more ways than
one to skin a cat, more ways than one to subvert the
economic order than by seizing its superstructural
armor from ruling-class control. But these alternative
possibilities Marx must—and does—believe to be im-
practicable in inferring the latter part of (2) from (1).
Then, even assuming all of (2) to be true—
notwithstanding alternative possibilities like the
above—(3) is true if and only if one believes, still
further, that great groups of men in society cannot be
enduringly united on grounds (such as humanist) other
than class relations of production or material interests.
This sort of alternative Marx in one way or another certainly entertained, but—again—firmly rejected as light-
headed, if not downright reactionary.

However, despite his general *rigeur de ligne* here, there
are a few largely ignored hints in Marx's mature work
that the schema we have set out above—reasoning from
the indispensability of the superstructure as a general
protector of the ruling-class economic order to the view
that class struggle is the only mode of action whereby
maintenance or change of the underlying "essence" of

society is secured—is not quite so restrictive as is generally thought.

To begin with, the possibility of specific superstructural agents not in fact protecting the ruling-class economic pattern, but being quite "free from partisanship," is not only allowed by Marx but described by him as having actually obtained, at the height of industrial capitalism (*CI*, 9).

Then again, he was well aware of the possibility that ruling-class members (such as the young capitalist Robert Owen) could disengage from their present economic interests; and, indeed, he openly called for, in his Preface to *Capital*, their promoting through the superstructure the interests of the working class: "Apart from higher motives, therefore, their own most important interests dictate to the classes that are for the nonce the ruling ones, the removal of all legally removable hindrances to the free development of the working class" (*CI*, 9).

Still again, he occasionally remarked on the possibility that the class struggle need not be violent, and that power might change hands from the capitalists to the proletarians peacefully: "We know of the allowances that we must make for the institutions, customs and traditions of the various countries: and we do not deny that there are countries such as America, England, and I would add Holland if I knew your institutions better, where the working people may achieve their goal by peaceful means" (*OB*, 494).

All these qualifications, however, are quite compatible with Marx's line of thought as we have formulated it. He recognizes and applauds superstructural agents, such as the "courageous" factory inspector Leonard Horner, who honor the state's claim to be the protector of the interests of all. But men such as Horner, he holds, are the exception, not the rule. He is impressed by the young millionaire Robert Owen's rising above economic interests to devote his life to industrial communes, but he observes that Owen remains élitist in his theory, and is not emulated, but vilified, by an increasingly defensive ruling class. He calls for "the classes that are for the nonce the ruling ones" to promote through the state the working class's "free development." But his appeal is not at all inconsistent with his line of thought, as it might first appear.[16] He emphasizes the possibility that "working people may achieve their goal by peaceful means," such as voting ruling-class representatives out of political office; but such possibility, so far as it effectively occurs or is allowed to occur, is still for him a "seizure" of the state from ruling-class hands, as it also is for them. In short, none of Marx's important qualifications here is inconsistent with his underlying argument. Rather, they disclose an openness and sophistication to his concept of the state that are not generally appreciated.

In summary, then, Marx conceives of the state as the indispensable "mask" and "weapon" protecting the ruling class's economic hegemony; holds that its existence

[16] G. A. Cohen, in personal correspondence, makes the following point here, worth citing *verbatim*:

The *Capital*, p. 9 quote is not puzzling when we read the context which shows why it is in the interests of the ruling class to allow the working class to develop itself: it is because then, when the revolution comes, there'll be less chance they'll have their heads chopped off. If you're going to be displaced, better "humane" than "brutal" displacers. Here, interestingly, something is in the interest of the people who are capitalists which is in no way in the interests of the survival of capitalism. Marx is saying that there is something in the interests of capitalists as individuals which they should consult against even their class interests, given the imminence of revolution. I don't want a deluge if it isn't going to be après moi.

as such requires its control by the ruling class to sustain this hegemony, and by some other class(es) to alter it; and maintains, in turn, that political class struggle is the only effective way of keeping or getting this control. This is, in brief, Marx's firm line on the legal and political superstructure and its disposition in all periods of history.

As we can readily discern, the importance granted to the superstructure in Marx's theory is very considerable. Indeed, he lays such great emphasis on it in his social philosophy (an inversion of Hegel's notion of the state as the bearer of the Universal) that one of the most moving criticisms of his position—exemplified by the anarchist Bakunin's opposition—is that he is an ultra-authoritarian, who betrays the working-class struggle in his German love for the state.[17] But whatever the merits of his position on the significance of the legal and political superstructure, we can see that—for all its dependence on the economic infrastructure—it is of central importance to Marx as a socio-historical factor. That it is normally in a "reflex" relationship with the economic "anatomy" underneath does not—as many have thought—render it somehow impotent or superfluous for him as a mechanism or phenomenon. On the contrary, the state is as vitally important for Marx in the

---

[17] Marx says, in a canonical text: "The movement of the proletariat is the self-conscious, independent movement of the immense majority, in the interest of the immense majority" (*CM*, 59-60). That is, the proletarian class struggle is a struggle of: i. the *immense majority* (i.e., all wage-dependent productive workers); ii. in a *self-conscious* way (i.e., comprehending itself as one class of such workers); iii. via an *independent* movement (i.e., not led by an external elite), and iv. for the *universal* interest, (i.e., the interest of all concerned). This is, it is clear, a radically democratic schema, not followed by Marx's most prominent successors, such as Lenin, who eschews at least principle (iii) (see Chapter 7), and rarely acknowledged by his most outspoken critics, including Bakunin.

ordinary life process of a society as defense mechanisms are for Freud in the ordinary life process of an individual. It is the historically constructed and visible hold whereby internal conflict is maintained in the grip of unseen (economic) structure: the so-to-say conscious "ego-formation" of society overlaying, regulating, and repressing the hidden contradictions beneath, in the defense of established but unacknowledged interests and their enslaving pattern.

# 5

## Ideology

As with all his other basic categories, Marx's concept of "ideology" has given rise over the years to a host of objections and decrials. A common interpretation, for example, has equated the term to mental activity as such, and then concluded from this an apparent major paradox in Marx's theory: namely, that while ideology is said, like the state, to be a mere "reflex" of the material mode of production, it must also be in its practical-scientific form a prime condition and constituent of the latter, inasmuch as productive forces necessarily involve the ideas of practical science in their construction and operation. But surely, this objection reasons, ideology cannot be both a mere reflex *and* a prime condition and constituent of the same thing.

Then, again, a not unrelated interpretation has construed Marx's notion of ideology as equivalent to "belief(s)" and, from this, criticized the notion in question on the issue of the relationship between belief and action in principle (e.g., Alasdair MacIntyre) and in the historical past (e.g., Max Weber): the former holding that, in principle, the two cannot be considered as separate phenomena, that is, belief "consists in" acting a certain way; and the latter holding that, in fact, certain beliefs ("the Protestant Ethic") gave rise to the economic form of capitalism, and do not, therefore, "reflect" it.[1]

[1] See MacIntyre's "A Mistake about Causality in Social Science," *Philosophy, Politics and Society*, ed. Peter Laslett and W. G. Runciman (Oxford, 1967), pp. 48-70; and Max Weber's classic *The Protestant Ethic and the Spirit of Capitalism* (London, 1968), p. 75. Weber seems

What we will show here, however, is that Marx's notion of ideology does not refer to mental activity or beliefs as such. Once this is shown, such criticisms as those
referred to above will be exposed as irrelevant to his
concept.

Marx's concept of "ideology" first leaps to prominence in *The German Ideology*, written with Engels in
1845-1846 as an attack on the then ascendent German
Idealist tradition. From the outset, ideology is conceived not as mental activity or belief as such but, as
Marx and Engels make evident in the opening sentence
of their work, *"men's conceptions of themselves"*: that is,
men's various articulated forms of social self-consciousness—from religious to economic, from moral
and aesthetic to legal-political. This same, strictly delineated concept of ideology—not at all ideas or beliefs
as such, but only special superstructural conceptions of
human matters or affairs from one or other
perspective—obtains throughout Marx's work, without
exception. Thus in his famous Preface to *A Contribution
to the Critique of Political Economy*, he says:

> In considering such [revolutionary] transforma-
> tions, the distinction should always be made be-

---

to include in his concept of belief not only—as is well known—
certain religious ideas, but also ideas involving the "rational organization of labour" (*ibid*, p.166), which for Marx do not belong to
ideology at all, but to the forces of production (see Chapter 2, p. 56).
Then too, Weber seems to want to subsume "ability and initiative"
(*ibid*, p. 179) and "purely mundane passions" (*ibid*, p. 182) under his
concept of ideology, when these are not even ideas and, accordingly,
never subsumed as such by Marx's more precisely delimited concept. In short, Marx's and Weber's concepts of ideology are radically
different, and hence what Weber shows about what he counts as
ideology does not, against almost fifty years of debate on the issue,
rebut what Marx shows about what *he* counts as ideology. They are
simply talking about different referents, as the following analysis of
Marx's position will make clear.

tween the material transformation of the economic conditions of production which can be established with the precision of natural science, and the legal, political, religious, aesthetic or philosophical—in short, ideological—forms in which men become conscious of this conflict and fight it out. Just as our opinion of an individual is not based on what he thinks of himself so we cannot judge of such a period by its own consciousness [i.e., what it thinks of itself].

And thus, in *The Eighteenth Brumaire of Louis Bonaparte* (p. 38), he says in a focal discussion of ideology: "And as in private life one differentiates between what a man thinks and says of himself and what he really is and does, so in historical struggles one must distinguish still more the phrases and fancies of parties from their real organism and their real interests, their conceptions of themselves from their reality." As Marx makes clear here, his concept of ideology is closely akin to our every-day concept of rationalization, only in his case the articulation and referent of such rationalization is social rather than "private" or individual, collectively rather than distributively construed.

Such public conceptions that men have about themselves are obviously not the technological ideas used to make material use-values. These ideas explicitly belong, as we showed in Chapter 2, to the domain of the forces of production. They are also not the ideas men have of things other than themselves. Thus "natural science" is explicitly excluded from consideration in a note in the first section of *The German Ideology* (p. 28).[2] They are,

[2] Where, then, does natural science belong in the Marxian model? Insofar as its conceptions and findings can be used to make material use-values (that is, generally), it belongs to the realm of productive forces. But insofar as its conceptions and findings are not thus us-

finally, not men's beliefs about themselves. One of the prominent qualities of much of the ideology that Marx discusses is its deliberate deceitfulness; thus, in these cases, not even public formulations of "belief," but of its opposite.[3] The referent we are dealing with in Marx's notion of ideology is not, in short, the all-inclusive range of cognitive phenomena that Marx's interpretors have hitherto held.

This important limitation in the referential range of ideology should not, however, be construed as downgrading its status as a sociohistorical factor. On the contrary, ideology's existence as the body of public self-conceptions renders it a kind of official currency of self-consciousness to which most or all other forms of

---

able, but are only men's conceptions of themselves in natural-science guise (for instance, "the brain is the director of the body corporation"), it is, in this respect, ideology.

Often, a body of natural science is both productive and ideological. Darwin's biology, for example, is essentially productive, formulating ideas and laws that are of immense technological use in, among other things, the breeding of plants and animals. But Darwin's biology is also ideological insofar as it articulates claims that are not so employable, but are only published conceptions of human affairs in disguise. Consider, for example, this not untypical passage in his masterwork, *The Origin of Species* (our emphases): "We sometimes see *the contest* [between varieties of plant species] soon decided: for instance, if several varieties of wheat be sown together, and the mixed seed resown, some of the varieties—*will beat the others*, and so yield more seed, and will consequently in a few years supplant the other varieties" (*The Origin of Species*, New York, 1909, p. 89). As Marx occasionally remarked of Darwin's biology, his natural science is overlaid with a Hobbesian political ideology (*SC*, 156-57).

[3] The public conceptions of ideology cannot, of course, ever be properly said to *be* beliefs. They might, on those occasions when they are not deceitful, be said to *express* beliefs (or, indeed, cause them to arise), but they can never themselves be properly counted as beliefs. Otherwise put, belief is an "interior" word, ideology an "exterior" word. For MacIntyre and others to talk about beliefs as all or even part of ideology is here, accordingly, akin to a category mistake.

cognition—including private (see *18thB*, 37)—are likely
to conform in one way or another, because man is a
"social animal." Indeed, Marx sometimes loosely talks
of "consciousness," with no qualifier, as being "determined"in the strict manner that the narrower realm of
ideology is determined, and this occasional conflation
has given rise to the mistake that he equates man's consciousness as such with ideology, and thereby holds a
tendentious philosophical position about the determination of ideas in general. But Marx makes it clear by all
the instances of ideology that he considers that it is not
man's consciousness as such to which he is referring
with this concept, but to its public modes;[4] though, we
repeat, he still regards these public modes—whether the
arcane philosophical publications of the German
Idealists or the contents of the popular press—as standard forms of human self-apprehension in any society
and, as such, pervasively influential.

Now that we have seen that Marx's concept of ideology is importantly limited in its referential range—not
only with respect to human (as opposed to nonhuman)
subject matter, but also with respect to its public mode
of existence—we schematize these and other observa-
tions into a set of criteria of ideology:
   1. It is constituted of *formulated ideas*, as opposed to
remaining merely on a subconscious, racial memory,
feeling, or spiritual level.[5]

   [4] For Marx's view of the determining influences on "consciousness as such," see our exposition, "Human Nature as Historically
Modified," in Chapter 1.
   [5] Formulated ideas could include more than linguistically formulated ideas, but Marx does not ever consider any further domain
(such as visual or musical arts) in his discussions of ideological
forms. See, however, John Berger's *Ways of Seeing* (London, 1972),
for an illuminating Marxian analysis of Western visual art since the

2. It refers to *human matters or affairs*, as opposed to nonhuman or natural phenomena.

3. Its content is *materially unproductive*, as opposed to being usable, in whole or part, to make material use-value.

4. It obtains in a *public mode*, such as any form of publication or public speech, as opposed to a private mode, such as personal reflection, conversation, or letter that occurs outside legal or political jurisdiction.[6]

5. It is *subject to state control*, by virtue of the approval of some sort, such as license or permit, required from the state for any public mode to ideate (whether publishing firm, official document agency, church, school, assembly, or whatever).[7]

---

Renaissance. Recently, the domain of spectator sport has been also analyzed as ideology, though, again, Marx himself never considers this area in any of his discussions of ideology, despite the presence of a substantial component of "linguistically formulated ideas," both oral and written, in this sphere of public ideation. For formative analyses of spectator sport as ideology, see our "Philosophy of a Corner Linebacker," *The Nation*, CCXII, No. 3 (February 1971), 83-85; "Smash Thy Neighbour," *The Atlantic*, CCXXIX, No. 1 (January 1972), 77-80; and "The Case against the Olympics," *Macleans*, LXXXVI, No. 1 (January 1973), 34-38.

[6] Otherwise put, ideology is constituted only of ideas that have reached *the public stage*. We suggest this alternative construction because Marx employs an implicit dramaturgical model throughout his work in his description of ideological phenomena. Just as the legal and political superstructure is implicitly construed by him in terms of stage performance, so ideology is similarly construed by him as stage speech. The composite is the "world-historical drama"— sometimes "tragedy" and sometimes "farce." Hence Marx's recurrent words for the superstructural realm—"illusion" and "pretence."

One way of catching the picture Marx is trying to present of the relationship between the economic base and the superstructure is, thus, to conceive of the former as man's private material interests, and the latter as these interests being acted out on the public platform to the audience of society's membership as a whole.

[7] That ideology is subject to state control is not only given *ad hoc* attention by Marx (for instance, when his *CPE* had to pass through

For anything to count as ideology, it must meet all five of these criteria.

The last criterion is of particular significance because it explains Marx's famous insistence that the ideology of a society is the ideology of its ruling class. The ruling class, after all, is held to control the state as its agency of collective self-protection; hence, inasmuch as ideology is subject to the superintendence of the state, it follows that it is subject to the superintendence of a ruling-class agency. Ideology is thus not only economically tied to the ruling class, but superstructurally tied, as well; as Marx knew well from his personal experience at the hands of state censors, and at the hands of publishers afraid to publish his work for fear of official repression. Hence, that the ideology of a society is said by Marx to be the ideology of its ruling class is not at all the philo-

---

state censors before publication in Germany), but follows from his conception of the state's essential function as a protective mechanism for the collective interests of the ruling class: which protection entails, among other things, protection of these interests in the realm of public ideation. Now precisely how, for Marx, this protection of the ruling class's collective interests is in fact secured in the realm of ideology, other than by the vigilance of individual owners of the "means of intellectual production," varies in accordance with specific sociohistorical conditions. With the case of published print in the United States, for example, the standard state "license or permit" is not required. But other realms of ideology here, a Marxian attention to specific sociohistorical circumstances would disclose, are subject to such state control (for instance, schools and television); and the sphere of print itself is subject to other forms of state control than the standard "license or permit" (such as antisubversion legislation and government "blacklisting," harassment of security, police, and tax officers and offices, information withholding either by secrecy acts or otherwise, selective withdrawal of legal protection, and so forth). An irresistible example here is the burning by the United States government in 1956 and 1960 of all journals published by the institute of radical thought's great complement to Marx, Wilhelm Reich (reported in *The Encyclopedia of Philosophy* VII [New York: 1972], 113-14). Reich himself, we might add, died in a U.S. prison in between these book burnings, in 1957.

sophically problematic claim it is often made out to be—for example, a claim about the nature and causation of ideas in general, which is subject to weakness of a general epistemological sort—but a plausible empirical claim about how ideas that reach the public stage are, in fact, subject to effective control by established social power, state as well as economic (see Chapter 7).[8]

These five criteria of ideology are not explicitly stated by Marx. But there is no instance of ideology that he treats—of the countless examples spread through his work—that does not satisfy all of them.

Yet although Marx's concept of ideology denotes a much more restricted domain than has been conventionally held, it must not be thought that the concept in question thereby loses its referential power. It still clearly includes within its ambit of reference mass-media, school, church, academic, legal, political, aesthetic, and all other forms of public communication;[9] and, as such, informs the private sphere of ideas with its content more or less exhaustively, depending on the extent to which particular individuals are influenced by the public realm. What remains outside this domain Marx properly regarded—its being merely personal idea-

[8] i. What, it might be asked, of societies where state superintendence of ideation extends beyond the public realm to the private realm too? Such extension, typical of those national boarding schools ironically called "Marxist societies," is conceptually permitted by totalizing the notion of what is "public" to include all discourse whatever.

ii. The corollary of this criterion of ideology—that it is subject to state control—is, of course, that what is not so subject is not ideology. This is one reason why the disappearance of the state and the disappearance of ideology go hand in hand in Marx's vision of communist society.

[9] Some forms of public communication (such as educational) are productive as well as ideological: productive insofar as the ideas they disseminate can be used to make material use-values, ideological insofar as the ideas they disseminate cannot (see pp. 125-26n).

tion—as unqualified for the status of sociohistorical influence.[10]

Though we now have a firmly delimiting set of criteria of Marx's notion of ideology, a very important issue remains unexplored. That is, throughout his work, essentially with regard to the theories of political economists, Marx draws the distinction between scientific and unscientific conceptions of human affairs; that is, between "classical" and "vulgar" Political Economy. Even though in these cases the works in question all satisfy the criteria of ideology we have proposed, their difference to Marx is so substantive that a case has sometimes been made for highlighting their difference by classifying only unscientific thought as ideological. If this line of interpretation is followed, then still another mark of ideology must be that it is "unscientific," in another sense than already implied by the criteria outlined so far. By this additional criterion, then, "classical" political economy and other "truly scientific" theory—especially Marx's theory itself—would count as nonideological.

Though there is evidence of a shallow sort to recommend such an interpretation—namely, Marx's generally pejorative use of the term "ideology"—we are not going to regard it as decisive, though many have. Rather, we are going to interpret Marx as regarding scientific and unscientific conceptions of human affairs as distinct subclasses of ideology. Our reasons for doing this are:

1. Only in this way can such scientific conceptions of human affairs as classical political economy be subsumed by Marx's general framework of sociohistorical explanation. Otherwise, these scientific conceptions are

---

[10] Of course, to the extent that personal ideation is publicly communicated, it does qualify as a sociohistorical influence.

quite excluded from such subsumption, and a major area of Marx's concern is thereby put out of reach of his own theoretical framework.

2. One may only suppose from Marx's persistent talk of "ideological struggle" that he counted "scientific socialism" as part of this struggle. Otherwise, he rules out the "true" representative of proletarian interests, scientific socialism, from, in fact, representing these interests in the public realm of ideation.

3. If scientific conceptions of human affairs such as Marx's cannot be ideology, then they cannot be repressed as ideology *via* economic determinism. Thus Marx's conceptions are not so repressed, and a central thrust of his economic determinism theory is thereby nullified.

4. The most persuasive reason for holding that scientific conceptions of human affairs are not ideological is that if they were ideological they could not be knowledge in the strict Marxian sense (see p. 79n). However, as we show in the course of this chapter, Marx's theory is properly conceived as both ideology *and* knowledge: ideology before it is enacted in socialist revolution, and knowledge with the occurrence of this enactment.

For these reasons, then, we conclude that Marx's concept of ideology subsumes scientific as well as unscientific conceptions of human affairs. We now ask what criterion or criteria he employs to distinguish these subclasses of ideology. If we are to understand the full complexity and import of his concept, this substantive distinction—which is basic to his harshly critical attitude toward almost all ideology (that is, ideology that is unscientific)—requires explanation.

Unfortunately, Marx never makes a general distinction between scientific and unscientific conceptions that men have about themselves, but only makes a specific distinction with respect to his most abiding concern, the conceptions of political economy. However, we can extend without distortion the principles he proffers here to historical, legal, and all other ideological conceptions. What he says with regard to Political Economy is this: that scientific Political Economy "investigates the real relations of production" (that is, the effective ownership relations) in a society, whereas unscientific Political Economy does not investigate such relations, but ignores or conceals them. In his own words: "Once for all, I may here state, that by classical Political Economy, I understand that economy which, since the time of W. Petty, has investigated the real relations of production in bourgeois society, in contradistinction to vulgar economy, which deals with appearances only" (*CI*, 81). Thus for Marx the work of David Ricardo, who "consciously makes the antagonism of class interests the starting point of his investigations" (*CI*, 14), belongs to the sphere of science; whereas the work of most political economists after 1830, which conceals or distorts or ignores these "real relations of production" (by, for example, representing the bourgeois economy as a harmony of freely choosing subjects) is not scientific, but merely "superficial," "trite," or—at worst—embodies "bad conscience and the evil intent of apologetic" (*CI*, 15). To render Marx's distinction here more general and systematic, then, we say that any conceptions of human affairs that attend to society's economic system in the following respects are scientific, whereas any conceptions that do not so attend are unscientific:

1. the real *relations of production*; that is, effective relations of ownership to society's forces of production;

2. the division into *objectively antagonistic classes* of these relations of production; that is, generally, monopoly ownership of the means of production by a

minority of society (the "ruling class") and little or no
such ownership by the rest of society (the "working
class");

3. the *laws of exchange* between these classes; that is,
generally, laws such that the class that has an ownership
monopoly is able to regularly extract from the other
class or classes unpaid labor.[11]

Certainly Marx's idea of scientific conceptions of
human affairs is not confined to these considerations
alone. He also insists in various places on the classical
scientific canon of empirical method (as in his assaults
on continental Idealism of all sorts); on the indispensability of an historical approach to human affairs, as in his
repeated repudiation of those who—like the otherwise
scientific Ricardo—ignore the universal principle of
"negation" or change in their conceptions of class division as a "social law of nature" (*CI*, 14); on the necessity
of "freedom from bias" (*PofP*, 19)—which, by the way,
he saw the working class, as opposed to the ruling class
and its "hired prize fighter" ideologists, as specially capable of by virtue of its membership's ownership of a
few or no material interests to distort their vision; and,
finally, on the theoretical imperative of explanatory
adequacy, as in his almost life-long obsession with full
explanation of the source of profits, which previous
economists—scientific or not—had, in his view, failed
to provide.

[11] Presumably, conceptions of human affairs that attend to these
related facts of effective ownership, class division, and laws of exchange would count as scientific for Marx, even if the precise classes
and laws of exchange discerned were, assuming accurate data, not
the same as those perceived by himself. Otherwise, of course,
Marx's distinction between scientific and unscientific ideology
would be subverted by his own unscientific assumption of
infallibility—not an altogether impossible assumption on his part,
we must acknowledge.

Nevertheless, when it comes to the question of distinguishing in ideology the scientific from the unscientific, Marx's most basic concern seems to be with whether or not the conceptions in question attend to the economic "essence" of all historical society—its relations of production, class structure, and laws of exchange. Indeed, he generally attributes failures in these other areas he mentions to a more fundamental failure to investigate critically this underlying "essence." Thus, for example, political economists before him fail to achieve explanatory adequacy in their work in consequence of a more basic failure to apprehend the real relations of exchange between classes—they find it "very dangerous to stir too deeply the burning question of the origin of surplus value" (*CI*, 516). And thus, too, failures to pursue empirical method, to adopt an historical approach, and to be "free from bias" are also, for Marx, outgrowths of a more fundamental negligence with regard to apprehending the economic foundations of the society in which the ideologists in question live. They fail in these various respects, he intimates repeatedly, because they are, on a deeper level, consciously or unconsciously *afraid* of examining critically the economic system that yields them the privilege of being ideologists in official favor, rather than toiling producers anonymously oppressed. From this basic "sellout" (a term that more or less exactly captures Marx's point), their other failures in scientific method derive. It is on this account that Marx is so deprecatory about ideology generally. For him, its typically unscientific nature is ultimately grounded on cowardly self-interest.

With the exception, then, of certain modern formulations of social science—"classical" political economy and his own theory, for example—virtually all ideology is for Marx unscientific. But Marx does not stop in his characterization of the mainstream of ideology with the attribute of "unscientific." Throughout his work, he alludes to other properties of the ideological mainstream that render it systematically misleading or, to call upon a number of his own particular terms, "illusory," "upside-down," and, more directly, "false." From his many and various descriptions here, we derive the following set of standard mechanisms of ideological deception:

1. Its categories are "empty generalities" rather than "determinate" and, as such, permit discourse to be "torn away from the facts" (*GID*, 53). For example, the contentless category of "man as such" (familiar in the Continental philosophy of Marx's day) detaches thought from "real, living, concrete individuals" in the here-and-now of the ongoing historical process; or, more specifically, the indeterminate categories of "Freedon," "Equality," and "Rights" in capitalist society mask by their generality the distinctions in the real world between the "Freedom," "Equality," and "Rights" of individuals who own nothing but their labor-power and individuals who own the wealth to buy, among other things, this labor-power for their own profit. Such "empty generality" of categories permits, as well, almost any signification whatever that might be convenient to ruling-class interests: see (3).

2. These same categories or ideas are not only "emancipated from the world" by virtue of their indeterminateness, but just as importantly are "transformed from predicates into subjects" (*GID*, 255), from general properties ascribed descriptively to the world, to the self-subsistent movers of the world (a Feuerbachian point, of course). For example, Platonists and German Idealists believe that the real world is the product of the "ideal world" (*GID*, 24); Proudhon believes that eco-

nomic categories precede and give rise to economic real-
ities; adherents to religion imagine that the properties of
a god they project rule human affairs as an omnipotent
force; and bourgeois apologists ascribe to their conceptions of liberty, rights, and law the magical role of independently operating authors of world-historical events.

3. The conceptions of ideology, insofar as they are
employed to refer to determinate social phenomena at
all, are selectively employed, so that they validate what
promotes the established social order, and invalidate
what challenges this order. For example, the conceptions that articulate an abhorrence of violence are generally applied in cases of people acting by force against
established material interests, such as rebels or communists, and generally suspended in the far more frequent cases of people acting by force for established material interests, such as political officials, police forces,
and armies. Or, similarly, the conceptions that articulate a fondness for "Law," "Order," and "Property"
figure very prominently in the ideology of a society
when what is involved is the protection of the ruling
class's material interests, but very weakly, if at all, when
what is involved is the ruled class's material interests
(for example, with illegally oppressive working conditions, "anarchial" insecurity of employment, and expropriation of centuries-old "commons" land rights).

4. The conceptions of ideology are historically distorted in that the language they employ, the phenomena
to which they refer, and the viewpoints they embody
are more or less tied to the past and, *ipso facto*, more or
less inadequate to the present. For example, the ideology of the mid-nineteenth century French political
struggle is permeated with "borrowed language," references to past circumstances and views of dead heroes
from the French Revolution of 1789. Or, again, the

ideology of maturely capitalistic England employs the phraseology of personal property, the circumstances of the yeoman past, and the arguments of Locke to justify the monopoly holdings of the modern big bourgeoisie. "The tradition of all the dead generations," Marx says in one of his more allusive and poetic utterances, "weighs like a nightmare on the brains of the living" (*18thB*, 10).

5. The conceptions of ideology generally tend to idealize human states of affairs by ascribing predicates to such affairs that "clothe" them in an inappropriately attractive guise. For example, the social positions that men hold by their superior command of material power are described as held from "divine sanction," "Social Contract," or "eternal necessity"; the material conditions into which men are born or forced are characterized as manufactured or chosen by acts of individual "will"; the untrammeled course of capitalist exploitation and accumulation is lyricized as "progress," "civilization," and "freedom"; and the successful securing of the economic interests of the ruling class is celebrated as the triumph of "Mankind," "Justice," or "the Absolute Spirit." The "aura," "intoxication," and "glamor" of such phraseology gives rise, in Marx's view, to an opiated ideological dwelling place where the perpetual conquest of force and fraud ever yields the inverted and romantic picture of some higher design regulating the world.[12]

These various mechanisms of deception of the ideological mainstream are not necessary attributes of

[12] Thus Marx says in one of his most telling descriptions of religious ideology (*YM*, 250): "Religion is the generalized theory of this world—its spiritualistic point d'honneur, its enthusiasm, its moral sanction, its solemn complement, its general ground of consolation and justification—it is the heart of a heartless world, as it is the spirit of spiritless conditions. It is the opium of the people."

ideology. Unlike the five criteria of ideology earlier outlined, they are simply standard duperies to which Marx
draws attention in his many provocative comments on
various ideological forms. But they are nevertheless informed by one essential and unifying function. That is,
all operate, in one way or another, to conceal the real
relations of production, class divisions, and laws of exchange of the society in question, and thereby exemplify
nonscientific ideology's principle of not attending to the
economic "essence" of human affairs.

By virtue of this unifying function—concealment of
the ruling-class economic order—mainstream ideology
is complementary in role to the state. That is, it forms
the rationalization component of the overall superstructural defence mechanism whereby, in Marx's account,
the ruling-class economic base is maintained intact.
What legal and political institutions do by organized
coercion and appearance of sanctity, mainstream ideology does by various forms of cover story in the realm of
public talk. Both sorts of phenomena contribute, in all
but revolutionary or prerevolutionary periods, to a
single, integrating end—protection of the underlying
economic order. They are both parts of the *super*structure, in its largest sense; both defenders, in various
ways, of the economic substructure, and indispensable
as such to the latter's historical persistence; both dependent, in Marx's view, on the inherent antagonisms
of this economic base for their existence; and both fated
to "wither away" with the end of class-divided relations
of production in communist society.[13]

[13] See G. A. Cohen's "The Withering away of Social Science,"
*Philosophy and Public Affairs*, I, No. 2 (Winter 1972), 182-203. We
add, however, that insofar as economic classes do remain in communist society (for instance, male adult vs. women and children)
such "appearances" of ideology as deified father figures might be
expected to persist.

Like legal and political phenomena, then, ideological phenomena are in the main for Marx a defensive "reflex" to the exigencies of the underlying economic base, rather than any sort of initiating influence. Indeed, with Marx's concept of ideology, unlike belief—to which it has been conventionally but mistakenly assimilated—ideology does not relate to action so much as inaction. None of the content of ideology can, by definition, be used to make a material use-value; none of it is, therefore, a productive force. Furthermore, it is not normally a motivator of economic behavior, insofar as it is typically constructed by noneconomic agents, formulated in terms other than those of material interest, and expressed outside the sphere of commodity exchange altogether.[14] So ideology in Marx's sense does not play a role in productive, nor, generally, even economic action. On the other hand, as public formulations sponsored by nonproductive agencies living off the society's surplus value, Marx conceives ideology as playing a very significant role in the inaction of society's members, namely, with regard to altering their economic arrangements. For insofar as it is normally a "cloak," "disguise," "veil," "shroud," and so on, of these arrangements, it blocks apprehension of their reality and, in this way, ensures their perpetuation. For it is difficult to socially change what is not socially seen. So the explanatory force of ideology is, for the most part, with respect to men's refraining from a certain sort of action—changing the economic substructure—rather

[14] Ideologies of national and racial superiority may appear to promote economic action—for example, imperialist ventures and foreign wars—but for Marx they merely hold on course (albeit as indispensable cover stories) what is ultimately determined by ruling-class material interests. It is in such cases especially that his distinction between the "appearances" of a society's ideology and the "reality" of its economic order is of striking explanatory import.

than to their undertaking this or any other sort of materially influential initiative. It is typically, as we have said, public rationalization of human matters and affairs and—like private rationalization of private matters and affairs—a justificatory concealment of underlying material interests.

In this way, then, ideology and the state are for Marx neatly complementary in both their nature and their function. One is public ideas (ideology). The other is public institutions (the state). Together, they make up one whole, the public realm. This is how they are complementary in *nature*. On the other hand, both serve one end, to protect the underlying ruling-class economic order from change—ideology by concealing it, the state by enforcing it. This is how they are complementary in *function*. Hence Marx sometimes refers to them as an integrated unity, as a "whole immense superstructure": the ideas and the institutions of one great public domain serving one great function, to maintain the ruling-class economic structure and its "law of motion" of surplus-value extraction intact.

However, just as the state operates as an agency of action with respect to changing the economic order before or during periods of revolutionary upheaval, that is, periods when the productive forces have "outgrown" their economic "integument," and require a change in the latter to ensure their own preservation and development, so ideology too becomes such an agency in these exceptional times of epochal transition. Ideology, like law and politics, is always part of the "class struggle"—its public consciousness side—and in these abnormal periods of revolutionary unrest a rising, hitherto repressed class's attempt to "seize" its influence is simply the cognate in the realm of ideas of the struggle to capture state power. In these periods, the class-ruptured economic order ceases to be maintained intact, and more or less "explodes" into open conflict by virtue of the superstructure as a whole being effectively claimed on all levels by a challenging class that in the past has been successfully kept from such levers of social power by the ruling class's control of them. Hence, just as the state ceases to hold the economic base in its established pattern to the extent that a formerly repressed class seizes its reins, so *pari passu* the ideology of the society in question ceases to exercise such a hold to the extent that *its* reins are seized; for example, by new and able critical conceptions of the social order in question, such as Marx's scientific theory itself, which achieve the status of ideology to the extent that new permission of state sanction is secured by the underclass's struggle on the legal and political level. In short, the ideological aspect of the superstructure, like the institutional aspect, reverses its normal role of defense mechanism for the economic infrastructure in prerevolutionary or revolutionary periods, and becomes a mobilizer with respect to altering the latter rather than—as in its typical function—an immobilizer; and, as such, it is qualified for the status of knowledge in Marx's *praxis* epistemology—unlike mainstream ideology, which cannot, in principle, so qualify.[15] Here ideology can and does truly, if exceptionally, spring men into economic action—its public formulations no longer merely the excuse, concealer, opiate of social rationalization, but penetrating to the secrets of the old economic system, as a sort of public self-recognition taking place in the final act of the historical dramas of the *ancien regime* and resolving its conflicts into a new, unwritten plot.

[15] We have now the missing link between Marx's thought as scientific ideology and as scientific knowledge: it is the enacting of socialist revolution (see Chapter 2, p. 70-71n).

For Marx, of course, it is only with scientific socialism that such "public self-recognition" that prefaces the death of the old order and the birth of the new may properly be regarded as being true self-recognition. For only here is the long-hidden tragic flaw of all historical human society—antagonistic class relations—fully apprehended. As Marx poetically puts it in one of his early works: "Communism is the riddle of history solved, and knows itself to be this solution" (*EPM*, 102). In contrast to the revolutionary ideology of the seventeenth-century bourgeoisie, which masqueraded as redemptive realization, but in fact merely sanctified the tragic flaw of class-division in another form to which it remained blind in accordance with bourgeois class interests, scientific socialism is scientific and, as such, adequately comprehends this flaw in all its depths and grip. The final resolving agent on the plane of public consciousness of the tragic flaw of historical society is thus, for Marx, the ideology of scientific socialism, which in the adequacy of its recognition spells the end of antagonistic class relations altogether. As in all classical tragic drama, its insight may indeed disclose to the stage's action the harbinger of bloody climax, but the new order whose dawn it signals is purged by it of the hidden *hamartia* from which the travails of classical tragedy have always sprung.[16]

Given that Marx's concept of ideology, like his concept of the state, allows for a quite different function in

[16] We extend our exposition of Marx into explicit dramaturgical model, here and elsewhere, not merely for explanatory flair, but to suggest the intensely dramatic nature of his work. Marx was a great devotee of classical drama—especially that of Aeschylus and Shakespeare—and the sociohistorical conflicts and flaws and rhetoric he describes are imbued with its archetypal power. Indeed, we wonder whether this, as much as his scientific penetration and sweep, is not responsible for the globe-moving influence of his theory.

prerevolutionary or revolutionary periods than the merely defense-mechanism function of normal times, we might ask what is the nature of man's public self-conceptions in that communist utopia that succeeds the last, the proletarian revolution.

First, we know that such self-conceptions are no longer ideological, inasmuch as there is no state by which their public mode must be sanctioned nor, re-latedly, any class divisions whereby an ascendant class controls the ideas in question as part of its mechanism of rule. Man's social self-conceptions, thus, become liter-ally dis-interested, that is, neither funded nor informed by class interest; and, as such, they neither conceal an antagonistic economic order—as mainstream ideol-ogy—nor penetrate behind such concealing *Schein*—as scientific ideology. All ideology disappears with the dis-appearance of class division: the former sort to the ex-tent that there are no longer any social ruptures to con-ceal, and the latter sort to the extent that there are no longer "appearances" to penetrate behind. Man's eco-nomic relations, being communistic, cease to furnish the antagonistic material conditions required for either scientific or unscientific ideology to arise. At this point, man's intrinsic *potentia* of projective consciousness is liberated in the realm of social self-conception (as well as elsewhere), and the "chains of illusion" binding the Prometheus of humankind are, with his other chains, "sprung into the air." Ideology gives way, in brief, to the emancipated ideas of public self-knowledge.

# 6

## Forms of Social Consciousness

Unlike the other general categories constituting the structure of Marx's world-view, this final category, "forms of social consciousness," has never, so far as we know, been singled out for critical attention. For though Marx very often talks of "forms of consciousness" or, in his later texts, "forms of social consciousness," he usually does so in such a way as to permit its interpretative conflation with "ideology" or "ideological forms." Published commentary on Marx has accordingly assumed an identity of sense here, counting the distinction in formulation as a mere difference of expression, and not sense. What we propose now, however, is that Marx's notion of "forms of social consciousness" is patently different in meaning from ideology. It is, we hold, a crucially distinct and path-breaking category of his thought—not only of signal importance in its own right, but indispensable to the understanding of Marx's theory of economic determinism,[1] as well as of germinal importance to the development of his philosophy of mind.[2]

In claiming for this category of "forms of social consciousness" a distinct and general status in Marx's explanatory model, we are relying on Marx's continual reference to it, as well as his occasional distinction between it and "ideology": for example, his distinction in

[1] See our discussion of economic determinism by "mapping" in Chapter 7.
[2] See Chapter 1, "Human Nature as Historically Modified," for the outline of Marx's general position here.

*The German Ideology* between "morality, religion, metaphysics and all the rest of ideology *and* their corresponding forms of social consciousness."[3]

Second, we are relying on the fact that the literal German here—*Bewusstseinsformen*—cannot without distortion of the word, and the Kant-and-after philosophical tradition associated with the notion of "forms of consciousness," be held as synonymous with ideology. Such conflation simply betrays defective translation and a limited grasp of philosophical history.

Finally, we are influenced by the theoretical sense the distinction in question makes when introduced into Marx's general categorical framework. It raises no problems, and contributes strikingly to the explanatory range and adequacy of his theory.

Given, then, that ideology and forms of social consciousness are discrete categories, precisely how do they differ? The answer is: the former is constituted of public formulations, whereas the latter are the *presupposed principles* of such formulations. The relation between these two, in turn, is such that the latter govern the former, as the underlying principles of a bigot govern the manifold of his specific statements. Consider, for example, the standard public formulation, "Columbus discovered America," and the presupposed general principle, *All human discernment is European*, underlying and governing this statement.[4] The former qualifies as ideology in

---

[3] *GID*, 38. See also *S-V III*, 483.

[4] Consider also such statements as "Orientals have no respect for life," "Africans can't govern themselves," "The only good Indian is a dead Indian," and so forth. In all such cases, the underlying, general principle, *All human discernment is European*, governs these specific statements as a syntactical rule governs a myriad of speech acts. It constitutes, so to speak, a rudiment in the grammar of white racism.

Interestingly, anticommunist ideology seems to have an homologous underlying principle governing it: namely, *All human discern-*

Marx's schema, whereas the latter qualifies as a form of social consciousness. With this concept of "forms of social consciousness," we have, in short, an historical materialist variation on Kant's *a priori* forms of understanding.

The relationship of "forms of social consciousness" to the forces of production or economic base is, however, no different from the relationship of ideology to these. The latter remain, for Marx, primary and determining (see Chapters 7 and 8). What is being suggested by the category in question is another level or sphere of "correspondence" between a society's mode of production and the rest of its life: here, the presupposed principles or "forms"—as opposed to ideological "expressions" or "products"—of its social consciousness.[5]

"Forms of social consciousness" and "ideology," then, are two levels—the governing form and the governed content—of published conceptions of human affairs. And though a society's ideology and forms of consciousness may be, as a matter of fact, at the same time the ideology and forms of consciousness of individuals belonging to this society, they are not necessarily or always so inculcated, and Marx makes no claim of this sort. As he makes clear in his talk of the "private" realm, the latter is outside his domain of analysis (*CI*, 9), and figures as a sphere of comparison rather than of

---

*ment is noncommunist.* Thus, such popular public utterances as "socialist hordes," "iron curtain," "communist slavery," "better dead than red," and so on, all conform to this *a priori* regulative principle, however various and manifold their appearance in ideology may be. That all white racists are also anticommunists may have something to do with the structural equivalence of the underlying principles governing the two ideologies.

[5] Because forms of social consciousness underlie ideology, the former is theoretically prior in Marx's overall model. Yet we have not maintained this priority in the order of our chapters because our explanation of the former presupposes our explanation of the latter.

subsumption (*CPE*, 21). All he is directly concerned with is consciousness that has achieved public exhibition of some sort or other, whether one is considering this consciousness with respect to its "products" (ideology) or with respect to its presupposed principles of regulation ("forms").

Having outlined the general sense of Marx's category of "forms of social consciousness," we now identify what these "forms" in fact are. Together these forms constitute the *public frame of mind* of all historical societies or—in Marx's language—"forms of social consciousness in general."[6]

Let us consider, as we have said, the "forms" in question as presupposed principles to which publicly exhibited ideas typically conform, whether or not these governing principles are discerned or—more likely—not discerned, by the ideological agents in question. Forms of social consciousness are like rules of grammar. They may regulate what is expressed without those who are using them knowing what they are, or even that they exist.[7] The "forms" of this sort that Marx implies as "in general" governing the vast manifold of ideological formulations from the times of the ancients to the present are:

1. *The existing social order cannot be qualitatively altered.* Thus it is ideologically represented as an "eternal necessity" that may possibly be made more internally consistent or "harmonious," but may not itself be changed.

2. *The existing social order is morally good.* Thus, in

---

[6] Marx says: "The social consciousness of past ages, despite all the multiplicity and variety it displays, moves within certain common forms" (*CM*,72).

[7] On the other hand, just as the grammatical rules governing language may be explicitly formulated as language, so the forms of social consciousness we are about to identify may be explicitly formulated as ideology.

ideological formulation, it is described as bearing the attributes of some ethical entity—"Divine Will," "Reason," "Justice," "Civilization," and so on.

3. *What does not comply with the existing social order is blameworthy*. Thus, in ideology, social protest is depicted as "extremist," reformers as "agitators," foreign antagonists as "barbarous," noncompliance with authority as "violence," spokesman for the impoverished as "demagogues," and so on.

4. *What promotes the social order is praiseworthy*. Thus, in ideology, undeviating submission to this order counts as "moral" and "high-minded," foreign conquest as "heroic" and "glorious," violent repression of opposition as "firmness" and "resolve," exercise of vested power over others as "duty" and "public service," passive acceptance of exploitation as "loyalty" and "reliability," and so on.

5. *Whatever rank is held by individuals in the social order represents their intrinsic worth*. Thus, in ideology, in successive epochs slaves are held to be slaves "by nature," the privileged as privileged by "noble blood," the unemployed as unemployed by "innate laziness," and so on.[8]

6. *The social order represents the interests of all in the society*. Thus, in ideological account, all citizens "will" it, "consent" to it, "benefit" from it, or whatever—the

---

[8] Consider such terms as "villain," "varlot," "knave," "vulgar," "yokel," "clod," "churl," and "red-neck." All these terms originally referred to low-rank positions in the social order; all have come to refer to intrinsic defects of character. On the other hand, consider such terms as "noble," "princely," "majestic," "high-class," "honorable," "gentleman," and "virtuous." All these terms originally referred to high-rank positions in the social order; all have come to refer to intrinsic merits of character. Here, then, we have a paradigmatic example of a form of social consciousness operating as a transepochal law of conceptual development.

multiform Social-Contract postulate—even if some of them "treacherously" or "irresponsibly" oppose it.

7. *A part of a society (or a social organization) must always represent the whole of the society (or social organization).* Thus, in ideology, a society without rulers or a workplace without a master is simply unintelligible, a state of "disorder," "anarchy," or "chaos."

8. *The social property of the ruling class is an independent, self-moving power.* Thus, in ideological formulation, the militarily held territory of the feudal lords is represented as "Landed Property," autonomously enjoining obligations and duties of all; the collective weapon of the ruling class as represented as "The Law" or "The State," independently and impartially subjecting all citizens alike to its rule; the private Capital of the big bourgeoisie is represented as self-governing subjecthood, which of itself "produces profits," "creates jobs," "brings prosperity"; and so on.

9. *Ultimate social agency resides in a nonhuman entity.* Thus, in the ideology of various epochs, ultimate responsibility for social phenomena is attributed to "Fate," "God," "Divine Plan," "Nature," "Gold," "The Invisible Hand," and so on.[9]

We now propose a number of clarifications to these "forms of social consciousness in general":

1. They are obviously very intimately related. This is why we have called them, together, the "frame" of social mind. As Marx's metaphor of a "camera obsura" suggests (*GID*, 37), they are like the layers of a unitary and inverting lens, through which the objective phe-

---

[9] Thus, those who hold that such-and-such a social pattern (such as war, hierarchy, private property, and so on) is but an expression of "human nature" are conforming to this form of social consciousness. For nature, not man, is the prescriber in any such claim.

nomena of human society pass and are organized prior to this or that ideological formulation.

2. This "unitary lens" or "public frame of mind," which organizes as an historically and socially developed *given* that which emerges ultimately in ideological formulations, is not necessarily the "frame of mind" of individuals in the society in question, even if the individuals concerned happen to be themselves ideologists. As we emphasized in Chapter 5, the ideas Marx is concerned with in "ideology" are only those ideas that achieve the social reality of public exhibition. As his imagery repeatedly suggests, these are the ideas of the sociohistorical stage; and one may adopt the "public frame of mind" required of a speaker on this social stage without being committed any more than any other hired performer, either to it, or to the ideological expressions it emerges in, as a private individual. It may be merely an in-role performance; and the histrionic nature of ideology and corresponding forms of social consciousness is persistently stated or implied in Marx's descriptions. (Consider his recurrent imagery of "masks," "costumes," "chorus," "platform," and so on, when talking of these phenomena.) However, it would be wrong to suppose that Marx considered or suggested that the various forms and expressions of thought of this public "drama" did not carry over into and impinge upon men's private mental lives. On the contrary, his massive emphasis on man as a "social animal," on man as a being whose consciousness derives from his "social being" and "social relations," urges the conclusion that ideology and forms of social consciousness are exceedingly influential in the formation of individuals' own cognitive lives. Such ideas and forms of public judgment constitute for Marx the socially accepted standards of ideation in any historical society, into which personal

consciousness more or less resolves itself as the price of social existence. It is in this way, among others earlier described, that the individual's consciousness becomes a "social product." Thus individuals, as a matter of fact, take on the various roles, postures, and lines of this public stage as their own—so that what exists in principle only in the realm of official superstructure comes more or less simultaneously to obtain contingently in individuals' own minds—what we today might call "brain washing." At this point, social "self-deception" (Marx's own phrase, *18thB*, 11) becomes individual "self-deception," and the important distinction in principle is conflated in fact ("All the world's a stage," to cite one great ideologist). This is why Marx is so often anxious to "drum into people's heads" his revolutionary mode of thought. He is trying literally to *break* the hold that ruling-class ideology and its governing forms of social consciousness have on the minds of their individual working-class victims and the latter's various representatives. His recurrent phraseology of "shattering illusions," it seems clear, most aptly applies to the ensconced forms of public consciousness, and it is these forms, with their "carry-over" effect on individual consciousness,—perhaps more than ideological formulations themselves—that Marx is concerned to challenge and usurp. More basically (that is, structurally) than anything else in the realm of consciousness, they allow for the identification of the individual with the ruling-class social order within which he lives, an identification that can and does approach the level of "organic," to invoke Gramsci's term. When such "forms of social consciousness" become part of the cognitive equipment of the individual himself (on the public "stage" or not), the remarkable possibility of one who is objectively exploited by the social order comprehending the persist-

ence of it as in *his* interests, achieves actuality.[10] A servil-
ity of the very mind structure is accomplished, which
accounts, in large part, for the invasive brutality of
Marx's polemic. He is struggling against society's
ruling-class framework as it has gotten into people's
heads, against the mechanics of public illusion as they
have been adopted as the individual's own.

3. The "forms of social consciousness" are a social
unconscious insofar as they are not recognized, but govern ideology as an undiscerned set of regulative principles. Since little or no ideology does in fact formulate
these principles, but is merely governed by them, we
might consider these forms of social consciousness as
historical materialism's version of the Collective Unconscious. The reach, thereby, of Marx's overall model
into the domain of the unconscious deserves pause. For
not only does it extend the referential range of Marx's
world-view into an extremely significant and generally
unsuspected realm, but it indicates important common
ground with that other central theory of human affairs
associated with the names of Freud and Jung.

4. The term *a priori* as applied to "forms of social consciousness" is similar to the term of the Kantian tradition only with respect to the idea that these forms govern consciousness as a given, existing prior to this or
that concrete judgment. It is not at all meant to imply
the socially independent and logically necessary regulation of understanding that Kant's *a priori* does. On the
contrary, the forms of social consciousness are:

    i. socially acquired;

    ii. historically grounded; how great a role history

---

[10] "The advance of capitalist production develops a working
class," Marx says, "which by education, tradition, habit looks upon
the conditions of that mode of production as self-evident laws of nature" (*CI*, 737).

plays in determining these forms is indicated by Marx's declaration that the "weight of all the dead generations weighs like a nightmare on the brain of the living" (*18thB*, 10);

iii. applicable in principle, though not in fact, only to the public realm of ideas;

iv. general but not absolute in their government; Marx's scientific ideology, for example, is not governed by them, and the rest of ideological formulations vary in the stringency of their obedience according to the permissiveness of the specific historical conditions in question;

v. defeasible, both in their particular historical form, such as feudal "forms of social consciousness" giving way to capitalist "forms of social consciousness," and altogether, that is, with the emancipated consciousness of the classless, communist society.

5. The same forms of social consciousness—even assuming thorough-going stringency of government—may tolerate very different ideological formations, depending on the historical circumstances of the ideological phenomenon in question. Indeed, even with respect to the same class at the same time over the same issue, no uniformity of ideological formulation or anything like it is being suggested—just that such formulations are generally governed by these several principles. The same grammar—and forms of social consciousness resemble in their governance a grammar—permits an infinite variety of language expressions.

6. Finally, the forms of social consciousness are neatly consistent with, and explanatory of, the various common characteristics of ideology outlined in the previous chapter. That, for example, ideological formulations, (such as those articulating an abhorrence of violence) are "selectively applied," corresponds neatly with the forms of social consciousness that presuppose what vio-

lates, or promotes, the social order as morally bad, or good, respectively, (that is, which *govern* the selective application which takes place).

Or, again, more generally, that mainstream ideology is systematically misleading can be logically accounted for by its regulation by forms of social consciousness, which are each and all begged questions, each and all *petitio principii*.

As far as the relationship between forms of social consciousness and the other categories of phenomena constituting Marx's general theoretical framework is concerned, the former corresponds felicitously not only with ideology, the state, and the economic structure, but with *human nature* as well. That is, the forms of social consciousness constitute the social mechanism—described in Chapter 1—"restraining the compass" of human nature's capacity of consciousness within the bounds of a definite, historical "functionable range": limiting such "functionable range" of consciousness by virtue of the established "public frame of mind" they constitute.[11] For example, the limit restraining Aristotle's thought from conceiving of the labor theory of value—the limit ultimately set, Marx says, by the economic conditions of slavery of Greek society—is penultimately erected by the existence of certain forms of social consciousness obtaining as a mediating mechanism between the economic order of a society and its members' natural capacity of creative intelligence: hence, Marx's talk in this place of the necessity of the notion of human equality achieving "fixity of a popular prejudice" (that is, form of social consciousness) before Aristotle or anyone else can "decipher the secret of the expression of value" (*CI*, 59-60).[12] In other words,

[11] See Chapter 1, pp. 43-45.
[12] Lest it be thought that the notion of human equality cannot,

Marx is indicating a middle-link role for the forms of social consciousness between the economic infrastructure and man's essential cognitive *potentia*, a role in which the compass beyond which the latter does not go is proximately determined by the frame that the forms together constitute.

In summary, then, "forms of social consciousness" in Marx's schema constitute a still further superstructural "hold," maintaining society's established economic structure intact. As the underlying principles governing public conceptions of human affairs (ideology), they bind the Prometheus of humankind on yet another, unseen level: the public frame of mind to which individual consciousness as a matter of fact generally conforms, and within which man's essential power of projective consciousness is likewise confined.

The forms of social consciousness are, in brief, the machinery of fixed public prejudice regulating ideas as an unseen grammar of ideological propriety, as a set of undiscerned rules of acceptable formulation on the public stage. Or, otherwise put, they are the cognitive mechanism of historical illusion, the underpinnings of Marx's special answer to the ancient problem of appearance and reality.

---

with consistency, be considered as a "form of social consciousness" as we have identified these forms, we suggest that it be considered as a historical modulation of the very form of social consciousness (5) that it seems to violate. That is, the form in question—"Whatever rank is held by individuals within the social order represents their intrinsic worth"—easily accommodates the notion of human equality insofar as the equality involved here is merely equality of right before the law (which equality is, of course, perfectly consistent with radical inequality of rank in other respects). Indeed, such a notion of equality before the law may in certain contexts be a necessary condition of intelligible ranking, in the way that equality before the track rules is a necessary condition of intelligibly ranking runners in a race.

# 7

## Economic Determinism

We now proceed to the set of ideas for which Marx is most famous.

No doctrine in our intellectual history has received more attention—critical, puzzled, and celebrative—than that of "economic determinism."[1] To catalogue adequately the literature on Karl Marx's epoch-making theory would require a considerable tome.

We are not, therefore, going to attempt such a task here, illuminating though it might be as a study in the history and sociology of ideas. Rather, we are going to outline an interpretation that will—if we are successful—be both faithful to Marx's texts, and immune to the standard philosophical criticisms that have hitherto been advanced against the theory: namely, that it is intolerably imprecise,[2] that it is indefensibly monocausal,[3] that it is refuted by historical fact,[4] that it is committed to

[1] Marx never himself employs the specific formulation "economic determinism"; but he talks so persistently through his mature work of the "economic structure," "economic base," and "economic form" in relationship to other factors of the sociohistorical process, such that it "determines" (*bestimmt* or *bedingt*) them, that the label is quite apt.

[2] This sort of criticism was reported in our Introduction, and met in Chapter 3.

[3] This is a claim advanced by Western social scientists generally: for example, R. M. MacIver and Charles H. Page in *Society: An Introductory Analysis* (Toronto, 1965), p. 563.

[4] This criticism, widely advanced in both popular and academic circles, generally refers to workers' rising wages since Marx's day, and/or the failure of proletarian revolution in advanced capitalist societies.

logically improper prediction,[5] and that it is incompatible with ethical and personal responsibility.[6]

Our interpretation will venture, as well, beyond what has been offered in defence of Marx in the century that has passed since his publication of *Capital*: for example, Frederick Engels' interpretation, which holds sway among orthodox Marxists to this day.[7]

To begin, we point out, against some well-known interpretations, what Marx does not mean by his landmark theory:

1. He is not saying that noneconomic phenomena are *uniquely* determined by the economic order. The widespread tendency to read "uniquely determine" when Marx writes "determine"—or, to be more exact, the German *bedingen* and *bestimmen*—is one of the great banes of critical commentary on Marx.[8]

2. He does not mean by "ideology" those scientific principles and theories that are technically utilizable in maintaining or improving productive output. These are

---

[5] K.Popper, *The Poverty of Historicism* (London, 1961), pp. v–vii.

[6] Isaiah Berlin, *Historical Inevitability* (London, 1957), *passim*.

[7] Engel's argument, given some years after Marx's death in his well-known letter to J. Bloch in 1890 (*SC*, 498-500), is essentially that the "economic conditions" are "ultimately decisive," that they determine action "in the last resort." This, unfortunately, tells us almost nothing.

[8] The question might arise here, "Well, if Marx doesn't mean 'uniquely determine' by his notion of 'determine,' then what *does* he mean?" In the next pages, we exhibit three specific uses of the concept by Marx, but do not reduce these uses to any single sense. We might appeal to the later Wittgenstein in defence of this strategy, and leave it at that. However, it is important to recognize that Marx's concept of "determine" is generally used in the sense of *limit*, a sense that is basic to both Eastern and Western philosophical traditions since the Upanishads and the pre-Socratics, respectively, and we might add, is the original meaning of the Latin "determinare" (see p. 161 ff. for our detailed discussion of this use). We might also point out here that such a use of "determine" is neatly consistent with Marx's concept of the economic order of a society as a *form*.

primary constituents of the forces of production, and are everywhere recognized by Marx as such (see Chapter 2).

3. He is not saying that those phenomena that are determined by the economic structure are inefficacious in their relationship to the latter. Throughout his work he draws attention to the great practical influence and, indeed, necessity of laws, politics, ideology, and so on, in maintaining the economic structure (see Chapters 4, 5, and 6).

With these points in mind, and maintaining the full conceptual underpinnings of Chapter 3, we now say that the economic structure "determines" by virtue of these principles that define it:[9]

1. Effective ownership by a small minority of most of society's forces of production, and effective ownership by a large majority of few or none of the forces of production is maintained intact, the proportion of the society who so control the means of life and the share they hold remaining constant, or becoming more monopolist still.

2. Surplus labor over and above the amount allocated to the producers for their survival is extracted, by and to the advantage of (1), from these producers by the ruling class, the amount of such tribute labor remaining constant, or increasing.[10]

Strictly speaking, (1) constitutes the economic struc-

[9] Of course, in any prerevolutionary or revolutionary stage, the economic structure is in the process of dissolution and, correspondingly, ceases to exert determining force. What happens in such stages, according to Marx, is that men reorganize their constraining economic structure through political action, a reorganization that is nomically necessitated by the growth of the productive forces beyond the limits of the economic order to accommodate them (see Chapter 8).

[10] Though the rate of profit in capitalist society declines, according to Marx, the mass of surplus labor grows (*CIII*, 219).

ture as such, and (2) is its "law of motion." But here, economic structure refers to both (1) and (2).

Remaining on the general level,[11] we now state how the economic structure determines individual behavior, as well as the legal and political superstructure, ideology, and the forms of social consciousness.

First, the economic structure determines individual behavior by:

i. compelling those who are without the forces of production they require to stay alive (the majority of society) to work and provide surplus-labor or service for others, those others being correspondingly compelled to follow their role of domination or sink to the same level;

ii. compelling those who work and provide surplus labor or service for others to pursue precisely and externally stipulated forms of activity in their work. This external prescriptive control of the individual's working life, extending as it often does to most of the activities of his waking hours, is perhaps the strictest sort of determinism that the economic structure exerts; those who hold the power to so stipulate other man's activities being correspondingly compelled, again, to sustain their hegemony or sink to the same level;

iii. restricting those who are not members of the ruling class within narrow limits in their non-work lives by virtue of:

a. placing severe consumer limits (by what is paid for labor or service) on what they may enjoy in the way of dwelling place, food supply, culture goods, luxuries, and so forth;

---

[11] We will not concern ourselves in this chapter with the multitude of particular laws of the capitalist economic structure.

b. excluding them from access to most of the natural and technological environment, which is owned by the ruling class;

c. so confining them in their work lives by extended repetitive labor that the possibilities of their nonwork lives are gravely curtailed (by virtue of exhaustion and mechanical habit).[12]

Second, the economic structure determines the legal and political superstructures, the ideology, and the forms of social consciousness by *blocking or selecting out all such phenomena that do not comply with it*.[13]

For example, in capitalist society, all of the following will be rigorously blocked from, or selected out of, existence:

1. a proposed law that guarantees an above-poverty income to all citizens;

2. a parliamentary party policy to convert profitable economic monopolist holdings to public ownership;

3. a mass-media advocation of the prohibition of unearned income;

4. an educational technique (or plant substance) that alters public consciousness toward noncompetitive outlook;

5. planned legislation to reduce profits.

The decisive extinction of each and all of these

[12] These constraining influences of the economic structure are reported by Marx throughout his corpus, especially in the *Economic and Philosophical Manuscripts, The German Ideology*, and *Capital*, Volume I.

[13] Marx consistently uses the German word *entsprechen* (meaning "correspond to" or "comply with") to describe the relationship between a society's economic structure and its legal and political superstructure, ideology, and forms of social consciousness (e.g., *PofP*, 95; *SC*, 40-41; *CPE*, 20-21; *CI*, 82 and 372; and *CIII*, 791). The implication is that what does *not* so correspond to or comply with the economic structure is ruled out by it.

superstructural phenomena is firmly predictable.[14] They do not comply or "correspond" with the economic structure. They are "blocked," therefore, from obtaining; or "selected out" before they can achieve effective hold.[15] Thus, says Marx, in his historical materialist variation on the basic dictum of Spinoza, *determinatio est negatio* (*CI*, 597).

Such "blocking" or "selecting out" of phenomena that do not comply with the economic structure is made possible by, essentially, the following conditions:

1. the supervisory prominence of ruling-class members in legal, political, and ideological agencies;

2. the power of ruling-class members to provide and withdraw economic support from parliamentary, educational and mass-media personnel who are not members of the ruling class;

3. the tendency of societies to sustain, simply as a

[14] If any of these phenomena did occur, then the main "law" of economic determinism as we have formulated and applied it here, would be *prima facie* falsified. Such apparent falsification, upon further investigation, would yield one of the following conclusions:
1. the economic structure of the society is in a state of dissolution: a revolutionary stage has been entered;
2. the phenomenon in question is, to use Marx's frequent term, "accidental," an exception to an otherwise firmly obtaining regularity;
3. the phenomenon in question does, in fact, "correspond" with the economic structure in a manner not yet evident;
4. the phenomenon in question, in company with other phenomena similarly recalcitrant, obtains and continues to obtain with no revolution ensuing, thus falsifying the main "law" of economic determinism.

[15] One of Marx's favorite illustrations of this "blocking" phenomenon is nineteenth-century Political Economy, which always remains "within *the bounds* of the bourgeois horizon," "within a *limited field* of expression." Once the class antagonism of the economic structure becomes manifest, then these "bounds" are more restrictive than ever. "It was thenceforth no longer a question whether this theorem or that was true, but whether it was useful to capital or harmful, expedient or inexpedient, politically dangerous or not" (*CI*, 15).

matter of entrenched historical "habit," the economic structure that is already firmly established;

4. the logic of collective action that, insofar as legal, political, and ideological activities can only be generated collectively, renders individual commission impossible.

It might be objected here that the concept of "complying" or "corresponding" with the economic structure lacks rigour, and that in consequence Marx's theory of economic determinism is not scientifically acceptable. However, such a caveat tells quite as forcefully against Darwin's similar, but scientifically accepted, theory of natural selection. Darwin, as we know, claims that "favorable species tend to be preserved and unfavorable ones to be destroyed."[16] But he never specifies set criteria of what it is for a species to be "favorable" or "unfavorable" or, otherwise put, "fit" or "unfit" for natural survival. Similarly, Marx does not sponsor such criteria for what it is for a superstructural or ideological phenomenon to be fit or unfit for social survival. (That is, compliant or uncompliant with the economic structure). In both cases empirical inquiry into the relevant concrete circumstances is required to generate a judgment of what in fact will be selected, or selected out, in the "struggle for life." But in both cases, reliable predictions or explanations can be deduced by application of the "law of selection" in question to the circumstances in question. Thus, just as Darwin can reliably predict that, say, dolphins in the Thames will suffer extinction (because the material succor they require is lacking in such a natural environment), so Marx can reliably predict that a bill for worker management of factories on the floor of British Parliament will suffer extinction (be-

---

[16] Marx, it is interesting to note, wanted to dedicate *Capital* to Darwin (who declined the honor). And Engels, in his graveside speech on Marx, focused on the similarity between the theories of the two men.

cause the material "succor" it requires is lacking in such a social environment). Marx's theory of social selection is, in short, no more problematic in its scientific form than Darwin's homologous theory of natural selection.

It might still be objected here that there are many historical occurrences that plainly falsify Marx's "law" that only what "complies" or "corresponds" with the economic structure is permitted social survival. For instance—we cast about for the most persuasive local example that this sort of rejoinder might muster—the Canadian volume *White Niggers of America* by the Quebec radical, Pierre Vallières, was in recent years permitted publication and wide distribution in two languages in Canada, though it called for armed overthrow of the government and the uncompensated expropriation of all large-scale capitalist enterprises. Here, surely, a critic might claim, is a clear case of empirical refutation of Marx's economic-determinist principle.

A convincing reply would be this. First, the book itself was published by a large capitalist firm and earned substantial profits for the firm, thus clearly reinforcing the economic structure. Second, state repression of its publication might have generated more challenges to the capitalist economic order than it prevented and, therefore, been inimical in the end to the preservation of this order. Thus, again, the book's correspondence to the economic structure. And finally, when circumstances arose such that this and similar literature did represent a clearer threat to the economic structure than hitherto, a special and decisive superstructural step was taken—invocation by the national government of the War Measures Act—whereby all support of the cause it embraced was subject to indefinite detention—an executive move that permitted, among other things, the extended imprisonment of the book's author. In short, an examination of specific historical circumstances leads plausibly to the conclusion that the apparent refutation here of Marx's economic-determinist principle is, on closer analysis, a confirmation of it. Other apparent refutations might be similarly subverted.[17]

We come to now the third sense in which the economic structure determines the legal and political superstructure, ideology, and forms of social consciousness. This sense of economic determinism complements the second sense discussed above. It refers to the *mapping*, as we will call it, that takes place between a particular economic structure and the particular legal, political, and ideological phenomena of a society (or, in short, its superstructure). In this mapping, definite economic-structural content is projected onto the superstructure, which, in our account, has already been shown to be constrained within a "limited field," that is, within bounds that comply with the economic struc-

[17] Nonetheless, we think there is a need for refinement of this "law" of economic determinism: namely, that whatever superstructural phenomenon does not corrrespond to the economic order is blocked from, or selected out of, existence. We propose, then, the complementary "law": *The extent of such blocking or selecting out is in direct proportion to the extent of the noncorrespondence in question.* That is, the more a superstructural phenomenon "contradicts" the determining economic order, the more thoroughgoing is its annihilation. Marx's exact arguments, for example, maximally contradict the capitalist economic order and are, accordingly, maximally blocked from and selected out of social currency in capitalist-society schools, courts, churches, mass media, and so on. Where they do not suffer such social extinction (that is, in some university curricula) their existence, according to our complementary "law," obtains only to the extent that their noncorresondence with the capitalist economic order is reduced, that is, via confinement to an elite audience, noncore program, refutive approach, prolix formulation, and so forth. Conversely, insofar as "contradictory" ideology is neither thus extinguished nor reduced, its survival signals impending transformation of the economic order.

ture. Thus, whereas in the second sense of economic determinism, we spoke of the determining *limits* beyond which superstructural and ideological phenomena could not go, now we speak of the actual *content* within these limits that the economic structure gives rise to.

Perhaps the most graphic way of explicating economic determinism by "mapping" is by illustration.

Consider a capitalist economic structure. It is constituted of "bloodless" exchange-value terms: abstract, equal, and homogeneous monetary units to which all use-values and economic roles in the society are increasingly reduced. This capitalist economic structure, says Marx, is qualitatively "reflected" in the political and legal doctrines of Equal Rights (*CI*, 176), the abstract religion of Protestantism (*CI*, 79), and the empty reified categories of German Idealism (*GID*, *passim*). Its transformation of social labor into cash-value terms, into the "social hieroglyphic" of money, is "mirrored" as an "image in men's brains" of commodities and forms of capital ruling the world as independent entities.[18] Its atomicizing of economic intercourse is reflected in moral doctrines of exploitative self-interest (*CI*, 176). Its principle of unlimited competition is projected onto Malthusian and Darwinist theories of human life as an eternal contest (*SC*, 157). Its indifference to human content is reflected in a scientific and religious rhetoric of "abstinence" (*CI*, 596-97); its inequalities of income in the popular notion of "God's elect" (*CI*, 646); its unrestricted extension into distant lands in the credo of "civilization" (*KMC*, 347); its reduction of the laborer to machine-appendage status in an ethic of "Work" and "Order" (*CI*, 228); and its removal of all hindrances to

[18] See especially Marx's section "The Fetishism of Commodities and the Secret Thereof" (*CI*, 71-83).

exploitation by capital in the laws and slogans of "Liberty" and "Freedom" (*CI*, 277 ff.).[19]

Although the above panorama of illustration could be unfolded indefinitely, it gives us no precise, regulative account of this mapping of economic structural content onto the superstructure. We know that the determining of "social selection" sets the limits within which superstructural phenomena must stay to survive; and that the determining of "mapping" involves projection from the economic process of concrete content upon this definite range. Now, we add, this mapping conforms to the underlying governing principles of ideology described in Chapter 6; or, more specifically, to the more determinate forms that these principles take in any particular historical epoch. These latter are *the rules whereby mapping proceeds*, and their systematic determination of particular superstructural configurations is what constitutes the formal aspect of mapping. How-

---

[19] The primacy of the economic structure in all these cases of economic-ideological correspondence is demonstrable for Marx by—among other things—the fact that economic interest generally or always prevails over ideological position. As he says in one of his wittiest epigrammatic thrusts: "The English Church will more readily pardon an attack on 38 of its 39 articles than 1/39 of its income" (*CI*, 10).

One of the most detailed accounts by Marx of the way economic-structural interests regularly assert themselves over superstructural and ideological considerations is in the pamphlet *The Eighteenth Brumaire of Louis Bonaparte*. Here too his wit flashes: "Thus the Tories in England," he says, "long imagined they were enthusiastic about monarchy, the church and the beauties of the old English Constitution, until the day of danger snatched from them the confession that they are enthusiastic only about—*ground rent*" (*18thB*, 38).

It is instructive to compare Marx's contrast between the "hidden" economic structure and the "visible" content of ideology to the psychoanalytic contrast between the "latent" and "manifest" content of dreams. Consider in this light—it is irresistible to add—the phenomenon called "the American Dream."

ever, as our set of examples makes clear, this mapping is not at all merely a formal operation.[20] On the contrary, it is initially and terminally concrete. That is, its ground lies in the material facticity of the economic process, and it is initial material facticity of the economic process, and it is this initial material facticity of the economic process that, in mapping, is translated *via* its formal regulatory mechanism into the terminal issuance of definite superstructural content. We have then, in summary, a precise range of superstructural possibility set by the economic-determining system of "social selection," and the specific content of this range projected onto it by the economic-determining system of "mapping." It is by virtue of this compound determining mechanism, social selection and mapping, that Marx is able to hold his striking methodological position that historical materialist science can deduce a society's ideological forms from its social relations of production:

> It is, in reality much easier to discover by analysis the earthly core of religion than, conversely, it is, to *develop from the actual relations of life the corresponding celestialized forms of those relations*. The latter method is the only materialistic, and therefore the only scientific one (*CI*, 372).[21]

[20] That the process of "mapping" is formally regulated in the manner described can be systematically demonstrated by comparing this of illustrative examples from Marx's work with the set of underlying principles of superstructural formulation identified in Chapter 6. The latter is indispensable theoretical accompaniment to the concept of "mapping" disclosed here.

[21] Take the capitalist relation of production: private ownership of instruments of production (i.e., fixed capital) such that their employment by wage-labor yields surplus value (i.e., profit). Applying our economic-determinist principles of social selection and mapping to this economic fact, we deduce that: 1. all conceptions of religious ideology will be within a limited field (that is, any such conception that does not correspond to this fact—for example, any dissanction

To summarize then, the economic structure determines *via*:

1. work-leisure constraints
2. social selection
3. mapping

Now, we ask, is economic determinism as it has been characterized here subject to the familiar charges made against it? If we consider again the standard objections that have been fielded against Marx's theory, we can see that none of them tells against the account that has been presented here. First of all, relations of production can in fact be clearly distinguished from the forces of production and legal superstructure, as we have seen in Chapter 3. And second, as we can now see, the claims that Marx's theory of economic determinism is indefensibly monocausal, that it is easily refuted by historical fact, that it is committed to logically improper prediction, and that it is incompatible with ethical and personal responsibility all clearly fail against the theory. They are, that is, all false. For economic monocausality

---

of private ownership or money profit—will not obtain); 2. the conceptions of religious ideology that are within this limited field will conform to the set of nine rules of mapping. Thus, for example, private ownership and profit will take on the form in religious ideology of sanctioned, or never dissanctioned, social practices. Then, within this definite range of ideological possibility set by social selection, the specific conceptions of religious ideology will be governed by the rules that private ownership and profit are inalterable structures of a Christian society; are morally upstanding (and their violation morally degenerate); endow all with the sacred obligation to protect them; allot to each individual his rightful station and/or spiritual desert in the social order; operate in the general social interest; establish the indispensable leadership of the social order; constitute the magistrature of Capital bestowing on man its material benefits; and, finally, are prescribed and guided by the divine agency of God.

That the original gospel of Yeshua is in this way transformed into its opposite shows how inexorably the "laws" of economic determinism regulate ideological conception.

is simply not claimed or implied here, or anything like it: the very charge, indeed, intimates a fundamental incomprehension of Marx's system of thought.[22] Then, too, putatively refutive historical events—such as rising wages, or failure of proletarian revolution in advanced capitalist societies—are not, in fact, critically relevant to the theory's claims: for the former is consistent with all its principles (including the "law" that surplus-labor extraction remains constant or increases),[23] while the latter is, in Marx's model, explicitly a matter of technological determinism, not economic.[24] Again, the sort of prediction that Popper accuses Marx of making is simply not a commitment of his economic determinist theory.[25] And, finally, the denial of ethical or personal responsibility that is said to be implied by Marx's economic determinism is not, in truth, so implied, as Marx demonstrates in his continual use of the vocabulary of blame for those who maintain the economic structure and its repressive determining mechanism.[26] In short, the standard objections against Marx's conception of eco-

[22] See, for example, Chapter 8.

[23] Marx was quite aware of real rises in workers' wages, and his theory explicitly accommodates this phenomenon (*CI*, 645). On the whole, his position is that the persistent heightening of material productivity in capitalism permits increases in both absolute profits and wages.

[24] See Chapter 8.

[25] It is interesting to note here, in addition, that the term "inevitable" sometimes improperly intrudes into English translations of Marx's work. For example, the well-known statement near the end of his first Preface to *Capital*—"It is a question of these laws themselves, of these tendencies working with iron necessity towards inevitable results"—makes no mention of "inevitable results" in the original German. This is an addition by Marx's translators, Aveling and Engels. See, however, 208-17.

[26] Consider also Marx's remark in *Capital* (*CI*, 9), where the "higher motives" of the ruling class are said to oblige the latter's support of working-class development (see pp. 232-39).

nomic determinism are in one way or another quite misaimed.

The theory of economic determinism now clear and intact, we proceed to final questions and clarifications of its explanatory power. We have seen that its essential gist is that of a social form[27]—a ruling-class pattern of ownership relations and its fundamental "law of motion" of surplus-labor extraction—coercively regulating all aspects of society (production, politics, ideology, and so on). We have also seen that more specifically, with capitalism, this determining social form is a matter of a ruling-class minority of capitalist owners presiding over the productive forces of society (all embodiments of capital) so as to return to themselves surplus-labor in the form of monetary profit with every production cycle—a determining social form to which all members of society must variously comply in work and leisure, and to which the legal and political superstructure must correspond, as well as public ideation. Without further traversing area already covered, we now say that for Marx this determining social form constitutes *the* structure of domination in historically advanced society, whose thoroughgoing dissolution through socialist rev-

---

[27] Marx repeatedly conceives of the economic structure as society's governing "form," and the forces of production as this form's material "content" (e.g., G, 267–68, 272, 304, 646, 680, 767, 770). His conceptualization here recalls Aristotle's basic distinction between "matter" and "form," but it elevates this classic distinction from an object to a social level. Consider also its similarity to Wittgenstein's concept of language as a "form of life" in the *Philosophical Investigations*. As we have suggested elsewhere, economic form is to action as grammatical form is to speech, only it is the form of life to which all others conform. Thus, for example, when in a capitalist society the rules of grammar conflict with the rules of profitmaking—as they regularly do in media publication and sales promotion—it is the former that fall, and the latter that hold.

olution must superannuate man's domination by man altogether.[28] For in Marx's account, other orders of domination (such as political) are wholly derivative from the capitalist economic form ("The bourgeois state is nothing but a mutual insurance pact of the bourgeois class both taken against its members individually and against members of the exploited class"), while, on the other hand, whatever domination survives the socialist overthrow of this determining capitalist form is simply a matter of the persistence of, and the dealing with, its "bourgeois remnants." In sum, the determining economic structure of capitalism accounts, according to the Marxian model, for virtually all human domination in historically advanced social orders.

This apparently extreme stature accorded by Marx to the determining economic structure of capitalism may, we suspect, lie at the heart of the myriad, if mistaken, objections to his economic determinism theory. But be that as it may, it deserves our consideration if we are to grasp the theory's full meaning and import. Perhaps the most intuitively compelling difficulty to its great claim to explanatory power protrudes from the course of history itself as it has unfolded since Marx's death. That is, in most societies where Marxist-led revolutions have apparently broken the capitalist economic form—both its ruling-class pattern of ownership relations and its profit-extracting "law of motion" of productive resources—there does not seem to have been even a proximate end to man's domination of man. So the question arises, how does all this square with Marx's economic determinist theory, which so focuses on the capitalist social form as *the* underlying framework of human oppression in historically advanced society?

[28] Marx makes this claim in, among other places, the *Grundrisse* (*G*, 749) and *Capital* (*CI*, 16).

The answer to this question might run as follows. First, what many might count as domination in these societies (such as the USSR) would not count as domination under Marxist criteria. For example, for individuals to be prevented from having private ownership holdings that require others' labor to be worked, or for individuals to be required to contribute their full share of personal labor to society's material reproduction process—these exactments might strike many people as "domination" of an intolerable sort, but they do not qualify as domination under Marxian principles. They qualify, instead, as necessary measures to *prevent* domination (see Chapter 3).

Second, the societies in question do not qualify as "historically advanced" societies until their productive systems are thoroughly mechanized and mass-worked—until, in a phrase, they have modern technology (see Chapter 8). But the societies in question have not been so technologically endowed until recently or, in many cases, not yet. Thus, the question does not even apply to them until recently or, in many cases, not yet. They simply fall outside the referential range of Marx's claim. Furthermore, it might be held, what has gone on in these societies prior to their material qualification as historically advanced societies—for example, "forced collectivization" and "consumer deprivation"—which may well appear to involve human domination of the most extreme sort imaginable, is not really human domination at all, but domination by material *needs*, which require great and rapid technological advance to be met in the entire population: which great and rapid technological advance requires, in turn, "forced collectivization" and "consumer deprivation" to be achieved. The "tyranny" of these societies, it can thus be argued, is, in fact, the "tyranny" of material want, of natural necessity—a "tyranny" that the measures in question precisely reduce by the technological leaps forward they effect.

Finally, this argument might conclude, what can neither be ruled out by Marxian criteria as domination, nor resolved into domination by natural necessity, can be understood as the "dictatorship of the proletariat," which Marx insists upon as a "transitional" requirement of revolutionary socialism (*GP*, 25). Therefore there is, in the end, no domination in the societies in question that cannot be plausibly accounted for by Marx's theory. What our question singles out as anomalous to his theory turns out, on closer analysis, to be ultimately explainable by it.

Though there is considerable explanatory promise to this three-step argument, we regard it as in principle inadequate to our problem. That is, the societies in question, what we now designate "state socialist" societies, decisively and systematically exhibit superstructural and ideological signs of a ruling-class economic order that are inexplicable in terms of the argument we have outlined. For example, we take it as an incontrovertible empirical truth that the direct producers of these societies cannot publicly (or privately, for that matter) oppose the established state or communist party as their one and only collective representative—not legally, not politically, not ideologically.[29] For, if they do

---

[29] The literature to support this claim is so copious, so varied, and from so astonishingly broad a spectrum of sociopolitical position that no report here can pretend to do it justice. Perhaps the most persuasive evidence, however, comes from eminent Marxists themselves. We speak here not just of floor-crossing Marxists such as Milovan Djilas (*The New Class*, London, 1966), but of core Marxists such as Herbert Marcuse (*Soviet Marxism*, New York, 1961), Rosa Luxembourg (*The Russian Revolution*, Ann Arbor, 1967), and Leon Trotsky (*The History of the Russian Revolution*, New York, 1932), not

so oppose—on any of these superstructural levels—they are subject to the full weight of the state's or party's repression in the way of forced relocation, public vilification, harrassment by spies, arrest, imprisonment, and so on. This draconian prohibition of productive workers' legal, political, and ideological activity on behalf of what they might construe as in their collective interests against the judgment of the small minority occupying state or party offices of power cannot be explained by any step of the argument outlined. Indeed, as we shall soon show, this superstructural governance of the productive worker class is in direct and fundamental contradiction with the principles of "proletarian dictatorship" conceived by Marx.

A most significant problem has emerged here. State socialist societies show a rigorous monopoly control of superstructural mechanisms by a small minority of that society, a monopoly control that is stricter, indeed, than in advanced capitalist societies. That is, *the entire minority in question is individually appointed in either candidacy for, or occupancy of, superstructural office by those already holding superstructural office.*[30] Yet this monopoly control

to mention a younger generation of "New Left" thinkers, such as Daniel and Gabriel Cohn-Bendit (*Obsolete Communism: The Left-Wing Alternative*, London, 1968)—all of whom have endorsed, and developed, the claim of legal, political, and ideological repression in state socialist societies. We might add, as well, that our experience in nine of these societies (including our trial by military tribunal in one, the USSR, in 1965) has yielded much confirming, and no disconfirming, evidence for the claim in question.

[30] To the extent that this principle does not apply to a state socialist society, to precisely that extent the monopoly of superstructural mechanisms that we are claiming here does not obtain. It may be the case, then, that certain state socialist societies fall outside the range of our reference here, though we are not aware of any that do (including, it is certain, the People's Republic of China: see *The Constitution of the People's Republic of China*, Peking, 1975, pp. 30, 37, 52.)

of governmental and ideological mechanisms has, it seems, no underlying ruling-class *economic* order in terms of which it can, and according to Marx's theory must, be explained (Chapters 4-6). Such a monopoly of superstructural mechanisms always "reflects" or is "raised upon," according to Marx, a ruling-class economic "basis"; but, in fact, neither a ruling-class pattern of ownership relations nor a "law of motion" of surplus-value extraction—that is, no economic structure—seems present here as this "basis." The means of production are, on the face of it, socially owned; and surplus-labor extraction is thereby, on the face of it, rendered impossible.

In view of all this, we have to ask, how, if at all, does Marx's theory of economic determinism apply here? We seem to have a preeminent ruling-class superstructure suspended, so to speak, in the air, with no underlying ruling-class economic infrastructure as its "foundation." We seem to have a strictly determined governmental and ideological apparatus, with no underlying economic structure determining it. We seem to have, in short, an exception to Marx's economic determinist theory of such historical magnitude and importance that the theory seems to be irredeemably refuted.

The irony of our quandary may appear irresistible—Marx's most celebrated theory falsified, it seems, by the insistent facticity of putatively "Marxist" societies. And the substance of its difficulty may appear irresolvable—the societies in question occupying almost half of the globe, steadily increasing their domain, and virtually all quite devoid of that private ownership of the means of production in terms of which Marx's analysis of historical societies' economic structures proceeds. Nevertheless, we judge that the problem here is by no means intractable. An economic structural analysis of state socialist society and, from this, an economic determinist analysis of its legal, political, and ideological phenomena, is, we propose, precisely securable. On behalf of this claim, we offer the following conceptual schema:

1. Marx's determining economic structure, the underlying social form that is said to coercively regulate all aspects of a society's life (work, politics, public ideation, and so on) is constituted of a ruling-class pattern of ownership relations, whose "law of motion" is the systematic extraction of surplus labor from that society's direct producers.

2. These constituting ownership relations of the economic structure are to be defined, in accordance with the argument of Chapter 3, as relations wherein social members have the power to use or exploit forces of production and exclude others from doing so, which relations "reveal the innermost secret, the hidden basis of the entire social structure" (CIII,791).

3. These constituting ownership relations of the economic structure are generally conceived by Marx as *personal* ownership relations, that is, "private property." That is, the owner-subject of the ownership relation is a person or, in cases of joint or corporate ownership, a set of persons. It is in virtue of this owner-subject being a person that he can privately sell or pass on by inheritance the content of "his" ownership. It belongs to him.

On the other hand, there can in principle and in fact be *official* ownership relations, that is, "state property," which Marx recognizes, but only in abeyance.[31] Here, the owner-subject of the ownership relation is a state

[31] Marx's standard conception of the state as only the organized superstructural representative of the collective interests of a ruling class of private owners (such as ancient slave holders, medieval landlords, modern capitalists) normally rules out any consideration by

office, whose occupant or, in cases of a set of occupants, whose chief occupant exercises the various powers of the ownership relation in question.[32] It is by virtue of the owner-subject being a state office (and the jurisdictions of state offices are as precisely stipulated and regulated as the territories of private property)[33] that its occupant or chief occupant cannot privately sell or pass on by inheritance the content of "its" ownership. It belongs to the office.

4. Because office ownership cannot be exercised except so far as the occupant or chief occupant of the office concerned so exercises it, it is the latter who effectively owns the productive forces in question. Thus, *qua* such office occupant and only *qua* such office occupant, he can use or exploit the productive-force content of the official ownership relation, and exclude others from doing so: that is, exercise its ownership powers, which is indeed,

---

him of state-office ownership relations as economic-structural in themselves. He simply did not have the knowledge we have of state socialist societies, or even fascist or "welfare state" societies, to render to the economic-structural analysis of state-office ownership the theoretical priority it has come to have since his lifetime. However, he does give fertile hints of such an analysis in *18thB*, 50-51, 104-105; and *G*, 472-74.

[32] Such chief occupants of state office would include first secretaries of communist parties, generals of armies, ministers of ministries, and so on (with top officials occupying several head-offices at once).

It is interesting in this connection to cite Marx's passage on the arrogation of social responsibility by state offices in postrevolutionary France (his emphases): "Every *common* interest was straightaway severed from society, counterposed to it as a higher *general* interest, snatched from the activity of society's members themselves and made an object of government activity: from a bridge, a schoolhouse and the communal property of a village community to the railways, the national wealth, and the national university" (*18thB*, 104).

[33] See, for example, Charles A. Reich, "*The New Property*," *The Yale Law Journal*, LXXIII, No. 5, (April 1964), 734-87.

we repeat, the only way the latter can be exercised at all.

5. To exploit forces of production means, we have seen, to extract unearned benefits from them.[34] With personal ownership, this means that the owner-subject extracts, say, *profit* thereby. With office ownership, it means the owner-subject extracts, say, *rank-remuneration* thereby.[35] In the former case, the profit belongs to a person as the subject-owner, and in the latter case it belongs to an office as subject-owner; but as the latter is and must be occupied by a person, it is this person occupant who, *qua* occupant, receives the unearned benefit. The underlying principle of persons extracting unearned benefits by virtue of ownership remains the same, only in the latter case this exploitation is mediated by the mask of state office.[36] As for the extent of the un-

[34] See, again, the analysis in Chapter 3.

[35] *i*. Where a state office is occupied, as it usually is, by a set of persons (such as the Ministry of —), it is the rank-remuneration of its chief occupant (such as the Minister of —), to which we refer.

*ii*. By the concept of rank-remuneration, we refer to both the salary and the set of perquisites attached to such occupance of a state office.

*iii*. Marx holds that socially standard payment for the materially productive labor a capitalist does is not to be counted as "profit," but as part of the labor-costs of production; for example, the labor of a small proprietor who inserts his own labor-power, instead of someone else's, into a necessary productive function in his workshop, for which he pays himself the going wage. The same proviso applies here, *mutatis mutandis*, to rank-remuneration. But the precise requirements that must be met to qualify activity as "materially productive" (see Chapter 2), as well as the restriction of payment for such activity to its socially standard cost (again, see Chapter 2), rule out applicability of the proviso to the owner-subjects we are considering. Where there is such applicability, and to precisely the extent, and only the extent, that these criteria permit, the owner-subjects in question are not under our account receiving "rank-remuneration," any more than capitalists are receiving "profit" under Marx's account, when these criteria apply to them.

[36] State-office ownership, however, may still constitute a world-historic advance in limiting private ownership of society's means of production. Just as the "bourgeois" revolution reduced such

earned benefit so extracted, in both cases it is in general in direct proportion to the extent of the ownership content in question. That is, the more a capitalist owns, the more total profit he in general extracts from the content of his ownership. Correspondingly, the more a state office owns, the more total rank-remuneration its occupant or chief occupant in general extracts from the content of its ownership. In both cases, as well, the unearned benefits extracted by virtue of the ownership in question are ideologically formulated as, on the contrary, earned benefits (see below, no. 7).

6.i. The totality of ownership relations to productive forces in a society constitutes, as we have said, its economic structure, the definitive feature of which is the ruling-class pattern of these ownership relations. Applied to a society in which all ownership relations to productive forces have as their subject-owners state offices, it is clear that the occupants or chief occupants of these state offices are the members of the ruling class,[37]

---

ownership from its permanent ties to ruling-class lineage to less ensconced but still inheritable ties of capital holding, so the "bolshevik" revolution reduced these latter ownership ties even further to office-holding alone.

In consequence of this limitation of ownership power, the productive forces over which state-office occupants preside cannot normally be sold off by them nor, when they can be, can the cash returns for such sale privately belong to them (to invest elsewhere, for instance). These restraints are the opposite of capitalist "freedom" (see p. 186), and constitute the basic advance of state socialist ownership structures.

[37] The question now arises as to whether Marx's fundamental distinction between the economic structure and the state superstructure can be maintained under this analysis. That is, the former seems included in the latter, thereby, on the face of it, nullifying the cardinal distinction Marx's theory draws between the two. However, consultation of Chapters 3 and 4 will show that the distinction still remains applicable here. That is, the difference between "power" and "right," upon which Marx's distinction between the economic base and the legal and political superstructure essentially depends, re-

and the rest of the members of that society the ruled class. In this way, a ruling-class pattern can be discerned in the totality of that society's ownership relations to its forces of production, and the extent to which such state-office occupants do not qualify as ruling-class members is for Marx the extent to which they are "elective, responsible, and revocable" (CWF, 41) by those who work the forces of production over which they variously preside.[38]

---

mains precisely securable. Every citizen in a state socialist society is thus by right a joint owner of this society's publicly owned forces of production; but only a small group of these citizens exercises in fact the powers of such ownership.

[38] i. Marx stipulates these radically democratic procedures as essential to genuinely socialist relations throughout *The Civil War in France*. "Nothing could be more foreign to the spirit of the Commune," he says, "than for 'hierarchic investiture' to supplant 'elective responsible and revocable' government in *all* branches of the Administration" (CWF, 40-43).

Compare Marx's preeminent concern here with "free and associated labor," with "really democratic institutions," with "government of the people by the people"—with, in short, the "true secret" of communism, the "self-government of the producers"—to Lenin's position:

The Soviet of Workers Deputies is not a labour parliament and not an organ of proletarian self-government, nor an organ of self-government at all, but a fighting organization for the achievement of definite aims. *Marx-Engels-Lenin/Anarchism and Anarcho-Syndicalism* (Moscow, 1972), p. 204.

To govern you need an army of steeled revolutionary Communists. We have it, and it is called The Party. All this syndicalist nonsense about mandatory nominations of producers must go into the wastepaper basket. *Ibid*, p. 323.

ii. Unlike his state-socialist heirs, Marx's position is intractably democratic and of primary importance at every level of his theory. It is central to his concept of a realized human nature (see p. 29); it is central to his concept of higher productive forces (see p. 69n); and it is central to his concept of the revolutionary supercession of production relations (see pp. 98-99), the state (see p. 121n), and ideology (see p. 144).

The idea of an undemocratic Marxism, whether advanced by disciple or detractor, is thus a total contradiction in terms.

ii. The economic structure is, however, not only defined by its ruling-class pattern, but also by its "law of
motion," whereby the ruling-class owners of the forces
of production "pump out" surplus labor from the direct
producers of society who constitute and work these
forces of production. Applied, again, to a society where
all ownership relations to productive forces have as their
subject-owners State offices, it is clear that the occupants or chief occupants of these offices "pump out"
surplus labor from the direct producers to the extent
that they receive from the material production process
more socially standard labor-equivalents (in the form of
salaries and perquisites) than the activities of their offices
contribute to this material production process.[39] In this

[39] i. Marx says, we may recall with our own emphases: "The
specific economic form in which *unpaid surplus-labour is pumped out of
direct producers*—the direct relationship of the owners of the conditions of production to the direct producers—reveals the *innermost secret*, the *hidden basis* of the entire social structure" (*CIII*, 791). Needless to say, those who receive such surplus labor by virtue of their
disability alone (via age, injury, or disease), or by virtue of their unproductive function alone (as for instance, one of the "hordes of
flunkeys" protecting the various interests of the ruling class) do not
thereby qualify for ruling-class membership. Such membership is,
for Marx, strictly determined by ownership of material forces of
production, and the surplus value this ownership yields. As we have
seen from (3), (4), (5) and (6i) above, state-office ownership of material forces of production gives the sole or chief occupant of such
office the exercise of its powers, which includes among others that of
surplus-labor extraction.

ii. To understand "socially standard labor-equivalents," one need
not know nor endorse Marx's labor theory of value. The calculable
answer to the ordinary reflection, "I wonder how many hours of
labor this item cost," identifies the precise meaning of the concept in
question. However, it is important to stress that activity that is not
materially necessary to the production of x is not a labor cost of it
(see the discussion in Chapter 2 of what counts as a productive
force).

Applying all this to the case of ruling-class office-occupants, we
may now say, in the simplest Marxian terms, that they receive a very

way too, a surplus-labor-extracting "law of motion" can be discerned in the operation of the ruling-class economic structure in question. Both of Marx's underlying general principles of economic determinism—a ruling-class pattern of ownership relations and a "law of motion" of surplus-labor extraction—can thus be disclosed from analysis of a society in which state office ownership of society's forces of production obtains. The extent to which this second basic principle of economic determinism does not operate in such a society is, in turn, the extent to which its state-office occupants or chief occupants do not regularly extract from society's material production process more socially standard labor equivalents than they contribute to it.[40]

7. It is by virtue of these two essential principles of a ruling-class economic structure and its "law of motion" of surplus-labor extraction determining all other aspects of a society's life—work and leisure, politics, law, and ideology—that economic determinism is said to obtain: a process that, as we have shown, is primarily a matter of social selection. That is, whatever corresponds to the requirements for maintenance of the ruling-class pattern of ownership relations and its surplus-labor extraction is permitted to survive. Applying this primary "law" of

---

great deal in the way of the results of others' directly productive labor, but do virtually no directly productive labor themselves; and the difference between what they get and give is the surplus labor they extract.

[40] Marx's basic principle of distribution for transitional socialism, *to each according to his work* (*GP*, 15), as well as his explicit insistence that administrative functionaries never receive more than "workmen's wages" (*CWF*, 40) are theoretically adequate provision against the "pumping out" of surplus labor by a ruling class of state-office occupants. His injunctions in this regard seem, indeed, to reveal his clarity about the danger of an administrative mode of surplus-labor extraction replacing the capitalist, if not effectively ruled out by these preventative measures.

economic determinism to societies in which there is state-office ownership of the forces of production, and the chief occupants of these offices are the members of the ruling class, we can deduce that, say, any ideological phenomenon that exposes or challenges the collective interests of this office ownership or its occupants, or either's fundamental social worth, or whatever, is fated to social extinction (as "counter-revolutionary"). Conversely, any public ideation that conceals or bows to these interests, or sanctifies them as the whole society's, or whatever, will be selected for survival (as "progressive").

We can also deduce, in accordance with the same "law," that any legal or political phenomenon that does not correspond or comply with these ruling-class interests or their "law of motion" of surplus-labor extraction—say, a proposed set of regulations to implement the measures dissolving office ownership defined in (6i), or formation of a political organization to pressure for the rank-remuneration subverting measures defined in (6ii)—will be effectively nihilated in the societies in question (and perhaps, as well, their sponsors). Correspondingly, we may again deduce that the expressed superstructural content of any of these societies will be in accordance with the rules whereby the form of economic determinism termed *mapping* proceeds—such as, "The social order (i.e., state socialism) represents the interests of all in the society"; "A part of a society (i.e., the party) must always represent the whole of society"; "The social property of the ruling class (i.e., the state) is an independent, self-moving power"; and so forth.[41]

---

[41] Thus, just as the maintenance of the collective foreign interests of the capitalist ruling class of the United States is mapped by this regulatory mechanism onto ideology as the "protection of the peoples of the earth" by the "leadership of the Free World" in ac-

With respect, finally, to work-leisure constraints of individuals in societies where state-office ownership of these societies' forces of production obtains, such constraints can be analyzed in the manner set out in part 1. Again here, it is the effective monopoly ownership by the ruling class of society's forces of production, and the "law of motion" of surplus-labor extraction from the direct producers by means of this monopoly ownership, that "determines individual behavior" in the set of ways delineated. Only in state socialist societies the monopoly ownership in question is a greater monopoly than in capitalist societies; that is, a larger proportion of the means of production are effectively owned by state offices in a state socialist society than by capitalists in a capitalist society. And thus the individual's behavior is here, correspondingly, more determined by such monopoly ownership; that is, a lesser proportion of society's means of production is available to individuals to use independently of ruling-class relations. It is, indeed, precisely this economic structural difference between state socialist and capitalist societies that provides the "real basis" to the standard claim of the latter's ideologists that the capitalist order is "freer" than the state socialist (the corresponding superstructural difference between the two orders being, in turn, the "reflection" of such infrastructural difference).

---

cordance with the "will of God," and so on, so the maintenance of the collective foreign interests of the state ruling class of the USSR is similarly mapped onto ideology as a show of "shining internationalism" by the "Party vanguard" in accordance with the dictates of "dialectical laws," and so on. In each case, needless to say, the spectacle of such ideological transformations of ruling-class imperialist facticity provokes derisory denunciation from the other ruling class's ideological representatives, which denunciatory material is then, in turn, employed by each ruling class to justify the maintenance of its domestic and foreign hegemony against the provable machinations of the other.

On the other hand, the monopoly ownership in question is ownership of a more limited sort than in a capitalist economic order. That is, the occupant of a state office is confined to a much narrower set of powers of ownership than a capitalist, with respect both to the use and the exploitation of the productive-force content of "his" ownership. Thus, the individual's behavior is, correspondingly, less determined by such ownership; that is, there are fewer ways in which it can be constrained and confined by ruling-class ownership of the forces of production and its "laws of motion" of surplus-labor extraction. And thus, it is this economic structural difference between state socialist and capitalist societies that provides the "real basis" to the standard claim of the former's ideologists that the state socialist order is more "humane" than the capitalist. Confinement of individuals to destitute unemployment; to cultural and educational disenfranchisement; to disease-producing conditions of work; to inaccessibility of medical aid; to impoverished old age; and—more generally—to an advertising-permeated environment; to chemical-ridden foods; and to a slaughterous travel system—all such work-leisure constraints are, more or less, ruled out by the nature of the ownership in question.[42]

[42] The state offices of state socialism can be illuminatingly compared to the baronial offices of feudalism. In both cases, a set of ownership powers conferred by office comes paired with a set of limitations of utilization of these ownership powers: in contrast to the set of ownership powers conferred by capital, which come "free" of such limitations. Thus, in ideology, "party duty" resembles "noblesse oblige," and state-socialist denunciation of capitalist "freedom" resembles feudal denunciation of the same.

It is by virtue of these limitations on utilization of the productive-force content of ownership powers that the ravages of more or less unlimited capitalist ownership powers—from vast material inequality and systemic starvation to gas-sports and throw-aways—do not obtain in state socialist societies.

In sum, the important differences in the extent of monopoly and the nature of ownership involved in the state socialist and the capitalist economic structures make for important differences in the work-leisure constraints they respectively impose. Nevertheless, such constraints are quite as adequately accountable for in the former as the latter by an economic determinist analysis. Here too, Marx's theory would seem to apply as well to the state socialist societies he never saw as to the capitalist societies he did.

In conclusion, it seems that Marx's theory of economic determinism commands a far broader range of sociohistorical application and explanatory power than he himself conceived. As it turns out, the epochal order of state socialism, too, operates in conformity to its essential laws of ruling-class ownership and surplus-labor extraction. The great historical struggle toward the "realm of freedom" where humanity is finally liberated from the shackles of coercive ruling-class form seems, then, more onerous still than Marx insisted. His error with the theory of economic determinism may be, in the final analysis, an error of underestimating its historical hold.

Marx, however, had complex reasons for his confidence in man's ultimate release from the fetters of economic determinism. To these we now turn.

# 8

## Technological Determinism

Just as Marx holds that the economic structure "determines" the legal, political, and ideological superstructure, so he holds that, on a lower level, the stage of development of productive forces "determines" the economic structure. So also, he calls the former the "basis" of the latter, and repeatedly says the two "correspond" with one another.[1] In other words, the relationship Marx posits between the productive forces and the economic structure is homologous to the next-step-up relationship he posits between the economic structure and the superstructure.

The determining relationship that Marx thus proposes between the productive forces and the economic order of a society is the essence of his technological determinism. Through this relationship, of course, the forces of production also influence the "whole immense superstructure"—determining the economic determiner, so to say. They also determine the needs and capacities of human nature, as we pointed out in some detail in Chapter 1. Then too, in the exceptional periods of breakdown of a mature social order, such forces, mediated by class struggle, impel superstructural changes on their way to "bursting" the economic structure, as we described in Chapter 4. Finally, Marx claims on a few occasions that productive-force content is di-

---

[1] This use of the terms "determine" (*bedingen* or *bestimmen*), "base" (*Basis*) and "correspond" (*entsprechen*) to characterize the relationship between the forces and relations of production is most persistent in *The German Ideology*, pp. 1-95. See also *CI*, 382-85.

rectly "mapped" onto the superstructure, just as economic content is—a determining influence we delineate later. But the relationship of a technologically determining sort with which he is most fundamentally concerned is that between the stage of development of productive forces of a society and its economic structure. Any discussion of his technological determinism has to focus, with Marx, on this fundamental relationship of his world-view.[2] Herein lies the complex conceptual linchpin of his entire system.

This pivotal relationship of "correspondence" that Marx claims between a society's technological stage and its economic order has been the subject—as with so much of his categorical framework—of considerable disagreement about what it means or whether it in fact obtains. As we saw in the Introduction , the relationship is for many critics intractably problematic. And since Marx's relevant texts fail, typically, to articulate the precise principles involved, we must press analysis beyond the raw letter of his corpus to ascertain the logic of the connection he affirms here.

Marx's own repeated characterization of the relationship is, simply, that "relations of production correspond to a definite stage of development of the material forces of production." We have already argued in the previous chapter that the implicit converse of "correspond to" is for Marx "selected out": that is, what does not "correspond to" or "comply with" the "base" (then, the economic order) does not arise or persist or is, in our parlance, "selected out" (then, superstructural phenomena). Here, we get precisely the same nomic pattern. Only now, it is the stage of development of

---

[2] Marx himself regards his discovery of the relationship in question as his primary contribution to human thought (*SC*, 86).

ductive faces that is the "base," and the relations of production/economic structure that must "correspond to" this "base," or be "selected out."

What Marx means by "corresponds to" here is the same as what he means by it elsewhere. It is the standard term for linkages in his theory, and implies:

1. there is a base factor;
2. there is a determined factor;
3. the determined factor corresponds to the base factor, or it does not arise or persist.

Now, we repeat, the base factor is the stage of development of the forces of production, the determined factor is the economic order, and the latter either corresponds to the former, or does not arise or persist.

For example, feudal economic arrangements cannot survive in a society with modern factories and machinery. Such economic arrangements do not "correspond" with the latter's requirements. Hence they are not a "live" option in such a technological environment. The selecting-out which thus occurs may be—adaptation aside—a matter of ruling out in advance, a failure in the attempt, an epochal revolution, or whatever. But the general principle that economic phenomena that do not correspond to the stage of development of the productive forces are economic phenomena that do not arise or persist—this general principle or "law" remains the same. Thus Marx says: "The hand-mill gives you society with the feudal lord; the steam-mill society with the industrial capitalist" (PofP, 95).

The determining relationship between the technological and the economic, then, continues to resemble the next higher determining relationship between the economic and the superstructural. In both cases, the latter either "corresponds" with the former (the "basis") or, as a matter of fact, it fails to come into, or to persist in, historical existence.

However, identifying such similarities between the principal determining relationships in Marx's system does not disclose the answer to the more demanding question before us—which is the precise nature of this technological-economic correspondence in terms of which technological determinism takes place. There is, of course, the still further question of the grounds Marx gives for the primacy of the technological in such correspondence, to which we later attend; but the more elementary, if long unresolved, problem before us is to identify the underlying principles of this claimed correspondence itself.

We propose that the following principles constitute the "laws" of this technological-economic correspondence Marx claims:

1. The relations of production/economic structure correspond to a definite stage of development of the forces of production insofar as the *units of effective ownership* involved in the former *correspond in scale to the units of technological integration* involved in the latter.

Thus, for example, if a society's stage of development of productive forces involves technological units of large-scale factories with machines and extensive work forces integrated into single great productive complexes, then the relations of production/economic structure must involve correspondingly large-scale ownership units (or, specifically, "great capital concentrations").[3]

[3] A technological unit may be defined as a set of productive forces coordinated by one productive plan. Similarly, an effective ownership unit may be defined as a set of productive forces related to one owner (individual or corporate). Otherwise put, the required technological-economic correspondence is a correspondence of unitary domains of ownership to unitary domains of productive plan.

If the scale of effective ownership units does not so correspond to the scale of technological units, the ownership units in question cannot—because the relations they entail are by nature exclusive—accommodate the technological units in question. There is a mismatch between production and ownership domains of integration: the technological units of productive forces are in "contradiction" with the economic powers over such productive forces by virtue of different scales of unification. Thus, in Marx's account, the small ownership units of feudalism "dissolve" in the face of large-scale industry, and "petty" capitalist ownership is "ruined" or "taken over" by the same process. Since the scale of their effective ownership units is unable to comply with the scale of the technological units prescribed by the stage of development of productive forces of the society in question, their ownership domains have to be somehow rendered into larger capital holdings that do so correspond in scale. By virtue of this same principle of scale correspondence between production and proprietary units, Marx also predicts the end of large-holding capitalism itself. That is, as technological units achieve an increasingly international scale, capital ownership units must correspondingly grow to comply with them: more and more beyond past national boundaries of ownership (thus increasing imperialism, national conflicts, wars among leading capitalist nations, and so on), until such technological economic correspondence of scale can only be stably secured through the conscious

---

This does not mean, of course, that one domain of ownership may not include more than one productive unit, as in present capitalist conglomerates. It means that domains of ownership must correspond to technological domains in the sense of being as large in scale as the latter, which is, of course, consistent with their being larger in scale.

regulation of a social plan of international communism.[4]

2. The relations of production/economic structure correspond to a definite stage of development of the forces of production insofar as the *social coordination of exchange and appropriation of products corresponds to the social coordination of the production of these products*.

Thus, for example, if the stage of development of the productive forces is such that masses of individuals cooperate in their work activities, then the relations of production/economic structure must be such

[4] Though Marx himself seems solely concerned with cases in which the scale of technological units has outgrown the scale of ownership units, as in late feudal and late capitalist modes of production, the principle of correspondence in question would seem also to cover converse cases, in which the scale of ownership units has overreached the scale of technological units, thereby involving a noncorrespondence or "contradiction" between forces and relations of production the other way round from what Marx considered the historically universal pattern ("No social order ever disappears before all the productive forces for which there is room in it have been developed" *CPE*, 21). Yet it would seem plausible that it is just such a converse noncorrespondence between forces and relations of production (not precisely converse, because ownership units may to some extent be of a larger scale than technological units without dysfunction of the latter, whereas the reverse is not possible), which explains the world-historic transition from the ancient Roman social order to the barbarian/feudal order. That is, briefly, there does not appear to have been here a case of productive units outgrowing economic units at all, as Marx says, in the above citation, as must be the case in all such epochal transitions. Rather, it was a case of economic units outgrowing technological units. Roman big farms (internally) and imperialism (externally) more and more extended the scale of ownership domains beyond the scale of productive force integration of the day (see K. D. White's *Roman Farming*, Ithaca, 1970), and ultimately suffered—because of such *over-reaching of economic control*—decline and ruin, with the smaller-scale ownership units of a new order taking over to resolve the "contradiction" in question. In this way, we propose, the principle of scale correspondence indicated by Marx can be inverted as an explanatory device of great fecundity, applicable, as well, to such contemporary phenomena as the failure of American imperialism in Vietnam.

that the exchange and appropriation of the products so made—more simply put, their distribution —is correspondingly mass coordinated: by some standard medium of purchase, such as a salary system, and so on. If the social coordination of economic distribution does not correspond with the social coordination of productive cooperation, then the relations of production/economic structure must either be adjusted so that it does (as by collective bargaining, charity and welfare programs, rationing, price controls, monetary schemes), or the economic order in question will be revolutionized (as by worker's revolt). Without such correspondence, the human parts of the productive mechanism have no assured form of material sustenance, and the products of the productive mechanism in question cannot be marketed in the manner required to regenerate the productive cycle. Such alternatives, however, though possible, are as a matter of technological imperative historically avoided in favor of maintaining or securing the correspondence of coordination between men's producing and men's receiving, even should this involve revolution of the established economic order itself. Hence Marx predicts in accordance with this principle that in capitalist society, as men's cooperation in production is maintained or increased, while at the same time the distribution of their product is progressively concentrated in ruling-class hands through the "laissez-faire" expansion of private capital, a noncorrespondence of social coordination between the forces and relations of production will increasingly obtain, which must ultimately culminate in a socialist revolution. This revolution will, in turn, reestablish the required correspondence between the social coordination of production and of distribution, by collective ownership. Here, as in all such "contradictions" between forces and relations of production, the forces of production are held by Marx to be ultimately overriding: their social coordination of labor-power will maintain its stage of development whether the established system of distribution is able to comply with such productive cooperation in its present form, or must be revolutionized into a new economic order to do so[5]

3. The relations of production/economic structure correspond to a definite stage of development of the forces of production insofar as *what is effectively owned* in the former (the "content" of the economic "form") *corresponds to the socially standard level of productivity* involved in the latter.[6] Thus, for example, Marx holds that in the transition from feudalism to capitalism, as machines, factories, and cooperative labor raised the so-

[5] Welfare-state capitalism might be understood, then, as a confirmation of this "law" of correspondence that Marx claims, though he does not seem to have anticipated the extent to which capitalist economic arrangements could be adapted to achieve the required correspondence of coordination between society's production and distribution systems. He was inclined to think, rather, that the capitalist economic order would before long require a revolutionary transformation to secure this correspondence. Hence his "law" seems to have been strikingly confirmed, but his inference from it disconfirmed, by the important twentieth-century phenomenon of welfare-state capitalism in West European and North American societies.

[6] Very briefly put, a productive force is at or above the "socially standard level of productivity" for Marx when it demands no more than the "socially necessary labor" to produce (or help produce) a certain quantity of material use-values. For example, a handloom is well below the socially standard level of productivity in 1850 England because it requires far more than the "socially necessary labor"—a prominently recurrent, if problematic, concept in Marx's work—to produce (or help produce) x yards of cloth. Thus ownership of a handloom in 1850 England is no longer a relation of production (consider the adjective *uneconomic* that might be used to describe such ownership), because its ownership content does not correspond to the "definite stage of development of productive forces" of the society in question.

cially standard level of productivity in European society, the ownership content of all less efficient forces of
production unavoidably dissolved through transformation, such as craft-skill to pliant factory labor power;
takeover, such as sale of feudal lands to capitalists; and
simple extinction, such as junking of old tools, of the
productive forces in question. Ownership obtains only
so long as its socially competitive productive efficiency,
which effective ownership may endure over long periods of time with the same productive force content (for
example, in the case of monopolist feudal guilds that
managed to keep the social stage of development of
productive forces more or less fixed by strictly enforced
regulations), or may endure for only short periods of
time with the same productive force content (for example, in the case of laissez-faire capitalism, where the social stage of development of productive forces spiralled
continually upwards in the competition among capitalists to make cheaper goods). But in all cases, what
productive force is effectively owned complies with the
socially standard level of productivity. Otherwise the
labor-power, instrument, or natural resource so pos-
sessed is rendered obsolete or "uneconomic." It is
thus in accordance with this principle of required correspondence between the ownership content of the relations of production/economic structure and the socially
standard level of productivity of the forces of production that Marx predicts a still further sort of increasing
"immiserization" of the majority in capitalist society.
That is, insofar as the socially standard level of productivity is continually rising, and insofar as only owners of
great amounts of capital possess the resources to update
their forces of production in compliance with such development, the productive force content of small capitalist ownership is constantly being rendered socially

uncompetitive, with insufficient economic holdings to adapt to society's ever higher stages of technological development. The "petty bourgeoisie" of society are thus increasingly plunged into the ranks of those who have nothing left to sell but their own labor-power. And like all other proletarians, they are able to sell this, in turn, only if it is, or is made, fit for the rapidly changing technological environment. The immiserization that thereby takes place is a matter of insecurity and loss of past productive-force ownership, such as small capitalists "going under" and skilled or unskilled workers being bereft of the value of their former labor power, as distinguished from—if complementary to—the relative immiserization that occurs with respect to the ruling-class capitalists who simply own more and more capital (see pp. 77-78). It is, indeed, because the ascending stages of development of productive forces in capitalist society so regularly require the increasing ranks of those who own only their labor power continually to reform the content of such ownership to maintain its exchange value that Marx holds that a "many-sided" labor-power is thereby increasingly enjoined by capitalism (see p. 224). This requirement, he further holds, must ultimately subvert the fixed division-of-labor framework of capitalism—yet another case of how Marx views the capitalist economic order as sowing the seeds of its own destruction:

> Modern Industry on the other hand, through its catastrophes imposes the necessity of recognizing as a fundamental law of production, variation of work, consequently fitness of the labourer for varied work, consequently the greatest possible development of his various aptitudes. It becomes a question of life and death for society to adapt the mode

of production to the normal functioning of this law. Modern Industry indeed compels society, under penalty of death to replace the detail-worker of today, crippled by life-long repetition of the one and the same trivial operation, and thus reduced to a mere fragment of a man, by the fully developed individual, fit for a variety of labours, ready to face any change of production, and to whom the different social functions he performs are but so many modes of giving free scope to his own natural and acquired powers. . . . There is also no doubt that such revolutionary ferments, the final result of which is the abolition of the old division of labour, are diametrically opposed to the capitalist form of production, and to the economic status of the labourer corresponding to that form. (*CI*, 487–88)

Note the connection here between ever-developing forces of production or technology and the fulfillment of man's natural capacities. It is in ways such as this that the mature Marx presupposes human nature and assimilates its development to that of the productive forces. In such manner, one could say, technological determinism is on another implicit level the affirmation for Marx of man's essential nature.

4. The relations of production/economic structure correspond to a definite stage of development of the productive forces insofar as *the mode of extraction of surplus labor* by the ruling class involved in the former *complies with the technological requirements* prescribed by the latter.

Thus, for example, if the stage of development of the productive forces (factories, machines, and assembly lines) requires that labor-power be present in unskilled form and elastic quantities continuously during the

working week, then the relations of production/eco-
nomic structure must correspond to this requirement by
a surplus-value-extracting mechanism that is sufficiently
indifferent to labor-power (no "gradations of skill,"
"personal ties," and so on), sustained in operation (not
the intermittent expropriation of a part of the working
week as in "corvée labor," but expropriation spread
throughout the week), embracing in application (not restricted to this or that retinue or craft, but with all the
"free" labor-power of society at its disposal, and so
forth, to answer to the requirements of the technological stage in question. Hence, in Marx's account, as the
stage of development of productive forces of European
society develops from individual plot tillage and small
craft shops to mechanized and mass-labor farming and
factories, the mode of expropriation of surplus labor
changes, and has to change, in accordance with such
development—changes, and has to change, that is, from
the "fixed hierarchy" and "personal ties" of feudalism,
which cannot accommodate such development, to the
"cash nexus" of capitalism, which can and does. It is
also in accordance with this principle that Marx projects
the inexorable dissolution of the capitalist economic
order itself. That is, an increasingly automated or
"self-acting" technology inexorably reduces the need
for human labor and, thereby, contracts the very source
of the capitalists' surplus value, while at the same time
swelling the ranks of the unemployed. Hence the rate of
surplus value accruing to capitalists must progressively
fall, predicts Marx, until the capitalist economic form is
no longer compatible with its labor-diminishing productive force base, and is revolutionized into a new economic order where extraction of surplus value by a ruling class disappears as an historically obsolete mode of
appropriation in the technological conditions of an au-

tomated society; that is, a society where labor can no longer be exploited to the extent that it is no longer technically required.[7] Simultaneously, Marx predicts, unemployment must increase as an ever-expanding sphere of "idle" human productive forces that either die or live parasitically, and therefore that cannot be used to lower the working day for those who toil—until, again, the capitalist economic order is inevitably transformed into a new economic form that can accommodate all society's forces of production as then developed. This new, socialist economic order, Marx holds, by transcending the former mode of extraction of surplus value, is able to employ all society's productive labor without any ruin or parasitism of workers, and is simultaneously able, thereby, to permit a shorter working day for all.[8]

These four general principles together reveal the correspondence Marx claims between a society's forces and

[7] For the most extended and interesting discussion of this process, see G, 692-706.

[8] i. Once again, it is important to distinguish this underlying general principle of required correspondence between technological stage and economic order—here, more specifically, the necessary compliance of the latter's stipulations of labor-power use with the former's—from the particular inferences Marx draws from the principle in question, such as his claim that a proletarian revolution must occur against advanced capitalism in order for such technological-economic correspondence to be secured. Here, as elsewhere, the principle of correspondence in question may hold true, and yet Marx's prediction from it, which is not a straight logical consequence of it, prove false—with, for example, the claimed correspondence being secured in other ways than proletarian revolution.

ii. We have focussed with Marx on the contradiction between highly developed productive forces and the private-profit "law" of utilization of labor-power. But consideration of natural resources here may reveal a more dramatic contradiction still. That is, the private-profit "law" of utilization of the water, the air, the earth, the forests, and so on, comes to a certain point, as we have seen more tellingly since Marx's day, where it threatens to ruin society's stage of development of productive forces by destroying planetary life itself, by global pollution and resource exhaustion. See *CI*, 507.

relations of production. Though they are all implied by Marx's texts in one way or another, their formulation here is new and invites, therefore, the following further clarifications:

a. These underlying general principles of the correspondence Marx claims between a society's technology and its economic order decisively refute the common criticism that such claim of correspondence has no grounds at all. Raymond Aron's standard objection, for example (see p. 15) that there "may be exactly the same technical organization of agricultural production whether the land is the individual property of a great landowner, the collective property of producer's cooperative, or the property of the state" would appear to suffer, as so much of the criticism of Marx, from missing the substance of his position altogether. That is, Marx's notion of production relations is, as we have seen, an incomparably more developed one than merely, say, ownership "by a great landowner." It makes all the difference, for example, whether such "ownership by a great landowner" is feudal or capitalist, or some other specific form, and Marx could hardly have emphasized this more strongly than he does. Yet Aron's wording is quite indifferent to such critical and labored distinctions. It seems difficult, therefore, to take such criticisms as his seriously, though of course one might well take them seriously as instantiations of Marx's claim that mainstream ideology is systematically misleading.

Suppose, though, that the objection here were less indolent in its understanding of Marx's position on the issue of technological-economic correspondence, and ran something like this: "There may be exactly the same technical organization of agricultural production whether the land is owned by a great landowner according to feudal economic arrangements, by a producers' collective according to socialist economic arrangements, or by a state according to capitalist economic arrangements." As soon as the objection is so rendered in a form that is not devoid of the fundamental distinctions Marx makes with respect to economic formations, it already loses its tenability. For example, ownership by a great landowner according to feudal economic arrangements is such that mass production methods of working the soil are clearly ruled out, as the exposition of the fourth principle above makes clear. Then, as for communist and capitalist economic arrangements being able to accommodate the "same technical organization of agricultural production," this part of the reformulated claim, so far as it is true, represents no objection to Marx at all insofar as it is his well-known view that capitalism's technical organization of production (mass-production methods) has to be adopted by socialism as the latter's requisite productive base. If, instead, the objection in question were to refer to another sort of state ownership of land than capitalist—say, ancient Asiatic state ownership—the objection would still remain without force, for then the state ownership in question would not be able to accommodate the "same technical organization of agricultural production" as socialist ownership, because, among other reasons, it does not have the mechanism of social distribution necessary to sustain methods of mass production (see the second principle above). In short, Aron's objection seems to fare no better when it is bolstered with substance than when it is left tilting at a strawman.

b. The four principles in question are, obviously, intimately related. Indeed, they are so closely related that one might properly wonder about their ultimate amenability to four-fold distinction. But one can sustain their discreteness as principles. (1) and (2), for example,

are distinct, dealing as they do with separate aspects of
the economic form (its scale of ownership units and its
system of distribution, respectively), not to say separate
aspects of the productive forces. (2) and (3) are easily
distinguishable insofar as (3) is concerned with the content of individuals' effective ownership, whereas (2) involves no such consideration. (3) and (4) may just as
clearly be held apart, and so on for all possible such pair-
ings. However, in any stable social order, *all* these correspondences between the stage of development of productive forces and the production relations/economic
structure obtain together, in systemic unison. It is, *inter
alia*, the historical prevalence of this integral intercon-
nectedness that leads Marx to talk often of human society as an *organism*, and of any "contradiction" between
its economic "anatomy" and its productive force "organs" as the signal of the impending birth of a whole
new body, the "birth pangs" of a new form of life
altogether.[9]

[9] It warrants an aside here that Marx's imagery of organic birth in
connection with revolution seems to be out of line with the latter
conceived as armed civil war: which, if we wish to pursue such imagery of organism further, seems more akin to amputation than
midwifery. Lest it be thought that this is mere play upon metaphor,
it's worth observing here that revolution by armed civil war may destroy in large part the very productive forces upon which such revolution is, according to Marx's theory, materially dependent.

On the other hand, Marx often remarked on the development of
productive forces *through* warfare—for example, the revolutionary
development of new modes of cooperative labor (e.g., *SC*, 118 and
218). Indeed, it is in this progressive aspect of warfare that the Marxian explanatory key to the success of twentieth-century peasant revolutions may lie, (e.g. China). Here, that is, armed civil war *forms* the
"organs" of the new social body. The latter is not "delivered" by
revolution, but comes into being through it, a mode of gestation that
accounts for the militaristic nature of such societies in their postrevolutionary development.

As for highly advanced industrial societies, such as the United
States today, their revolution by armed civil war is, on the face of it,

c. Correspondence between a society's developed forces of production and its relations of production/ economic structure is, for Marx, what one might call a general law of collective human survival. During much or most of a society's existence, the problem of noncorrespondence or "contradiction" in this regard simply does not arise: correspondence obtains without complication as the necessary material foundation of any society's reproductive stability. Even when noncorrespondence or "contradiction" between the technological and the economic does threaten or obtain, typically in the late stages of a social order, it still must, according to Marx, be somehow rapidly resolved, somehow rapidly engineered back into correspondence again, either tenuously and haphazardly through superstructural interventions, conquests of new markets, destruction or waste of productive forces, and so on; or a social revolution that alters the production relations/economic structure into a new form where the required technological-economic correspondence is more decisively secured. Marx seems also to have believed that the former piecemeal resolution "inevitably" leads to the latter, thoroughgoing resolution. But be this as it may, he was committed to the view that in some way correspondence between forces and relations of production has to be secured if men are to collectively survive. In this law of technological-economic correspondence, indeed, lies the nub of historical materialism: social stability, instability, and revolution are all primarily accounted for by Marx in its terms.

---

technologically ruled out. That is, the concentration, interconnection, and refinement of such a society's productive forces would seem to render armed civil war both too difficult for the dispossessed to prosecute with the means accessible to them, and too ruinous of these forces to be compatible with Marx's basic "law" that the stage of their development is always preserved.

d. As far as the *primacy* of the stage of development of productive forces in its relationship of correspondence with the relations of production/economic structure, such primacy is held by Marx on the following grounds:

i. The former is in some form a necessary material condition of the latter, but not vice versa. In other words, men cannot have a private-property economic order without a stage of development of productive forces (which they require to reproduce themselves); but they can have a stage of development of productive forces without a private-property economic order (for instance, with communism).[10] The former is an "eternal, Nature-imposed necessity," but the latter is a defeasible historical construction.

ii. A stage of development of productive forces that yields a surplus product is a necessary material condition of a ruling-class economic form (to support the ruling class's nonproductive existence: *CI*, 511–12), but not vice versa. With communist economic arrangements, for example, there exists and must exist a stage of development of productive forces yielding a surplus product, but there does not and cannot exist a ruling-class economic form. The former is the indispensable material basis of the latter, but the latter is only one mode (albeit historically prevalent) within which the former can obtain.

---

[10] We emphasize: communist society has no relations of production/economic structure.

*i*. Relations of production are exclusive ownership relations to society's productive forces, and no such relations obtain in communist society (Chapter 3).

*ii*. That the state (S) withers away entails that the economic structure (E) "withers away." For $S \supset E$ (Chapter 4). But if $S \supset E$, then $\sim S \supset \sim E$.

What takes the place of exclusive ownership is agreed-upon usufruct; and what takes the place of ruling-class economic structure is democratic social plan.

iii. *In all cases where correspondence between a society's stage of development of the productive forces and its relations of production/economic structure cannot be secured without the forfeit of one or the other, the former is preserved and the latter is annihilated and replaced by an economic form that can so correspond.*

Hence Marx says:

> As the main thing is not to be deprived of the fruits of civilization of the acquired productive forces, the traditional forms in which they were produced must be smashed (*PofP*, 107).

> Men never relinquish what they have won, but this does not mean that they never relinquish the social form in which they have acquired certain productive forces. On the contrary, in order that they not be deprived of the result attained, and forfeit the fruits of civilization, they are obliged from the moment when the form of their commerce no longer corresponds to the productive forces acquired, to change all their traditional social forms (Letter to Annenkov, *SC*, 41).

Some paragraphs back, we suggested that the nub of the historical materialist doctrine was the general "law" that a society's stage of development of productive forces and its relations of production must correspond. Here we have the further and complementary "law" that when such correspondence cannot be secured without the forfeit of the former or the latter, it is the former (the existing stage of development of the productive forces) that is preserved, and the latter that is forfeited (revolutionized into a new form to accommodate such preservation). Thus while the first "law" stipulates a multifaceted correspondence between the technological and economic factors in a society, the second "law" claims the primacy of the technological factor in this relationship.

Now it is crucial to clarify the concept of productive-force primacy that Marx proposes here. As he has formulated it here, such primacy refers only to those occasions when either the stage of development of the productive forces or the economic order must be *"forfeited."* It is quite consistent with this claim that the productive forces are *"fettered"* by the production relations/ economic structure—and in this sense subject to the latter's primacy, so long as such "fettering" does not involve relinquishing an established productive stage, giving up the achieved level of material productivity of the society in question. Hence, for example, the production relations/economic structure of advanced capitalism may since Marx's day have hindered technological development and, indeed, involved the outright wastage and destruction of productive forces on an increasing scale (through growing unemployment, nonproductive use of labor-power, destruction of commodities, unused factory capacities, decimating economic wars, and so on); but nevertheless, since during the same period the level of productivity of the societies in question has been preserved and, indeed, has enormously increased, there has been during this time no forfeiting of the achieved stage of development of the productive forces, no relinquishing of the "fruits of civilization" of historically developed technology.

In other words, the general principle or "law" under discussion is sufficiently restrictive in its reference that the course of development of advanced capitalism since Marx's writings has not, against common opinion to the contrary, falsified its claim. Cases where correspondence between the stage of development of the

productive forces and the relations of production/
economic structure cannot be secured without the forfeit of one or the other, cases to which alone the "law"
under discussion applies, have in advanced capitalism
simply not arisen (as opposed to late feudalism where, it
seems, at least in Marx's account, the situation was such
that either the stage of technological development or the
feudal economic order did have to be sacrificed—hence
the "thunderclaps" of the bourgeois revolution).

But it would be disingenuous to leave the impression
that Marx made or implied the distinction between "fettering" and "forfeit" on which our argument in favor of
his principle of productive-force primacy is based. It is
fair to say that he quite conflated the concepts of "fettering" and "forfeit"; and that, in consequence, he sometimes (as it turns out, mistakenly) anticipated a revolution of the advanced capitalist economic order by virtue
of its "fettering" of productive forces alone: "At a certain stage of [productive force] development it [the economic order] brings forth the agencies of its own dissolution . . . but the old social organization fetters them
and keeps them down. It must be annihilated; it is annihilated" (CI, 762).

It is this latter, less discriminating view of productive-force primacy that plunges Marx's theory into its
notorious problem of premature revolutionary forecast.
But since Marx's wording in such places as the passages
cited above supports the salvaging distinction we have
made, and since, besides, he himself allows for "fettering" of the stage of development of the productive
forces to obtain extensively under the capitalist economic order *without* the latter's "annihilation," (that is,
during the many decades of his own life when, as his
own descriptions made clear, this capitalist economic
order persistently and without dissolution inhibited full

productive-force utilization), we think his "law" of revolution and productive-force primacy can be maintained. That is, it is sustainable if the inchoate distinction in his work between "fettering" and "forfeit" is made.[11]

[11] i. It is worth formulating this distinction more explicitly. As we have already suggested, to "fetter" is to impede full use of the productive forces, but not thereby to diminish the quantity of use-values ("the fruits") that these forces produce. On the other hand, any case of decline in the achieved level of productivity is a case of "forfeit," and it is here that the distinction between "fettering" and "forfeit" lies: the former does not imply this decline, whereas the latter does.

Is, then, a "depression"—insofar as it involves a decline in level of material productivity—a forfeit of the stage of development of the productive forces? As we have so far characterized "forfeit" and "stage," yes. To avoid this difficulty, and at the same time to capture better the ordinary force of the concepts "forfeit" and "stage," we add the further provisos: that the giving up of the achieved level of material productivity must be both permanent (to count properly as "forfeit") and of qualitative significance (to count properly as relinquishing of a "stage of development"). As to the latter, where the giving up of productivity goes from quantitative to qualitative significance—where, otherwise put, the forfeit is of a full "stage" of development—Marx seems to mean by this the forfeit of a distinct type of productive force that is, at the same time, capable of a distinct level of material productivity (e.g., a steam engine versus a hand mill.) In other words, the notion of forfeiting a stage of development of productive forces is, when unpacked, sufficiently strict that a "depression" falls clearly outside its range of reference.

ii. The definition we accord here to "forfeit of a stage of development of productive forces," though it may salvage Marx's general historical "law" with respect to depressions or recessions, raises an obvious problem insofar as the epochal transition from the ancient Roman order to the so-called "Dark Ages." For here there does seem to have been an authentic forfeit of the stage of development of productive forces. Is then Marx's general historical "law" falsified by this particular but crucial case?

As we observed earlier, the transition in question is one with which Marx himself never seriously engages. It is a definite weak link in his technological determinist account of history. One could, though, meet this problem in one of the following ways:

a. The transition from the ancient Roman order to the "Dark

Such a distinction, we might add, while a refinement of theoretical importance, does not at all violate the logic of Marx's theory of revolution. It simply explains the precise point at which periodic crises and "contradictions" between a society's forces and relations of production can continue no longer: identifies, that is, exactly when a "qualitative" change or revolution of the economic structure must occur. It must occur, we have now seen, when the economic "fettering" of productive forces has reached that threshold point where either the achieved stage of development of these forces or the established economic order has to be forfeited.

Marx himself talks about such a threshold limit to the economic structure's "fettering" of the forces of production. Thus in *Capital*, he proclaims: "The monopoly of capital becomes a fetter upon the mode of production. Centralization and socialization of the means of production at last reach a point where they become incompatible with their capitalist integument. This integument is burst asunder" (*CI*, 763). Elsewhere, he re-

---

Ages" is indeed refractory to Marx's general historical "law" that a civilized society never forfeits its stage of development of productive forces, but it does not thereby falsify this "law": the latter is simply true in most cases but not all, a statistical "law" or firmly obtaining regularity.

b. Marx's general historical "law" here is really meant to apply only to post-ancient Western society; that is, it is applicable to the last thousand years of Western civilization alone.

c. The transition from the ancient Roman order to the "Dark Ages" does not, in fact, involve a "forfeit of the stage of productive forces" at all insofar as the basic productive complex of food and shelter goes, but on the contrary salvages these basic forces of production from increasing ruin within the economic form of Roman imperialism (see our earlier discussion on p. 193). Only, for the most part, the production of luxuries and military installations of the ruling class is forfeited in this transition, and hence the falsification of Marx's general historical "law" is only apparent. The basic forces of production of the society as a whole are secured from dissolution, and Marx's "law" is thus confirmed here rather than refuted.

We favor (c).

fers to "a certain stage" when "the depth and breadth" of economic-technological "contradictions" and "antagonisms" finally necessitate the economic structure's transformation (*CIII*, 883–84). Still elsewhere, he refers to "a situation" being reached, at last, "which makes all turning back impossible" (*18thB*, 14). But in all these cases, it is not clear precisely what this "point," "certain stage," or "situation of no return" is. What our refining distinction between "fettering" and "forfeit" does, simply, is define this "point," "certain stage," or "situation of no return" and, by so doing, rehabilitates Marx's widely dismissed prediction of "inevitable" revolution.[12]

[12] i. As we have refined Marx's "law" here, revolution of the capitalist economic structure necessarily occurs when maintenance of it requires forfeit of a technological stage of development. But such an occasion, as we have pointed out, has not yet arisen in advanced capitalist societies. Therefore, the "law" in question has not yet been falsified, or confirmed, in these societies. It remains perfectly consistent with the facts, then, to continue to predict a "necessary" or "inevitable" revolution in these societies when the determining conditions to which this "law" applies have occurred—that is, conditions such that either a society's technological stage or its economic structure must be forfeited.

Marx, as we have emphasized, seems sometimes to have believed that such determining conditions would soon be, or even had been already, fulfilled by mere economic "fettering" of productive forces alone, "fettering" that had not yet reached that threshold limit of *forfeit*. In consequence, his forecast of "inevitable" revolution is sometimes premature. However, with our salvaging development of his inchoate distinction between "fettering" and "forfeit," no such problem in the prediction of "inevitable" revolution in advanced capitalist societies arises. The prediction remains unfalsified (but still falsifiable), because the determining conditions stipulated by the "law" from which this forecast is made have not yet occurred.

ii. There is, of course, another, *long-range* sense in which Marx believes revolution of the capitalist economic order is "inevitable": as a corollary to the well-founded belief that "all things pass," or, as a dialectician might put it, that all phenomena are subject to the law of negation. In this long-range sense, Marx's prediction of "inevitable" revolution of the capitalist economic order requires no rehabilitation: though for some bourgeois ideologists, to whom this capitalist order would seem to be an eternal social form, even this distal version of his forecast is impossible to accept.

Now this principle or "law" that the stage of development of the productive forces is preserved, and the existing economic form is destroyed, in cases where one or the other must be forfeited, is a limited version of a still more general principle or "law" of Marx's that the stage of development of its productive forces is *never* forfeited by a society[13]—whether in conflict with the obtaining economic order or not. That is, "Men never relinquish what they have won."

Indeed, in this more general "law" lies the ultimate ground of Marx's entire system. It is essentially this embracing "law" that earns the state of development of productive forces the predicate "base" in Marx's discussion of technical-economic correspondence, and similar attribution elsewhere. And it is, as well, in terms of this principle that for Marx the determination by "selection" of economic arrangements (and, indeed, all other factors of his socio-historical ontology) takes place.

Accordingly, the more limited principle initiating this subsection might be formally broadened into the more inclusive form: *No civilized society ever forfeits its stage of development of productive forces, including cases where the production relations/economic structure must be annihilated and replaced by a new economic form to avoid such forfeit.*

iv. Any case of dissolution or revolution of the established relations of production/economic structure is causally dependent on an outgrowing stage of development of the productive forces. Thus Marx's famous interlocking general claims of the Preface to *A Contribution to the Critique of Political Economy*: "No social order

---

[13] Marx's phrase "fruits of civilization" in the passage I have been drawing upon indicates that the wording here might more properly be: "the stage of development of its productive forces is never forfeited by a *civilized* society." When we use the open term "society" here and elsewhere, it is with this qualification in mind.

ever disappears before all the productive forces for which there is room in it have developed," and "New higher relations of production never appear before the material [i.e. productive] conditions of their existence have matured in the womb of the old society." Now, granting these are not mere tautologies (as they might be unsympathetically read), and granting, in addition, they are claims for the causal dependency of change of the economic form on an outgrowing stage of productive-force development, these statements might furthermore be interpreted as together constituting a neatly complementary "law"to that adduced in subsection (iii) above. That is, Marx holds, according to (iii), that the stage of development of productive forces is never forfeited by a society and furthermore—here is the theoretically integrating complement to this "law" we suggest he provides by the interlocking claims in question—a society's production relations/economic structure never "disappear" or are revolutionized into "new, higher relations" *unless they must be so negated or transcended to avoid such forfeit* (that is, the forfeit of a higher technological stage). Note that we retain here the distinction in (iii) between "fettering" and "forfeit." Thus, according to our interpretation, to say that "no social order ever disappears before all the productive forces for which there is room in it have developed" means, more explicitly, that no society's production relations/economic structure ever disappears before the stage of development of productive forces can no longer obtain within these production relations/economic structure without forfeit; that is, *the "room" for growth ends where the "forfeit" starts*. And thus, under our reading, to say that "new, higher relations of production never appear before the material conditions of their existence have matured in the womb of the old society" means, along the same lines, that new, higher relations of production/economic structure never appear before the stage of development of productive forces to which they correspond must be forfeited under the old relations of production/economic structure within which they have developed; that is, "higher" relations because they require no forfeit of technological stage whereas the old relations, within which this stage has arisen, do. In both cases, with our integrative rendering, change—dissolution or revolution—of an established economic form is held to be causally dependent on an outgrowing stage of development of productive forces that requires such change for its preservation. It seems then that, if our interpretation is accepted, Marx here is proposing a "law" of the causal dependency for change of the economic form on technological development that can be simply stated as follows: *No production relations/economic structure is ever dissolved or revolutionized before it must be so dissolved or revolutionized to avoid forfeit of a stage of development of the productive forces.*[14]

As we have it, then, this "law" links felicitiously with the "law" of technological primacy disclosed in (iii): namely, that a society never forfeits its stage of development of productive forces. Here we have the complementary "law" that it is *only* when the persistence of the economic order enjoins such a forfeit that it will disappear or appear in a new higher form.

---

[14] Applying this "law" to post-Marx circumstances, we might say:

i. The old order in Russia only disappeared with electrification of the countryside.

ii. Chile's prerevolution failed because before it could secure a higher stage of production to burst its capitalist economic form, the society's transport system was sabotaged and, in turn, its gestational modes of cooperative production (such as housing) annihilated by systematic terror and murder.

This complementary "law" of technological primacy may appear, however, to be more easily falsified than our first "law" of technological primacy. That is, cases of dissolving or revolutionizing an economic order seem as a matter of historical fact not always causally dependent on cases of an outgrowing technological stage. Let us, therefore, propose two pairs of simplified examples and explanations, which show a rather firmer and broader hold of this "law" than historical criticism here may initially discern.[15]

1. Britain conquers India and then introduces to the latter a radically new stage of development of productive forces. India's relations of production/economic structure are dissolved and/or revolutionized.

Turkey conquers Transylvania and then introduces to the latter no new stage of development of productive forces, but merely exacts tribute in produce. Transylvania's relations of production/economic structure are not dissolved and/or revolutionized.

In the first case, India's economic order changes because an outgrowing technological stage has been introduced by Britain (positive confirmation of the "law" in question). In the second case, Transylvania's economic order does not so change, because such an outgrowing technological stage has not been introduced by the conqueror (negative confirmation of the "law" in question).

2. "Reds" and "Whites" vie for power in Russia. The Reds win and introduce a new stage of development of productive forces. Russia's relations of production/economic structure are dissolved and/or revolutionized.

"Labour" and "Conservatives" vie for power in Britain. Labour wins, and introduces no new stage of devel-

[15] See G, 97-99 for the paternity of what follows.

opment of productive forces. Britain's relations of production/economic structure are *not* dissolved and/or revolutionized.

In the first case, Russia's economic order changes because an outgrowing technological stage has been introduced by the Reds (again, positive confirmation of the "law" in question). In the second case, Britain's economic order does not so change because an outgrowing technological stage has not been introduced by the victorious party (again, negative confirmation of the "law" in question).

These examples illustrate the power of the "law" under present scrutiny. Cases like the Russian Revolution of 1917 or the British conquest of India, which might seem at first to be cases of old economic orders disappearing and new economic orders appearing by virtue of other than technological causes, are shown, on the contrary, to obtain because of technological causes.

Applying now this "law" of causal dependency of social revolution on outgrowing technological stage predictively to contemporary North American circumstances, we can forecast that a social revolution will not occur here (whatever the problems, whatever the dreams) until it must occur to avoid forfeit of a stage of development of productive forces. If, on the other hand, a situation arises such that economic-structural transformation must occur to preserve the achieved stage of technological development, then we can predict that such a revolution will occur (whatever the concessions, whatever the anxieties to evade it).

This schematic position, we hasten to add, is not at all fatalistic, as will be presently demonstrated. On the contrary, it simply delineates the precise nomological parameters within which social-structural preservation, or revolution, must proceed. For example, it is quite consistent with this "law" of causal dependency of revolution on technological development that an organized workers' movement (with vast votes, vast consumer demand, vast pension funds) deliberately engineers this development to a stage (more automation, shorter hours) where either this technological stage or the capitalist economic order must be forfeited: in which case and only in which case, according to the "law" in question, transformation of the capitalist economic order will necessarily ensue. [16]

[16] i. Other ways in which a higher stage of development of productive forces might be established in revolutionary contradiction to the capitalist economic structure would be: the implementation of full employment (for example, by shortening the work week), the cost-reducing development of labor-power, (for example, by worker self-management replacing administration), the substitution of collective goods for private commodities (for example, in job-transit and leisure spaces), and the social regulation of capital (for example, by criteria of method safety and investment relocation).

ii. Marx, as we have already observed on several occasions, conceives the revolutionary "contradiction" of forces and relations of production always in terms of the former outgrowing the latter (as above), and never in terms of the latter out-reaching the former (as in the transition from Roman to barbarian society: see pp.193, and 209-10). Yet the latter sort of revolutionary noncorrespondence might be as likely as the former to occur in advanced capitalist society: with revolution ensuing to avoid forfeit of a nongrowing technological stage (such as of fresh-air and fresh-water production) by continued maintenance of overreaching economic relations (such as capitalist empires). Both sorts of revolutionary noncorrespondence, however, are subsumed by Marx's general "law" in its refined form—no production relations/economic structure is ever dissolved or revolutionized before it must be so dissolved or revolutionized to avoid forfeit of a stage of development of productive forces.

iii. The foregoing "law," and what it subsumes, might be instructively considered, in a Fabian rather than Marxian way, as admitting of degrees: so that in place of "dissolved or revolutionized" we put "significantly changed" (as by social insurance), and in place of "avoid forfeit" we put "improve" (as by more productive labor-power).

The implication of all this for a Marxian revolutionary strategy is, of course, crucial. It means that the way a revolution against advanced capitalism must proceed is through this situation, where either technological stage or economic order has to be forfeited: revolution by, say, seizure and consolidation of state power alone must prove abortive, lacking as it does the required material conditions for success.

We have explicated the principal relationship of Marx's technological determinism: the relationship of correspondence between a society's stage of development of productive forces and its relations of production/economic structure. We have argued that this relationship of correspondence obtains in accordance with a set of four principles of "laws," and that the stage of development of productive forces is primary, is the "base" in this relationship: by virtue of, essentially, the "law" that it is never forfeited by a society, whereas the economic order is, when either it or the former must go. We have also proposed, finally, that it is in terms of this "law" of preservation of the technological stage that the productive forces may be said to determine all else. That is, whatever in a society is not compatible or does not correspond with the preservation of the stage of development of its productive forces is "selected out" (including, most importantly, the economic order itself). Just as, to follow Marx's own course of analogue, the individual is governed before all else by the natural law to preserve his "organs" of person, so society is governed before all else by the historical law to preserve its "organs" of technology. That everything in a society thus conforms to the preservation of its technological stage, of its "productive organs" (*CI*, 372), is not only the "law" whereby Marx explains the dissolution or revolution of the economic order itself, but also the "law" by virtue of which he judges utopian communes, return to craft labor, romantic anarchism, and so on, as historical impossibilities—to identify just a few of the cases in which he most plainly invokes it.

All in all, it seems for Marx—to translate his position into cosmological terms—that technology has replaced Divine Will as the ultimate arbiter of history, fating whatever does not conform to its dictates to death or ruin, with Marx as the secular prophet of its design. Only here, Marx truly "descends from heaven to earth." Man, not God, is the Maker. And human production, not supernatural grace, is the agency of salvation.

Having schematized the essential principles of Marx's technological determinism, we move now to other less central sorts of determining influence that he claims the productive forces exert. We have already discussed in Chapter 1 the relationship Marx posits between men's needs and capacities, and the forces of production. So there is no need to recount here how he sees the latter as expressing capacities and answering needs and, in so doing, determining such needs and capacities in dialectical turn. This is not to say that the prospects for working through this line of thought, for exploring the full richness and complexity of the mutually determining relationship suggested by Marx between the productive forces and human nature, are not extremely inviting. In the dialectic between human nature and productive forces, after all, lies for Marx the essential process of man's *self-making*, and in its explication may also lie one of the most promising frontiers of investigation opened by his thought:

> "For not only the five senses but also the so-called mental senses—the practical senses (will, love, etc.)—in a word *human* sense—the humanness of the senses comes to be by virtue of its object, by

virtue of humanized nature [i.e. production]: The *forming* of the five senses is a labour of the entire history of the world down to the present" (Marx's emphases: *EPM*, 108).

Nevertheless, we shall not further cultivate this area of discussion, however fecund, beyond our outline in Chapter 1 of the set of principles underlying Marx's treatment. We now confine our consideration to two types of determining influence Marx claims the forces of production to have with respect to the elements of the superstructure. Marx does not say very much in this connection, and what he does say is elliptical and desultory, but the following two principles identify the substance of his position:

1. The *methods of the forces of production of a society map onto the methods of the legal and political superstructure and ideology*. For example, Marx says in *Capital*: "The principle, carried out in the factory system of analyzing the process of production into its constituent phases . . . becomes the determining principle everywhere" (*CI*, 461). And he says in *A Contribution to the Critique of Political Economy*: "There is in every social formation a particular branch of production which determines . . . all other branches as well. It is as though light of a particular hue were cast upon everything tingeing all other colours and modifying their specific features" (*CPE*, 212).

Though in neither of these passages does Marx explicitly develop the force of "everything" beyond merely other materially productive sectors, it is reasonable to infer that part of what he meant by his celebrated remark in the Preface—"The mode of production of material life determines the general character of the social, political and spiritual processes of life"—was this mapping of the methods of production onto the superstructure. That is, the method of the capitalist forces of production of "analyzing into constituent phases" is mapped onto its state bureaucracy and modes of publication, which reflect just this method in their progressive resolution of legal, political, and ideological processes into assembly-line-like series of detail-functions.[17]

2. *Practical control achieved by the forces of production displaces supernatural control by mythical forces in the society's ideology.* For example, Marx says in *A Contribution to the Critique of Political Economy*: "All mythology subdues, controls and fashions the forces of nature in the imagination and through imagination; it disappears therefore when real control over these forces is established. What becomes of Fama side by side with Printing House Square? . . . is Achilles possible when powder and shot have been invented?" (*CPE*, 216).

It is by virtue of this principle of technological control diplacing supernatural control in a society's ideology that Marx counts such things as the British conquest of India and the victory of the bourgeoisie over feudalism as historically progressive. That is, the technological advances that were introduced by the victors in these cases rid the societies concerned of ancient superstitions "enslaving" public consciousness and, for this, as well as simple increased production of the material means of life, the brutal takeovers in question were in his view steps forward in the onerous labor of human history.[18]

[17] This mapping is, we propose, in accordance with the same principles of "mapping" discussed in the previous chapter. That is, content from the domain of the production process (such as its assembly-line methods) is mapped onto the range of legal and political superstructure (such as its system of due process) in accordance with the rule set defined in Chapter 6.

[18] As for the paradoxical possibility of technology itself in some way taking on the status of a mythical force in a society's ideology ("Technology will destroy us"), if we consult our rule set of "mapping" here, we can see that such ideological conceptions are in neat

## CONCLUSION

There is a radical change of emphasis by Marx in the development of his social philosophy after 1845. Up until *The German Ideology*—most strikingly in the *Economic and Philosophical Manuscripts*—his concern is with man's nature and its material fulfillment, and he deplores the capitalist economic order for its systematic violations and repressions in this regard. Here the technological factor is viewed as the "open book of man's essential powers, the exposure to the senses of human psychology" (*EPM*, 109) and is valued as such, *in terms of the realization of human nature*. In his mature work, however, though as we argue he maintains his concept of human nature, his concern with the capitalist order's violations and repressions is generally worked out *in terms of the realization of technology*, condemned because it derogates in various ways from the productive forces of labor-power and thereby from technological development. That is, the riveting of men to detail-functions must be replaced, for Marx, not so much because it is an offence to human nature, but because in such offence it fails to utilize labor-power properly for technological development. Wrongs to man's nature seem now, in his concern, subordinate to wrongs to man's technology. Now this is an appropriate shift in emphasis in Marx's thought, inasmuch as his post-1844 epistemology commits him to a concern with what men materially *do* rather than what they constitutionally *are*, while at the same time the basic "law" of history in his mature theory is that the stage of development of a society's productive forces is preserved before all else. Furthermore, since Marx conceives the instruments of technol-

---

accordance with rule 8, namely, "The social property of the ruling class is an independent self-moving power."

ogy as man's historically acquired "organs" (*CI*, 372), the shift in emphasis to them rather than human nature can be conceived, in the end, as simply an extension of his former central concern. The distinction between the early and later Marx thus turns out to be not so clear-cut as it may first appear. His concern with the preservation and development of technology is ultimately his concern with the preservation and development of human nature; for the former is only the extension of the latter.

Nowadays, however, a number of prominent thinkers, notably Jacques Ellul in *The Technological Society*, argue that the requirements of technology are in contradiction with the needs of human nature.[19] So we might properly press here the theoretically basic complemantarity which Marx, on the contrary, declares between them.

Because Marx was familiar with neo-Luddite lines of thought, his work abundantly caters to their refutation. In a sentence, he construed their distress at technology as, demystified, distress at the capitalist law of utilization of technology. Thinkers like Ellul, he would say, fail to distinguish between *productive-force* demands and *capital* demands, and thus saddle the former with the terrors of the latter, which is quite in conformity with the economic structure's determination of ideology.[20]

But is this really all there is to it? Cannot we discern conflicts in requirement between the needs of human nature and technological development? Is the perfect correspondence Marx holds between these requirements, perhaps the key to his entire *Weltanschauung*, really so

[19] Jacques Ellul, *The Technological Society* (New York, 1964), *passim*. Ellul is merely the most systematic purveyor of this point of view. It is widespread in contemporary social thought, and in nomic accordance with the capitalist economic structure's determination of ideology, as shown in note 18.

[20] See Chapter 2, pp. 68–69, and Chapter 7 *in toto*.

sustainable as he supposes?[21] Let us consider the most telling criticisms that can be directed against the Marxian position here, and the counters that it can generate in return.

1. Modern technology's essential method is "analysing the process of production into its constituent phases" (*CI*, 461): that is, in more familiar terms, converting the production process into a series of assembly-line detail-functions. But human nature's need is for "variation of activity" and "many-sided labor" (see pp. 33-34). It follows, then, that the requirements of modern technology and human nature are in fundamental contradiction.

*Answer*: Modern technology's assembly-line method increases material productivity, thus increases the material use-values available for the satisfaction of human needs, thus strictly corresponds to the requirements of human nature.

As for modern technology's systematic confinement of human labor-power to detail-function, Marx's theory makes a basic distinction between technological division of task and economic division of labor (see pp. 69 and 80). Division of task does not confine any one labor-power to a detail function, but may be—must be, with the development of modern industry—fulfilled by society's members "many-sidedly" alternating produc-

---

[21] Every factor of Marx's theory normally corresponds to the stage of development of productive forces. But in any period preceding social transformation, this multiple correspondence is rent into multiple "contradiction," which is only restored to correspondence again with the completion of such social transformation. However, with the relationship between human nature and the stage of development of productive forces, there is never any contradiction or conflict: the two are always in systemic correspondence. It is this perfect correspondence Marx holds between the two that we now subject to a set of challenges in terms of his own theory.

tion places (*CI*, 487-88).[22] Division of labor, on the other hand, does confine labor-power to detail-function, but it is an economic constraint, not a technological one, and is to be dissolved altogether by the transformation of the capitalist economic structure into communist social plan.[23]

In sum, the requirements of technology and human nature are not in contradiction but, on the contrary, doubly correspond. The apparent conflict between them is, on closer analysis, their complementary conflict with the economic order.

2. Modern technology's method is standardization of the production process. But the essential need of human nature is to produce in accordance with self-raised projects (Chapter 1). Therefore, there is contradiction between modern technological method and human-natural requirement at the very core of Marx's concern.

*Answer*: Standardization only qualifies as technologi-

---

[22] Marx considers this method necessary to meet modern industry's increasing demand for versatile labor-power "fit and ready to meet any change in production" (*CI*, 488).

Today it might be considered necessary, as well, to prevent the social-service costs of fixing individuals to detail-functions from bankrupting society; that is, the costs of medical attention of all sorts for those so fixed, the costs of unemployment and welfare support for those thereby kept out of work, and the costs of law-enforcement for those preferring criminal activity to either such fate.

[23] Thus Marx says in one of his most famous passages (*GP*, 17): "In a higher phase of communist society, after the enslaving subordination of the individual to the division of labor, and with it also the antithesis between mental and physical labor, has vanished, after labor has become not only a livelihood but life's prime want, after the productive forces have also increased with the all-round development of the individual, and the springs of cooperative wealth flow more abundantly—only then can the narrow horizon of bourgeois right be crossed in its entirety and society inscribe on its banners: From each according to his ability, to each according to his needs!"

cal method insofar as its use makes men able to produce a quantity of material use-values they could not produce without it (Chapter 2)—thereby, by definition, a method able to fulfill more of men's needs or provide more free time for their leisure. In either case, the technique in question and human nature are at one in their requirements. Only the ownership and utilization of such need-realizing benefits of technology by a ruling class renders them, on the contrary, need-denying misfortunes; for example, labor-replacing machinery not reducing society's working day, but rather depriving workers of their livelihood.

Furthermore, any method of production, standardized or not, is "truly human" for Marx only insofar as it is projected as constituent of a workers' plan, only insofar as it is a formula that productive labor gives to itself (see p. 27). Thus, again, it corresponds, rather than conflicts, with man's essential need to produce in accordance with self-raised project. And thus, again, it is the economic order, whose ownership arrangements exclude the direct producers from so determining production methods, that underlies the apparent conflict between the requirements of human nature and the stipulations of modern technology.[24]

---

[24] To argue that direct producers will not adopt the most efficient methods of production when they necessarily stand to benefit from such methods in either increased goods or a lower working day, is to argue that direct producers are irrational. Marx argues, on the contrary, that direct producers resist the introduction of more efficient methods of production only when the ruling-class owners of the means of production receive the benefits of such introduction (such as higher profits) while they, the direct producers, bear the costs of such benefits (such as loss of livelihood). To claim that such worker resistance to labor-saving methods, which is rational in some circumstances, will occur in fundamentally different circumstances, where it is irrational, is, as Marx was wont to describe such maneuvers, an "ideological sham."

3. Technological development causes human needs to grow and so, by Marx's own admission, expands the "realm of necessity" (*CIII*, 820). But Marx holds, as well, that material circumstances only permit the full realization of human nature insofar as they release man from "the realm of necessity."[25] Therefore, by Marx's own account, the need-expanding development of technology is in contradiction with the necessity-releasing demand of human nature.

*Answer*: Marx never considers the real possibility that technological development might expand the "realm of necessity" by need expansion more than it contracts it by labor-saving devices. Yet this real possibility, so far as it obtains, means that technological development, in even socialist society, must increase society's working day rather than, as Marx presumes, its free time. How-

[25] By "necessity" here is meant what must be done *for* something else. For example, food, clothing, housing and all other object-productions must be done for man's material survival at a certain sociohistorical standard (Chapter 1). Each is, thus, a "necessity," and all constitute together "the realm of necessity." On the other hand, that which is done as an end in itself is not a "necessity," such as artistic "composition" performed for itself, and not for something else. These latter types of activity are, for Marx, "free," and together they constitute "the realm of freedom."

In fact the realm of freedom actually begins only where labour which is determined by necessity and mundane considerations ceases—With man's development this realm of physical necessity expands as a result of his wants; but, at the same time, the forces of production which satisfy those wants also increase. Freedom in this field can only consist in socialized man, the associated producers, rationally regulating their interchange with nature, bringing it under their common control; and achieving this with the least expenditure of energy and under conditions most favorable to, and worthy of, their human nature. But it nonetheless, remains a realm of necessity. Beyond it begins that development of human energy as an end in itself, the true realm of freedom, which, however, can blossom forth only with this realm of necessity as its basis. The shortening of the working day is its basic prerequisite. (*CIII*, 819-20)

ever, Marx's presumption that technological development must increase society's free time, needs only to be made explicit as a conscious regulating principle of production under social plan, and the potential contradiction here is dissolvable by his heirs.[26]

It is in this way, indeed, that the world-historical visions of Buddhism and Marxism merge. For both hold that all attachment to need-objects is to be progressively divested of its constraint, that humankind is to be increasingly emancipated from its ageless chains of want. But for Marxism, the way is not the internal way of need relinquishment, but the external way of need-satisfaction by technological development under social plan (albeit social plan informed by conscious regulation in place of unconscious presumption).

4. Technological development since the dawn of history has been largely, if not essentially, the development of weaponry, and so too its determinism (*SC*, 118 and 218). Is not, then, at least this aspect of technological development in clear conflict with human nature as essentially creative?

*Answer*: By man's essential creativity, Marx means man's unique ability to raise and realize creative projects. Weapon construction instantiates this ability, and is not, then, in conflict with it.

Furthermore, for Marx, the employment of weaponry by man against man in the sociohistorical condi-

---

[26] The regulating principle required here can be simply formulated as follows: A new product, x, is to be produced if and only if x's production does not add to society's total necessary labor-time. Thus x qualifies for production if: a. it replaces another product that requires the same or more necessary labor-time for its production; or b. it does not exceed in the necessary labor-time it requires the amount of labor-time liberated elsewhere by some labor-saving device.

tion is to be systematically explained as, and only as, the mechanism of violence whereby material ownership relations are protected and advanced: essentially, the material ownership relations of the ruling class whose collective representative, the state, perpetrates or has perpetrated the preponderance of all weaponed conflicts, repressions, and wars in human history. But Marx proposes the nihilation and transcendance of all such ownership relations and, thereby, the nihilation and transcendance of all employment of weaponry by man against man. In sum, then, technology's weapon construction is not in conflict with human nature's creativity, but is, on the other hand, to be altogether sublated through dissolution of its essential cause, ruling-class ownership of the material means of life.

5. Technological development, it is known, increasingly destroys as it advances the exquisitely complex web of ecosystem interconnection developed over tens of millions of years of natural evolution. It thus increasingly robs human nature of the very grounds of its material possibility until, in the end, the final judgment on this debate over technological development and human nature is pronounced by the extinction toward which such development inexorably hastens us.

*Answer*: Natural resources constitute, for Marx, the "natural presupposition," the "conditions," the "materials," the "storehouse," the "laboratory" of all human production: in a phrase, the fundamental "body of human subjecthood" (*Pre-C*, *passim*). Technological development thus requires the preservation and improvement of natural resources as the most fundamental condition of its realization. Indeed, one of his major pioneering concerns is the "plundering" of "the very roots of life" by capitalist exploitation of nature's elements (*CI*, 507), a "plundering" that he counts as the direst possible threat against technological development. Accordingly, it is precisely because of this destruction of natural resources, among other things, that Marx regards the revolutionary transformation of the capitalist order as "inevitable"—to preserve, that is, society's stage of development of productive forces. In short, nature's ruin by technological development is, under Marx's conceptualization, mere absurdity, a contradiction in terms.[27]

The systemic concurrence Marx holds between the requirements of human nature and technology seems, then, sustainable against critical attack. In the language of metaphysics, human nature and productive forces are, for Marx, *the interior and the exterior modes of one human substance, with their respective requirements in perfect correspondence with one another*: always allied, and always progressing in mutual reinforcement and growth. The course of history is, in this light, the continuous ad-

[27] i. Such a contradiction in terms, that technological *development* incurs the *ruin* of nature (that is, the primary prerequisite and constituent of technology), is in neat accordance with the economic structure's determination of ideology. That is, by shifting the blame for nature's ruin from ruling-class owners' use of technology (that is, use to maximize their profits), to technology as such, the economic structure is protected from alteration (see Chapter 7).

ii. Marx's position on a "higher" relationship between man and nature is perhaps best expressed in this passage from *Capital*, Volume III:

> From the standpoint of a higher economic form of society, private ownership of the globe by single individuals will seem quite as absurd as private ownership of one man by another. Even a whole society, a nation, or even all simultaneously existing societies taken together are not owners of the globe. They are only its possessors, its usufructuaries, and like *boni patres familias*, they must hand it down to succeeding generations in improved condition. (*CIII*, 776)

vancement of this one human substance to ever higher, corresponding levels of human-natural and technological development, "bursting" one epochal economic "form" after another in accordance with the inexorable laws of productive-force maintenance and growth: until the birth of communist society sheds altogether the ruling-class economic form within which this human substance has hitherto historically developed, and the "realm of freedom" for humankind's full self-realization is achieved at last:

> In fact, however, when the narrow bourgeois [economic] form is peeled away what is wealth if not the universality of needs, capacities, enjoyments, productive powers, etc. of individuals, produced in universal exchange? What if not the full development of human control over the forces of nature—those of his own nature as well as those of so-called "nature"? What, if not the absolute elaboration of his creative dispositions, without any preconditions other than antecedent historical evolution which makes the totality of this evolution —i.e. the evolution of all human powers as such unmeasured by any previously established yardstick—an end in itself? What is this, if not a situation where man does not reproduce himself in any determined form, but produces his totality? Where he does not seek to remain something formed by the past but is in the absolute movement of becoming? (*Pre-C*, 84-85)

This strict coupling of the human-natural and technological factors, this conception of them as, so to speak, the internal and external modes of one human substance in progressive historical development that culminates in the absolute human self-fulfilment described above, constitutes the primal pattern of Marx's thought, from the *Economic and Philosophical Manuscripts* of 1844 to the *Gotha Program* of 1881.[28]

As we showed earlier (Chapter 1), the material realization of human nature proceeds *pari passu* with the development of productive forces. As we have shown here (Chapter 8), the development of productive forces always holds or advances, and never regresses. It follows, then, that the material realization of human nature always holds or advances, and never regresses. The realization of human nature and the development of productive forces are, in short, theoretically yoked. That the stage of the latter, by the basic "laws" of technological determinism, always holds or advances, and never regresses, entails that the realization of the former always holds or advances, and never regresses.[29]

[28] Thus Marx says in his *Theories of Surplus-Value* (his emphases): "Production for its own sake means nothing but the development of human productive forces, in other words the *development of human nature as an end in itself*" (*S-V II*, 117-18). In the same passage, Marx goes on to say that "at first this development of the capacities of the human species takes place at the cost of the majority of individuals, and even classes." But, he adds, "in the end, human development breaks through this contradiction, and coincides with the development of the individual": a coincidence of species and individual development which he elsewhere celebrates as "the realm of freedom."

[29] In some cases, recession or depression for example, the stage of development of productive forces is maintained (see p. 209n), but, because of restriction of its normal use by economic impediment, the realization of human-natural capacities and needs does not, to the extent of such impediment, correspond to it. In such cases, the correspondence of human-natural realization to technological stage suffers a temporary lag, by virtue of extrinsic economic "fetters" which, if persistent, it is the function of revolution to "burst asunder." Does, then, revolution occur on account of economic structural impediment to correspondence between human nature and technological stage as well as, if not more basically than, on account of impediment to the latter's preservation alone? We think, yes. This is for the later Marx an unspoken point, but underlying, we suggest, his calls for and forecasts of revolution not necessitated on technological grounds alone.

But, as we pointed out at the conclusion of our first chapter, there is a first major ethical premise of Marx's thought: men *ought* to materially realize themselves.[30] Now we see that it follows from Marx's basic "laws" of technological determinism, and the correspondence of human-natural and productive-force development, that through history men *do*, in fact, materially realize themselves to an ever greater, and never lesser, extent. That is, with each progression of the stage of development of productive forces, there is a corresponding progression in the material realization of human nature. And as it is for Marx a nomic necessity that the stage of development of productive forces is always holding or advancing, and never regressing, it is also for Marx, by implication, a nomic necessity that the material realization of human nature that corresponds to such progression of productive forces is always holding or advancing, and never regressing. Therefore, Marx's ultimate ethical imperative is, in fact, by the operation of the ultimate historical "laws" of technological determinism he discerns, necessarily and progressively fulfilled.

[30] There is a patriarchal bias to Marx's work insofar as it focuses almost exclusively on the lot of men in the sociohistorical process, and has little to say about women and the young. Outside the sphere of the wage-place, these classes' productive labor (p. 61n), their economic domination (pp. 97-98n), and the superstructural "reflexes" of their economic domination in state regulation and ideological formation (p. 139n) are all neglected by Marx. However, as we already have proposed in the chapters cited, his theory in principle, if not in application, subsumes the lot of women and the young in the sociohistorical process, in all these respects. The same holds true of the material self-realization of mankind that his ethical imperative demands. It applies, in principle, if not in application, to women and the young as well as to men in the narrow sense of this term. Thus when we say "men" here and elsewhere, we mean by it people, men in the largest sense of this term, though all the while acknowledging the extent to which this sense of men involves an inferential extension of Marx's literal concern (not to mention exemplifying a patriarchal bias of ordinary language itself).

It is only with thoroughgoing communist society, of course, that full material realization of human nature, of human needs and capacities, is achieved.[31] Thus, it is only with thoroughgoing communist society that the ethical imperative demanding this material self-realization is, in fact, fulfilled. But the fulfilment of this ethical imperative proceeds by degrees throughout the course of history prior to communist society, as a necessary concomitant of the "laws" of technological determinism. The "ought" here is necessarily and progressively rendered "is" on the way to its "inevitable" full realization in the communist society of the future, where the gap between "ought" and "is" is transcended altogether.[32]

We might say, then, from all this, that Marx's ultimate ethic is, in the end, a higher-order generalization of his ultimate "laws" of technological determinism: a transepochal grasp and prefigurement of what the latter inevitably and progressively effects. It is this scientific basis of his ultimate ethical imperative that makes the latter what might be called a *scientific ethic*. Its commended object—humankind's material self-realization—is at the same time the nomically necessitated consequence of the "laws" of productive force development empirical science discerns.

On this account, we can see why Marx's normative talk in a putatively positivist thesis, why his disdain for ethical positions while he embraces one, is not, in the

---

[31] We do not, of course, mean to say that for Marx humanity's material self-realization terminates its development with communist society. On the contrary, humanity's full material self-realization is conceived by him, as we have seen, as an absolute movement of *becoming*.

[32] Thus the force of Marx's implicit "ought," underpinning the continual denunciations and acclamations of his work, remains operative so long as communist society has not yet been achieved.

end, paradoxical. What Marx's ethic demands is in strict accordance with what the "laws" he identifies ultimately necessitate. The former is, in part, a prediction of what the latter must eventually effect.

It would be a mistake to conclude from this, however, that Marx's "laws" of technological determinism are disqualified thereby from scientific status (as, say, a sort of wishful thinking). On the contrary, these "laws," as we have shown, are universal,[33] empirical generalizations that are subject to scientific procedures of confirmation, or disconfirmation, by factual evidence. Whether they are sound or not is to be determined, thus, by subjecting them to retrodictive or predictive empirical test, not by *a priori* rejection of the moral progress that their operation, if they are true, must effect against established economic interests.[34]

On the other hand, it might be held that even if Marx's "laws" of technological development are not disqualified from scientific status on account of their ethical import, at least his ethic is disqualified as an ethic

[33] It is generally held that a necessary condition of any scientific statement proposed as law-like is that it be a universal generalization. Marx's basic "laws" of technological determinism, which have as their subject all historical societies, satisfy this necessary condition (with the qualification of p. 82n). In contrast, the preponderance of contemporary social science articulates empirical generalizations about merely *particular* societies, at merely *particular* times—that is, fad reports—and thus radically wants the nomic substance that Marx's theory has: though the elaborate mechanisms of quantification employed by these sciences is apt, like a *camera obscura*, to make the opposite appear to be the case.

[34] As we have seen, the law-like advance of technological development, and corresponding human-natural realization involves, with Marx's theory, the "inevitable" destruction of ruling-class economic structures. Ruling-class economic interests, thus, *ex hypothesi*, dictate resistance to such advance, which resistance selects, in turn, corresponding ideological formations, such as dismissal of claims of such advance as "illusory," "unscientific," "value-ridden," and so on.

insofar as its commended object is necessarily effected by these "laws." After all, if the ethical object of mankind's material self-realization is nomically determined—if, that is, communist society wherein this ethical object is fulfilled is "inevitable"—then any *choice* in the matter seems, thereby, ruled out, and the name of "ethic," in consequence, a misnomer. For the standard position here is that an authentic ethic is such by virtue of its pursuit or violation being chosen by the moral agent or agencies in question. Thus, an end that is inexorably determined—namely, humanity's material self-realization—cannot at the same time be a properly ethical end.

A well-known Marxian counter to this kind of objection is that there is no incompatibility between choice, or free will, and nomic necessity. On the contrary, in the words of Plekhanov, via Hegel and Engels, there is "identity between freedom and necessity."[35] But as we do not find this position or the arguments supporting it to be either true or illuminating, we do not adopt it here. We consider, instead, Marx's repeated, if cryptic answer to this problem, which is, unpacked, that there *is* a choice with respect to society's "inevitable" transformation to a socialist and, eventually, communist order in which humanity's material self-realization is achieved. And the choice, in its simplest terms, is this: to "shorten the birth-pangs" *or* not to "shorten the birth-pangs" of the transformation in question.

Most, if not all, commentators on Marx's thought have failed to discern that this concept of "shortening the birth-pangs" of society's "inevitable" revolution, because it implies the possibility of not "shortening the birth pangs" of such "inevitable" revolution, implies thereby a choice between these alternative, general

[35] "The Role of the Individual in History," reprinted in *Theories of History*, ed. Patrick Gardiner (Glencoe, Ill., 1960), p. 143.

courses of action.[36] In consequence too, of course, they have failed to discern that within the range of each of these two general possibilities of ethically elected commitment, because each admits of indefinite degrees, are

[36] Put in more precise terms, the general choice here is between the advancement or retardation of society's "inevitable" transformation, a choice which is not, of course, confined to the transition from capitalist to socialist society alone, but is in principle applicable to any social transformation, such as from feudalism to capitalism. What in general *advances* such social transformation, we know from the preceding chapters of this study: i. productive force development incompatible with the obtaining economic structure, such as, in the case of capitalism, many-sided labor-alternating productive roles; ii. alteration of the effective ownership relations and "law of motion" of surplus-value extraction of this economic structure itself, such as, in the case of capitalism, socialization of capitalist ownership or profit; and, relatedly, iii. reformation of the state mechanisms protecting this economic structure and/or of the ideological forms justifying it, such as, in the case of capitalism, direct producer "seizure" by, say, electoral victory of major state offices, and/or generation of published conceptions that expose the fraudulence of the established ideology sanctifying this social order. On the other hand, what *retards* social transformation is refusal to participate in, or active resistance to, (i), (ii) and (iii). The basic choice, then, is between such advancement(s) or such retardation(s) of social transformation. This basic choice, in turn, can be made by a person in the form of engaging in political class action, the only issuant of choice to which Marx seriously attends (see Chapter 4), or in some other activity.

An important instance of "some other activity," which Marx ignores but which would seem to be of crucial, if complementary, import in the advancement or retardation of society's "inevitable" transformation to a socialist order, would be the domestic upbringing of children, which is under the effective private jurisdiction of parents, the immense majority of whom are direct producers, and which is, thus, radically subject to their individual choice, whether or not they recognize this. Herein lies the main substance of society's production of labor-power, not to say, the primary process of its formation of legal, political, and ideological habits. Consequently, what transpires here is of great significance in the advancement or retardation of society's transformation to a higher order and may indeed be, as we have earlier suggested, the "long-missing link" of society's successful transition to authentic communism. We might even say, without undue exaggeration, that here society's members choose, with wide permission to their choice, the revolution or the counterrevolution in their every action.

an indefinite number of possible subclass choices, which radically enrich the scope of elective, moral options available. What first appears to allow no moral choice whatever—Marx's claim of "inevitable" revolution and, by deduction from this, mankind's "inevitable" material self-realization—allows, then, on the contrary, a substantive and broad range of moral choice. To clarify the great ethical substance which is involved in this basic choice, we offer the following three-step argument which, though not present in Marx's work, underlies the profound moral conviction with which he recommends the socialist revolution that is, under his theory, "inevitable" in any case. The argument, in its starkest form, is this:

1. To "shorten the birth-pangs" of society's transformation to a higher order is to hasten this transformation by an indefinite number of years.

2. On the one side of this transformation lies the immense suffering of hundreds of millions of people, through deprivation of needs and frustration of capacities. On the other side of this transformation lies the material realization of these needs and capacities.[37]

3. Therefore, to "shorten the birth pangs" of society's certain transformation to a higher order is to eliminate the immense suffering of hundreds of millions of people for an indefinite period of years.

We can see, then, that the basic choice between shortening, or not shortening, the "birth pangs" of society's certain transformation to a higher order—between, more precisely, advancing or retarding this certain transformation—is, for the Marxian world-view, a choice of supreme ethical import. And, if we recall

[37] The rest of this study can be viewed as the disinterred argument of Marx for the truth of these two propositions.

Marx's concept of knowledge—a conception, x, is knowledge if, and only if, x is used to alter the world in accordance with human needs—we can see that it is also a matter of supreme epistemological import. For just as to maximally advance this social transformation is, for Marx, the maximal *good* that can be ethically chosen, it is also, in accordance with his criterion of knowledge, the maximal *truth* that can be scientifically achieved (see pp. 70-71n).

In non-Marxian parlance, but according to Marxian principle, the Good is, when realized, the True. The ancient equation of value familiar since Plato and before, thus, assumes here its historical materialist form. And the middle term of this equation is social revolution.

# INDEX

feudal society (*cont.*)
  cally necessitated transition
  to, 193n, 209n
Feuerbach, Ludwig, 23n; theses
  on, 24n, 30n, 70n; and
  "species being," 28; critique
  of idealism by, 136
food, 21; need for, 21, 33; historicization of, 21, 38, 40-41,
  48-50; capitalist adulteration
  of, 25n, 68, 92, 186; preparation of, 61n; productive force,
  62; lever of exploitation,
  83-86, 89-90; class differences
  in, 160; in state-socialist and
  capitalist societies, 186; revolution for lack of, 193-95,
  203n, 210n; and realm of
  necessity, 227n. *See also* farming
force, 74-76. *See also* violence
force and fraud, law of, 115n;
  ideology of, 138
forces of production, *see* productive forces
foreign investment, 92-93. *See
  also* imperialism
form and content, 171n, 195
form of life, 171n. *See also* economic structure; economic determinism
forms of social consciousness,
  9-10; unrecognized general
  category of Marx's model,
  9-10, 14, 145-56; distinguished from ideology, 146-
  47; and racism, 146-47n; association with and differentia-
  tion from Kant's *a priori* forms
  of understanding, 146-47,
  153-54; transhistorically governing principles of published
  ideation, 148-50; identification of, 148-50; determination
  of personal consciousness by,

151-56; as social unconscious,
  153; permission of, 154;
  mediating mechanism be-
  tween economic structure and
  human nature, 155-56; as
  grammar of illusion, 156; and
  economic determinism, 156,
  165-68; religious ideology deduced by means of, 168-69n;
  state-socialist ideology deduced by means of, 184-85n;
  underlie ideology of anti-
  technology, 221-23n, 230n
frame of mind, 148-52
frame of reference, 45
freedom, 5; criticism of Marx
  for denial of, 16; based on
  human nature, 22-27; realized
  in work, 27-32; ultimately
  realized in leisure-time creative activity, 27-28, 36-52,
  199-200, 227-28; technological determinism as man's
  self-determination, 39-66,
  216-17, 219, 225-39; of ethical
  decision, 53, 234-39; and
  communism, 52, 98-99, 227n,
  231; repression of by economic structure, 59-80, 161-
  87; bourgeois ideology of,
  133, 135-39, 166-67, 180n,
  184n, 186; capitalism and state
  socialism compared on, 186;
  by technological advance,
  199-200, 227-28, 230-39; and
  inevitability, 216-17, 234-39;
  defined, 227n; to choose the
  revolution or the counterrevolution, 233-39. *See also*
  freedom and necessity; free
  will and determinism; revolution; self-realization; worker
  self-government
freedom and necessity, 51-52;
  realms of, 51-52, 187, 227-28,

Library of Congress Cataloging
in Publication Data

McMurtry, John Murray, 1939–
    The structure of Marx's world-view.

    Includes bibliographical references and index.
    1.  Marx, Karl, 1818–1883.     2.  Communism.
3.  Dialectical materialism.    I.  Title.
HX39.5.M29        335'.4'1        77-85552
ISBN 0-691-07229-9
ISBN 0-691-01998-3 pbk.

## DATE DUE